THE
PRESSURED
CHILD

THE PRESSURED CHILD

HELPING YOUR CHILD FIND SUCCESS IN SCHOOL AND LIFE

Michael Thompson, Ph.D.
with Teresa Barker

BALLANTINE BOOKS NEW YORK

To my brother, Peter B. Thompson, Ph.D.
—*MGT*

To Steve, Aaron, Rachel, and Rebecca
—*THB*

A Ballantine Book
Published by The Random House Publishing Group

www.ballantinebooks.com

LIBRARY OF CONGRESS CATALOGING-IN-PUBLICATION DATA
Thompson, Michael.
The pressured child : helping your child find success in school and
life / Michael Thompson with Teresa Barker.
p.   cm.
Includes bibliographical references.
ISBN 0-345-45012-4
1. Education—Parent participation.   2. Academic achievement.
I. Barker, Teresa.   II. Title.
LB1048.5 .T54 2004
371.19'2—dc22   2003065514

Text design by Julie Schroeder

Manufactured in the United States of America

First Edition: August 2004

2   4   6   8   9   7   5   3   1

Contents

Acknowledgments

There is no possible way that I can thank every child who has opened up his or her world to me and helped me to understand the nature of his or her struggle. However, the following young people, through their honest reporting and writing, helped make this book a reality: Daniel Flaherty, Cameron Sereno, Aaron Weiner, Erin-Claire Michaels, Serena Steele, Cindy Dutra, Rachel Cognata, Joanna Thompson, Nathan Belkin, Heather Chabot, Rachel Weiner, Ariel Zuckerman, Will Thompson, Thankgod Nwafor, Rebecca Weiner, Miranda Gerzon, Emily Kenfield, Barbara DeFlorio, Eric Steele, Jonathan Copithorne, Nikki Scotti, Lauren McPherson, Sonia Piers, Colzie Crump, Ben Cohn, Erik Lambert, Harry MacDonnell, Lily Morris, Beth Brown, and Emily Kagan. I want to recognize Erin-Claire Michaels. Her story ended up on the cutting-room floor in the final edits of the book, but her steadfast e-mails were enormously helpful to me, as was her optimistic view of school. I wish I could have included all of your stories, but many interviews and quotable quotes had to be cut in order to bring the manuscript down to a manageable size.

I am similarly in debt to many teachers and school administrators whose insights have enriched me over the years. I cannot list them all, but I would be remiss if I did not mention the support of Father Bill Campbell, Jim Sadler, Kathy Schultz, Bill Harrington, Steven Woodcock, Kristen Vanderveen, Father Simon Smith, Richard Melvoin, Cliff Goodband, Elaine Foisy, Bill Gerwitz, Bill Polk, Jerry Katz, Mark Segar, Bruce Shaw, Debbie Callahan, Donna David, Joan Stoner, Meg Maccini, George Rizkallahi, Kathleen Doyle, Susan Gurry, Linda Nathan, Debra Stacy, John Thomson, David Ladd, David Bachmann, Peter Rosheger, Vivian Powers-Richard, Mary

Gina Stilwell, and Joanne Gurry. I would like to thank the wonderful teachers at the Belmont Hill School who have worked with me and *trusted* me for seven years even though they must have had the uncomfortable feeling that whatever they said around me was likely to end up in a book!

I have the most vivid memories of my conversation with—and a file full of penetrating e-mails from—the "mothers' group" in Chicago: Kathy Flaherty, Jamie Sullivan, Sara Kurensky, Kathy Powers, Leslie Rowan, Loree Sandler, Kathy Slezak, Barb Hickey, Linda Oliva, Jean Luchini, Sherry Laten, Beth Kerr, Christine Huszagh, Sherry Laten, and Kathryn Ingraham. I am grateful to Steve Weiner, Peter Thompson, and Neal Michaels as well as the members of my men's group—the "So-Called Healthy Group"—for sharing their strong feelings and obvious love of fathering.

Perhaps in sympathy with my subjects, I struggled more with this book than any other that I have written. There were many stretches when I found it hard to believe that in my own flawed experience as a parent I had anything to offer my readers. Happily, I have been surrounded by supportive, concerned mothers! *The Pressured Child* exists because of the confidence and faith of my gifted collaborator, Teresa Barker, who held on to the thread of the book during those times when I had lost it. Her command of language and her experiences as the mother of three children are in the fiber of this text. The original idea for the book came out of a conversation between Teresa Barker and Gail Ross (both parents of beginning high-schoolers five long years ago). Gail is a sensational agent, an encouraging friend, and a real-life worried parent. Did I mention that Nancy Miller, the supportive and talented editor in chief of Ballantine Books, is also a concerned parent? My administrative assistant, Elizabeth Diggins, keeps my calendar, organizes my life, and worries out loud about her enchanting daughters, Devynn and Danielle. Bless all the mothers and their worries; I learn so much from them! When it comes to my knowledge of parenting, however, my greatest teacher has been my wife, Theresa McNally, whose thoughtful and loving support of our children through their school struggles has been literally awe-inspiring.

Tom Doelger, a gifted teacher of English, read a copy of the manuscript and helped sharpen my writing. Larry Cohen and Catherine

O'Neill Grace, my *Best Friends, Worst Enemies* coauthors, also read drafts of the manuscript and made thoughtful, supportive comments that improved the book. My wife, Theresa, a prodigious reader of fiction, had to put up with my insistent requests to "please read this section." She was always an honest and loving audience of this book.

I have felt totally supported by Gilly Hailparn and the publicity department at Ballantine Books. Lissa Dutra did early research for this book and was succeeded by Lindsay Garre, who brought passion, energy, and her experience as an elementary school teacher to the job of making sure that my "wisdom" was supported by research.

Finally, I need to mention once again my children, Joanna and Will, who have shared so generously of their experiences, and enlarged my life and my understanding of the nature of both school and childhood.

NOTE: To protect the privacy of the children and teachers whose stories are shared in some detail in this book, many names or identifying information have been changed. Some wished their names to be used and we have done so. In reproducing students' e-mail journals and correspondence, we have left typing and grammar as they are, which is typically (for many children as for adults, even the most accomplished academic contributors) a hodgepodge of misspellings, typos, slang, and creative abbreviations. In this and all other ways possible, we have attempted to preserve the authenticity of children's stories and expression.

Introduction

One Friday afternoon I picked up my son, Will, from his new school. It was late September and he had just started seventh grade. For the first three weeks of school he had been pretty content. He liked his new friends, he had some welcoming teachers; he was a happy guy. All that changed at the end of his fourth week. When he climbed into the car that day he looked whipped and discouraged. He threw his books across the seat and said, "I hate my life."

"School pretty tough?" I asked.

"Yeah," he answered.

In an attempt to be clever, and perhaps to elicit a smile from him, I followed up with the observation, "So the honeymoon is over?"

"What did you expect, Dad?" he shot back. "It's school."

This book is titled *The Pressured Child,* but it is written for *the struggling parent,* which is every loving parent, no matter what kind of student your child is. All children struggle to manage the pressures inherent in learning, growing, and developing. There are no exceptions. They struggle in life and in school. Learning-disabled children struggle every day with lessons and teaching methods for which their brains are not well suited. School is too much for them on a daily basis. Brilliant children suffer from boredom and loneliness, from feeling misunderstood, from being labeled as "nerds." School is not enough for them. The "average" child, for whom, presumably, the school experience should be just right, still struggles with mastering new material, with sitting quietly through a long day of classes, with good teachers and bad, with being more popular or less popular with her peers. As the great comedienne Gilda Radner used to say on *Saturday Night Live,* "It's always something!"

As parents, all of us struggle at times with feelings of helplessness, frustration, and anger over our children's school lives. All loving parents want to see their children succeed in school. We want them to learn well, study hard, make good grades, have good friends, and make their way from kindergarten through high school with as much success and as little pain as possible. They want that, too. When their efforts or their results fall short of expectations, or even threaten to fall short of expectations, parents and kids alike struggle.

Most of all, we cannot bear to see our children suffer. If we had it in our power to protect them from the disappointments, the unhappiness, or the true misery we experienced as children or saw around us, we would do so.

Many parents try. Some complain about even modest imperfections in their children's schools or teachers, routinely attempt to get their unhappy children shifted to new classes, buffer their kids at every turn, and help them excessively with their homework. They try to make childhood easier and to spare their children the struggles that they themselves endured, or whatever new version of struggle their children may confront. Some of us accept that this is all part of life, certainly part of growing up, but, just like the others, we can't accept the helplessness that comes with watching our children learn the hard way and suffer the emotional and academic bumps and bruises that come with it.

We all want to feel competent as parents, and that means when things aren't going right, our impulse is to jump in and fix them. We spend a lot of time and attention as quality-control managers, watching for snags or flaws we can fix in hopes of making our children happier, smarter, stronger, more competitive.

Despite our best efforts, and even with improvements, our children still struggle and sometimes suffer under the pressures of school and life. It makes many parents feel totally miserable and helpless. Our own discontent can fill our conversation and drive our behavior in respect to our children's way of "doing school."

It is my hope with this book to introduce a new kind of conversation about kids and school. I have written *The Pressured Child* to remind parents and teachers how life for children plays out in school. In my experience as a school consultant and psychologist, I see that often parents and teachers have forgotten what school actually feels like for a child, and why children struggle with both their own development and the environment of school. I want parents to remember how children live their lives in school, how they attempt to manage the endless pressures of the school environment, the infinite imposition of school, how they endure and how much resilience and wisdom they have and are willing to share with us—if we will listen.

Once upon a time, we were all kids in school and we understood completely the pressures on us from school, classmates, and parents. We forget because as we grew older those experiences receded into the past. We forget because we hope we can save our children from painful experiences, and it is difficult to admit to ourselves how much they have to struggle in order to grow. And we forget because when children challenge or frustrate us—as parents or as educators—we want to forget the complexity of their struggle so we can focus on simplifying our own.

To write this book, I had to go back to school. I shadowed children through many different grades in a variety of schools. I learned from them how they solve the problems of school—the problems they may never mention to a busy parent or even an inquiring one—and how they assess their own development. As I watched them encounter trouble and find ways to solve it, I watched them reach down and find their own resilience time and again.

My hope is that *The Pressured Child* will draw you into your own memories of school and deliver fresh insights, give you a more intimate understanding of your child's psychological and developmental experience of school, and lead you to discover your own capacity, your own competence, to respond in loving *and* effective ways.

1

If You Believe What Children Say

I know that school is meant for learning and expanding
your personality but adults either don't think
you're trying hard enough or they don't care.
—*Sixth-grade girl*

Of making many books there is no end,
and much study is a weariness of the flesh.
—*The Hebrew Bible, Ecclesiastes 12:12*

The question "How was school today?" may be the most-asked and least-answered question in America. It is the question that all parents are compelled to voice every day sometime between three P.M. and bedtime.

"*How was school today?*" No matter how gently you ask it, no matter how cleverly you phrase it, 99 percent of children don't give you the information you crave. "Fine," they reply, or "Okay." Younger ones may give you some details; a child who is a real talker, a born journalist, may give you an extended news report. But such kids are rare. Most children don't share the kind of information about school that parents want to hear. Besides, they know that if they made the effort, you'd just ask again the next day. You'd never be satisfied. That's the way it is with all of us parents, and as our children get older they may protest being asked the "How was . . ." question. "Mom," they declare through clenched teeth, "it was *fine*." What they mean is: "Don't bug me!"

Still, we cannot help ourselves. We were so connected to our children when they were little. We watched everything they did; we charted their developmental progress daily. We phoned our closest friends when our eleven-month-old seemed ready to walk. "She's cruising around the living room holding on to chairs and the coffee table." Nothing escaped our vigilant attention and eager celebration.

Then off they go to school and suddenly we're starved for information. We can't see what they're doing or what's happening around them or to them. We're cut off from much of our children's lives. We want scraps, quiz grades, gossip about the teacher's personality— *anything*. I once asked an audience of parents what they would ask for if they had "the teacher of their dreams."

A mother said, "I'd like my son's teacher to call me every day and tell me about his day."

"In what grade is your son?" I asked.

"Tenth grade," replied the mother without embarrassment, as the entire audience laughed.

But what do we really hope to learn from that question we keep asking? I imagine a parent asking a child, "How was school today?," and the child answering with something like this: "Mom, I'd like to tell you, I really would, but it is all too complicated to put into words. I don't know where to begin. The truth is that you're not asking me about school really, you're asking me how my life is going, and I don't have any perspective on that. I'm trying to develop into a person here and sometimes the school seems to be something of a help and at other times it feels like it is totally in the way of my becoming a person. Besides, why do I have to tell you what school is all about? Didn't you go to school? Don't you know what school is like? Why keep asking me?"

Of course you did go to school, but what does that have to do with your child's education? The aim of this book is to take you into the minds of children as well as back into your own school memories in an attempt to put you back in touch with the gritty reality of being a child in school. I hope I can help you appreciate the extraordinary psychological journey that constitutes every child's institutional education. But first, let's start with you.

Have you recently thought about your school years, what it really felt like, down to your bones? How did it feel to sit on those hard wooden or plastic chairs for hours, to stand in line to go to music or PE? What about eating lunch in a crowded, noisy cafeteria? Do you remember struggling to master a concept? Do you remember how it felt to get bad grades? Or perhaps you never received an F or a D or even a C. Were you ever afraid of the possibility? Did you come home from fifth grade and find yourself anxious until you finished your homework? Did you ever feel sick just thinking about going to school, or at the end of a school day? I know a talented physician who was, as you might expect, an accomplished student in school. Many days, however, his take on his teacher's demands made him so anxious that he threw up when he got home.

Did school ever bore you? Do you remember what a difference it could make in your daily life if the teacher really liked—or seemed to hate—you? Do you remember PE class? Did you love it or fear it? Do you remember the texture of it: the exciting, scary games like dodgeball (if you liked it) and the stupid games like dodgeball (if you didn't)? Were you afraid of being picked last? Were you nervous about the way your body looked or about changing your clothes in front of other children? Do you remember the endless amounts of wasted time in school?

Did your parents care about school? Had your mom or dad been good in school? Do you remember a teacher whom you loved? A teacher who seemed to care deeply about you? Do you still think of her from time to time? Was school a refuge from your family? Did it seem a calm and organized place in comparison to the chaos of home?

There are a million questions I could ask, hoping to make you remember things you haven't thought about in years. Why would I want to dredge up those memories? As a psychologist, I am fascinated by the lives people lived in school. I am also committed to reminding parents about the day-to-day experience of school so that they can *really* comprehend what their children are experiencing daily. Every child's school experience is an intricate, exciting, sometimes painful, often boring psychological journey. We should all be aware of that, but that's not what parents describe when they talk to me about their children's school experiences.

PARENTS HAVE LOST THEIR MEMORIES
OF WHAT SCHOOL IS REALLY LIKE

As a psychologist who works in schools, I spend much of my day with the unhappiest, least successful, and sometimes most bitter children in the building. When I finally sit down with a child, there is the hope and assumption that I will get him back on track in some way, that I will find the key to motivate him, that I will learn some secret about his family life—teachers always speculate that there are problems at home—that will remove the obstacles from his path and help turn him around.

Sometimes I am able to do exactly that. I find the key and I share that information with the child's educators. Most of the time it is not that easy. Generally I succeed in doing something less magical but more substantial. I learn how a child perceives school, in what ways school might not be a good fit for her, and, most important, I come to understand what she has to do every day to survive school.

My understanding of a student's school journey, of his strategy for negotiating school, is perhaps the most important thing I can learn from a therapeutic encounter with a child. This goes beyond any simple diagnosis, and beyond testing for a learning disability, though either of these may be an important part of the journey. Just the act of a child communicating to me how he feels he fits or doesn't fit into the school environment may change his experience of school entirely: simply being heard and understood can be healing or encouraging. If I can find a way to convey a portion of what I have learned from the child to my colleagues, and they respond helpfully, and to a child's parents, that too may change the nature of the child's experience in school.

After twenty years of working this way with parents and children, I am convinced that one of the greatest barriers to helping children in schools is the fact that parents don't have an accurate view of school. It's paradoxical: Since parents spent time in schools when they were kids, they should, theoretically, have such information available. However, it has been my experience that adults have lost touch with the texture and meaning of their own educational experiences. As a result, children feel that their parents are "out of it," that they don't understand. Parents tend to focus on grades and how it is all going to turn out and miss seeing the realities of their child's life as it is lived day to day.

This happens for a number of reasons: Our childhood memories are often lost or repressed. Also, perhaps starved for information about a child's school day, parents are condemned to focus on their child's future. Doing so, they may overlook important aspects of their child's present.

Even the most thoughtful parents of school-age children tend to hold the simplistic view that their kids operate at just two speeds: working hard enough or *not* working hard enough. Parents all too often use mechanical metaphors to describe children. We say that a child may need to "get her act into gear," or "put the pedal to the metal," and get her grades up. Sometimes, indeed, it is the case that a child isn't working as hard as she theoretically might. However, she cannot just be shifted into higher gear, or given a "kick in the butt" or a "jump-start," as many parents have said to me. If we're going to think about children as having gears, we should compare them to the most sophisticated mountain bikes. Children have at least twenty-eight gears and are constantly making minute adjustments as they go up and down the hills of the school day.

Every parent *should* know this because every adult lived through the demands of school life. When I was discussing the ideas for this book with a friend of mine, a woman in her fifties, she said, "Oh, school . . . I was scared every day." Even if you weren't frightened or worried every day, there were lots of times in childhood when you felt overwhelmed and little—precisely because children are small. One wit once said that the most powerful person on earth is a kindergarten teacher on the first day of school. As a child, it didn't feel as though you were making things happen. You were under the control of other people and most of it was happening *to* you.

We repress much of what happened to us in our childhoods. Perhaps Freud's most original insight was that we are all capable of locking up some childhood memories in our unconscious mind, memories upsetting or socially unacceptable to our adult psyche. Freud thought we repressed much of our childhood experiences because of sexual thoughts. However, I think we tend to repress memories of being helpless and out of control. People selectively remember their childhood experiences. If a parent loses touch with her school experience, she will be at a loss to fully support her own children in their school struggles. One of the goals of this book is to help you, the reader, remember what happened to you in school.

Adults often have a selective—sometimes romanticized, sometimes caricatured—view of their own school experiences. We condense many years into a set of war stories, anecdotal chestnuts that have been polished by repeat performances. If you have attended a high school reunion or college reunion, you have almost certainly swapped stories with former classmates about the popular kids, the tragic suicide or car accident that carried away a member of your class, the most boring or outrageous or sexy or pathetic teachers. Those communal stories need to be shared. But did you tell one another the inside story about being in school, perhaps how angry or miserable you were? Have you ever told someone how incredibly competitive you felt? Have you ever told someone how much you adored a high school teacher?

Many unconscious feelings about school experiences have never really been put into words. I interviewed a very successful real estate developer. He was bitter about his school experience from the first grade onward, even though he acknowledged the importance of education. "Everybody ought to know a certain amount about everything, but God, sitting through a year of it, stuff that you just hate, and so many—probably fifty percent of the class—is basically out of it a lot of the time. . . . I wasn't the only one feeling that way."

Did this man's parents know he was disengaged and angry when he was in school? Did they know his suffering came about because of a huge discrepancy between his native intelligence and a very real but undiagnosed reading disability? Did his parents not know what to do?

"School isn't too much different from a small country. Each school has its culture, its figureheads, its politics, its lower class, and its oddities. What you get out of it is really not totally yours to control. You live your life and deal with the various twists as they come. By the time it's over you are different in some respects. School changes your life, for better or for worse." (Twelfth-grader)

It is not only children given the label of learning disabled who struggle and suffer. "Gifted" students (many of whom also have learning disabilities or problematic gaps in their skills) may feel desperate for a genuine challenge or for social companionship among peers. They may wish other skills came easier or feel burdened by others' assumptions, hopes, or expectations. Some of the unhappiest children I have known have been highly gifted honor-roll regulars. It has been said that all great gifts come with a cost. What does it feel like for a child who lives it?

What about the average, or so-so, students? Just as there are no so-so human beings, no child is average once you get to know her. Is your best friend average or above average? Is a child who shows only mild interest or aptitude for schoolwork only mildly affected by the difficult challenge of school, by an argument with her best friend, by divorce or illness in her family, or by the way everyone compares her to her brilliant sibling?

What about children who cut themselves or use drugs and alcohol to self-medicate their unhappiness, or who end up in emergency rooms after suicide attempts? No one self-destructs over a history test, but the school day and school experience are hardly irrelevant. School is always a contributing factor to the quality of a child's life.

The more I thought about the school experience of the students who came to my office, the more I realized that, despite my own record as a successful student at excellent schools, I had experienced most of the things I was hearing about from these unhappy young reporters, though perhaps not to the same degree. I came to the conclusion that *even the very best school is a difficult place for a child*. In the words of my daughter, you have to put up with a lot of crap in school.

While this may not seem like an earthshaking observation, I found it helpful. Working with teachers and administrators, we operate every day on the implicit assumption that we have created a safe, healthy, and supportive environment for students, and that if the students struggle, it is due to factors inside *them*. However, students convey to me that even if school is a supportive environment, it is all too often a barrier to their own growth, development, and sense of self. They tell me that it is difficult to trust school. They have to be on their guard much of the time and are constantly searching for ways to be successful, to make school a good fit, and to get something out of the educational environment.

If you are reading this book, you probably have been looking for an answer to your question "How was school today?" The question you are really asking is: "What is school *really* like for my child? Is he okay?"

CHILDREN HAVE THE ANSWERS

As a psychologist my advice is simple: If you can find a way to ask children how school is for them, they will tell you. (I hasten to add that when it comes to talking to children, it is easier being a psychologist than a parent—more on that later.) Children tell me why school is scary. They tell me when they are bored. They tell me when teachers are hypocrites. Without fail, when interviewing a student, I always learn something that no adult was able to tell me about that child's functioning in school. I often learn something insightful about the school itself.

This past year I interviewed a boy who was in serious trouble for plagiarizing a paper in his senior year. The school was upset, his parents were distressed, and the boy was ashamed. He had been a good student, and when I asked what had happened to him he said, "This school is all about rhythm and regimen, and I've been out of rhythm for over a year." Not only was his characterization a brilliant description of his academically high-pressure school, it struck me as absolutely accurate on a psychological basis. He was out of rhythm with the demands of school. Haven't we all felt that way at some time during our school careers?

I have never heard from a student a life-at-school story with which I could not personally identify. A student describes her fury at the drama teacher who humiliated her in front of the class by saying, "Some people in this class are too shy," right after she had done her pantomime in front of her peers. I remember something like that. A disgusted third-grade boy becomes irate because the teacher supervising the playground made them stop playing soccer after just one near-fight between two boys. Of course that would make him angry. I cannot tell you how many times, when sitting with a child, I have wanted to shout, *"That's* the reason you're doing so badly. *Now* I understand why you can't concentrate!"

Sometimes the issue has nothing to do with classes, teachers, or homework. A tenth-grade boy with chronic headaches was having a stressful breakup with his girlfriend. This was taking up all of his mental energy. His parents' insistence that he work harder at school was falling on ears clogged with emotional pain.

That's a problem with being a parent. When your child tells you that he's doing badly in school because he's breaking up with his girl-friend, the parent side of you is compelled to say, "Don't make excuses!" or, "Well, I'm sorry that things aren't working out, but school is your future and you must not let everything go to hell in a hand-basket over your first love relationship." Such an exchange usually brings the discussion to an end.

A psychologist doesn't need to reproach or remind children of what's important. We need only to understand their inner life. This is why it is easier to get the story as a psychologist. Fearing a parent's judgment, children shut down in anticipation.

Almost invariably, I come away with the feeling that the child understands her school situation better than her parents do—even the most concerned and compassionate parents. Time and again, I have sat in my office with parents who are surprised as I explain what school is like for their child. They say, "We didn't realize she felt frightened every day," or, "We had no idea he hated his teacher so much. We didn't think things were that bad."

In eighth grade, I hated my teacher. I thought he was a real jerk: vulgar, slothful, self-indulgent, and mean to kids. I complained to the principal, fantasizing that I could get him fired. Two years later, I conducted a campaign against my tenth-grade French teacher, one of the most boring and petty human beings it has ever been my misfortune to know, hoping I could drive him into retirement. That didn't work either. Instead, I kept getting lectures and detentions for my efforts. Other years, I was detached, ashamed, or anxious. This, despite a level of academic success that took me to Harvard.

Throughout eighth grade, my parents repeated the adult mantra "You have to learn to work for people you don't like." I wanted to scream back: "It's not just that I don't like him. I don't respect him as

"School can be a great place to be because you get to learn new things and you get to see your friends. But school can be a hard place when you're confused, frustrated or just having a very hard time and it could be anything—like a test or reading in your text book." (Sixth-grader)

a human being and I'm forced to spend *all day* with him. Do you know what that feels like?" I wanted my parents to understand what it felt like to be in this man's classroom every single day, to understand that, even though I was doing reasonably well academically and was in many ways a "good student," I hated it. Every day, I hated it all over again.

A friend reported this to me after an open house at her seventh-grader's school, where parents attended a mini-version of their student's day—just five minutes in each class: "At one point, in the math teacher's presentation, I realized I was not paying attention. I tried to remember what I had been thinking about in those moments before I realized I wasn't listening and was lost in thought. Here it is: I was thinking about my driving schedule for the next day. I'm not sure I would ever have thought there is anything more boring than thinking about my driving schedule, but I guess there was: the math teacher. We were so relieved when we got out ninety minutes later—and we skipped last period!"

My daughter, Joanna, kept telling me that her tenth-grade science teacher was unbelievably boring. I was certain that she was overstating the case until I went to school with her on parents' visiting day. After fifteen minutes of listening to her teacher drone on in his deadly fashion, I wanted to scream, pass notes, daydream, or—as the Monty Python folks used to say—"Run away!" For me, the best thing about his class was that I did not ever have to return. Sadly, my daughter had to go back four times a week for seven more months. All I could do to help her was to get over that difficult threshold of adult loyalty and acknowledge the truth: "You're right, Joanna, he *is* incredibly boring."

My friend Jim Sadler is the headmaster of a small school in the Virgin Islands. Because his school is so small, he is personally responsible for evaluating all the members of his faculty. With a faculty of 70, he visits each teacher's classroom twice a year, for a total of

140 classroom visits. He tries to distribute the visits evenly across the academic year, but sometimes after a long recruiting trip to the mainland, he returns to the island and has to double or triple up his visits. "When I face a day in which I am scheduled to go to three classes, I just dread it," he told me. "Isn't it amazing that we ask kids to do something we wouldn't do? I can hardly bear going to three classes, yet we require kids to go to seven classes per day, five days per week." A total of thirty-five classes, week after week.

School is a rich and interesting world in which children live most of their young lives, yet we don't give them enough credit for what is going on inside their minds. Many parents think life begins after school. That couldn't be farther from the truth, both as a psychological matter and as a mathematical matter. If a college-bound girl is going to live to the age of eighty, her time spent in school and college represents 28 percent of her life. School occupies more waking hours of a child's life than home does. Every child in school has an intense psychological journey that must be lived—happily or unhappily—inside the school building. Inside those brick walls is where kids may feel excited, exultant, furious, or disappointed. Children know this very well. They sit at their desks and feel the passage of time. Some teenagers have said to me, "At this school, I don't have a life!" The phrase has haunted me.

Did you have a life in school? If so, what kind of a life was it? Or did you have a life outside school, in spite of school? If you want to understand what your child is experiencing, you need to recover authentic memories of your life in school. You have to focus on the unique psychological journey you took through school. Did your education touch your soul? Did it appeal to your authentic self? Did you discover yourself in school? What *did* you discover?

I asked a gifted scientist about his elementary school years. He immediately began to relate stories from fifth grade. When I questioned him about his first five years in school, grades kindergarten through four, he couldn't remember anything. I pressed hard, and he couldn't bring much back. He did know that he was slow in learning to read. "I didn't learn to read until third grade. In fact, I was about to be held back," he said. He then remembered that in fourth grade he went to the library and took out a book on Ohm's law to try to calculate resistance for parallel circuits.

He remembered more:

> When I was in sixth grade I was supposed to do a science report
> and, not being a very good listener and pretty active, I did it on
> electricity, and I thought I had to invent electricity. I thought I had
> to do experiments and *invent* both static and dynamic electricity.
> Needless to say, I never finished the report and got an F. One of
> the great traumas in my life and nobody realized that I went down
> to my basement workshop and tried to invent it.

And when his teacher was going over addition he had to do something to entertain his mind:

> A dominant memory is watching the clock and counting in my
> head to see if I could predict—'cause it had a minute hand that
> would click at every minute—and see if I could predict when it
> would move because I was so dreadfully bored. And I remember
> in mathematics, in doing arithmetic and so on, that I gave each of
> the numbers a personality, so if I was adding 13 and 54, it was "1"
> was the elephant and "3" was Mickey Mouse and see what they
> would combine, so I'd make stories about adding the numbers
> 'cause it got to be boring.

Was anyone aware that inside this boy's head he was trying to invent electricity and making up animal stories during boring arithmetic lessons? One of my aims in this book is to reacquaint you with the survival strategies children employ—some of which you might have used—to survive the school day.

THE PSYCHOLOGICAL ASPECT
OF EDUCATION IS MISSING

There is something missing from the public discussion in this country about education for children. Amid all the furor about state and federal testing, teacher accountability, teacher shortages, special education, and school funding, few people talk about the psychological dimension of school. It may surprise you to hear me say that. After all, aren't there truckloads of books by health professionals about aspects of school functioning? Take, for example, Mel Levine's splendid *A Mind at a Time,* or Edward Hallowell and John Ratey's valuable *Driven to Distraction.* Each of these books takes you inside the minds of children, examining how learning differences affect school performance and self-confidence. These books are based in research on the nature of the brain and learning. While they are indeed psychological and very helpful, I want to offer you a different psychological story.

There are books by psychologists that tell you how to motivate your child to achieve better grades or boost school performance. Other books by journalists have looked at the texture of life in schools. Some follow children through a school year. There are also revolutionary-style books that attack schools for being boring and for wasting kids' time. As interesting as these books may be, I deeply believe in the enterprise of schooling and am supportive of the teachers and administrators whose lives are dedicated to making schools work for children. I am out to accomplish something that is not revolutionary. I want to remind the reader what it is that kids do every day to keep themselves intact and psychologically alive *in* school.

We always talk about what we're trying to teach children in school, and whether they are learning what they need. However, this is only the first of three different levels at which children experience school: The Lesson, The Strategy, and Self-knowledge.

The Lesson is the adult agenda for children. The Strategy is what children develop in order to cope with both the reality of The Lesson and the many other things they are interested in learning from school.

As important as The Lesson is, it is terribly incomplete. Nevertheless, as adults we cannot stop thinking about it. The mother of a seventh-grade child told me that her daughter said in late July before her eighth-grade year, "I can't wait to get back to school . . ." Delighted, the mother waited expectantly for the girl to say something about her favorite classes coming up the next year. Instead, her daughter finished the sentence, ". . . to see how much taller the boys have gotten." Well, of course! That would be the most interesting thing about school for an eighth-grade girl or boy in the middle of puberty.

For adults, The Lesson is paramount. It is a basic assumption. The importance of school is obvious and undeniable, as is the inevitability of school attendance. Children *must* go to school. Children *must* learn to read and write. Education is good and a college degree is almost essential in the Information Age. These truths are so obvious that we do not question them. We forget that children are not indentured servants and are not machines. For children, school is not automatic. It doesn't come easily for any of them—even the ones who make it look easy—and it comes at great cost for some. We forget that a great deal of the learning in schools—perhaps a majority of it—is not provided by adults.

> "Sometimes I feel discouraged about school. It's not really about school but what happens to me there."
>
> (Fifth-grader)

The Strategy is what children bring to the school experience: their attempts to deal with the demands of school, the kind of learning style they have, the expectations of their parents, and the complex social requirements of their peers. Every child, no matter how disinterested or out of it he seems about the demands of school, is constantly refining a strategy for holding these intense and conflicting forces in place.

Self-knowledge is what children actually achieve in school. Most are the better for their school experiences. Kids in the mainstream emerge with confidence and a passionate interest in something. However, sometimes the self-knowledge is painful, not at all what the educators intended. For example, sometimes talented African-American kids who have been given scholarships to traditionally white elite private schools find themselves among a painfully few children of color. They emerge with a first-class education, as well as the profound feeling that they do not fit in anywhere. What kind of education is that exactly? The question I ask of children throughout this book, and in my work with them, comes down to "What did you *really* learn about yourself in school?"

I'll go first. From second grade through twelfth grade I wore a blazer, a button-down shirt, and a tie to school. I was blessed with a pretty good school brain and was an excellent test taker—a recipe for reasonable academic success. But inside, I knew that I was just a very good game player. I worked reasonably hard for teachers whom I loved and I played the game of school for the rest, jumping through the required hoops with dramatized effort.

For me, school was a game: Could I do what *I* wanted to do while still satisfying the demands of the authorities? At my high school—a small boys' boarding school in Dutchess County, New York—I was the king of extracurricular activities. School provided me with a place to practice public leadership and to pursue my passions. I maintained an aquarium of twenty-five fish tanks and edited the school paper. My junior year I was director of the dining hall, which meant that I supervised the student waiters and dishwashers. I also enjoyed watching TV with the professional cooks back in their lounge (TV was severely restricted in a boarding school; I got around those rules by using my leadership position). Writing papers for class and studying for French tests were far down on my list of things to do. While I generally got them done satisfactorily, I never pushed myself academically until I arrived at the University of Chicago to get my Ph.D. at the age of twenty-seven. That's when I started to really work in school.

My children have introduced me to an entirely different experience of school from the one I lived. Their schooling has been a profound challenge for both my wife and myself, both of us having been academically able and sufficiently compliant to stick with education long enough to earn our doctorates. My kids, Joanna, age seventeen, and Will, age eleven, have radically different strengths than I had—my daughter is an athlete and my son an artist—and more academic difficulties than I ever faced. Both of them have significant learning disabilities. Joanna is dyslexic and despises reading. Will has a grab bag of processing and sequencing problems, along with dysgraphia (terrible handwriting), which make school an ordeal at times. It would be an understatement to say that my own school experience of completing academics in an offhand, last-minute fashion prepared me badly to parent these two wonderful children through school.

When it comes to my own children, I can never get out of my own way. I always trip over my own anxiety, ambition, love, and confusion about how much they are like me or not in their needs and wants. I can never remove my set of parental blinders when it comes to my own children because my vision is always affected by history and hope, and by love, too.

Every parent shepherding and coaching his child through school

ﾁ has to take a hard look at his own history. What was the reality of
your school experience? What kind of genetic package of skills did
you bring to the front door of that brick building where you spent so
much time? Does your personal history have to do with the strategies
that your child is developing *right now* to survive in school? Finally
and most important, what did you learn about yourself in school? Did
you come away with the sense of yourself as a confident, successful
person, or did you come away from high school feeling a bit like a
failure? Did you drag yourself across the finish line, relieved just to
get out of there?

Do you want your children to walk out of school drawing the
same profound lessons about themselves that you did, or do you want
something different for them? Is it even your choice?

WHOSE LIFE IS IT?

Jake's mother stares at me as if I am crazy. Here is her son, wanting to
leave an excellent private boys' school to attend his local public
school, and she expects me to intervene to stop him. I can tell from
their faces that both she and Jake's father were clearly hoping that I
would say something wise or psychologically astute to make him re-
consider. Not only am I *not* saying the things they hoped to hear, I am
encouraging Jake to tell his parents why he wants to leave the school.

"I miss my friends," he tells them.

"But you get to see them on weekends," his father replies.

"I know, but I'm not going to school with them; I'm not playing
soccer with them."

"You could have friends here. There are great kids here and you
haven't made an effort to get to know them, not in three years," his father insists.

Jake shrugs. "They're not my kind of kids."

"You're doing much more demanding work here than you would
be doing in the high school. You'll have a shot at better colleges,"
says his mother.

"I'd be in AP courses in the high school. Kids tell me you've got
a better shot at the top colleges if you come from public school," Jake
responds evenly.

"But what about the faculty here? They're great." Jake's father is starting to sound desperate. He knows he is reaching for straws. Both he and his wife look to me, silently pleading for assistance. I see their pain, feel their pain, and wish I could help. I cannot. I believe that Jake knows what is best for him.

Before I met Jake, who is fifteen years old, he had been described to me by various teachers as talented, academically gifted, hard-working, detached, and arrogant. A kid who "thought too much of himself," one teacher told me; someone who did not have a "realistic view" of his own athletic ability, one coach said. He had been a student at the school for three years and had never made the kind of emotional commitment to life there that you need to make if you are going to thrive in that environment. Many boys become symptomatic when they find that their school does not fit them, either by falling apart academically or by getting into disciplinary trouble. Jake had done neither. He continued to be a well-prepared student, with B's and A's on his report card, and he participated in sports. But it was obvious that he was withholding his heart: He had closed himself off from both his classmates and his teachers. It is not an easy thing to do and, despite my empathy for his parents, I admired his discipline and loyalty.

His parents had sent him to see me after his teacher had raised concerns about his detachment. His parents knew the reasons all too well: Jake had never wanted to attend the school and had become increasingly upset at the prospect of staying. In my two meetings with him prior to our family session, Jake, characterized as "detached" by adults, movingly articulated his deep affection for and loyalty to his friends. After hearing him out all I could say was, "You've been carrying the torch for your friends for three years. I think you've been unwilling to make friends here because you refused to allow anyone into competition with your old group. You're incredibly loyal."

Boys seldom discuss their intense attachments—they often avoid the term *best friend,* which girls so eagerly embrace—but they certainly have such friends and they will always defend their friendships in the strongest possible terms. If you ask a boy why another boy is his friend, he will say, "He has my back." That is, that boy would leap to his defense in case of physical danger, and he would reciprocate.

Once Jake had explained to me the power of his friendships and his loyalty to them, I was satisfied that he had a compelling reason for his behavior. I agree that kids don't always make the right decisions, but they usually signal when they know what to do when they are in emotional conflict. If I had thought Jake was depressed or anxious or in an emotional bind that he couldn't negotiate, I would have handled it differently. The truth was, he was in an emotional bind and he knew what he wanted to do about it. His choice was reasonable: The school and the friends he wanted to be with were perfectly respectable. There was no reason to believe the move would be any more of a mistake than to remain at a school where he felt emotionally detached and profoundly isolated.

Jake's parents had invested a great deal of hope (and money) in the idea of a private school. They believed that he would get a better education, better college preparation, and a more powerful network of friends at the school. They had also made relationships with parents in the community. No wonder they looked to me to back them up. I was sorry to disappoint them, but I was convinced that Jake had the intelligence, self-knowledge, and determination to resolve his dilemma. The best solution, whether that would be to stay the course or make the change, would be found in a fuller understanding between him and his parents.

Jake's parents' anxieties about his present and his future began to pour out: their fears about an open campus, drinking and driving, the large class size, the lack of personal contact with an adviser. Most especially, they emphasized that most of his soccer-playing friends were not his intellectual equals, that they did not value school as much as Jake did, certainly not as much as Jake's family did. Would he be able to resist the downward pressure he would experience while hanging out with them? Would he be able to remain a good student even when his friends were less committed to academic achievement? They articulated powerful arguments, but the words fell on ears that were certainly unreceptive, though Jake listened intently.

The conversation degenerated, and Jake and his parents began to fight about grades. Was he really the independent student he claimed to be, and if so, why hadn't he gotten A's? He tried to defend himself, but they expressed skepticism about his ability to manage the freedoms at the high school and maintain high grades. In the end, Jake's parents created a set of conditions before they would allow him to end his relationship with the school.

"If you want us to believe that you'll get a good education at the high school, if you want to be able to leave here with our blessing," his father said, "you have to get all A's at the end of the year."

"I can do it," said Jake.

And he did. He earned himself the right to leave the school and return to a school with the friends who had stood with him the three years he was away.

At last word, Jake was taking AP courses and getting A's and B's, the same grades he received routinely in his private school. He wasn't working as hard for those grades as he had at the private school, but he was still a good student, staying out of trouble in the town and playing varsity soccer. He had not yet applied to colleges, so I cannot honestly say whether he hurt his college chances by shifting, or whether he and his parents are happy with the outcome.

> **"You've got your friends so you don't have to go through school alone."**
> (Eleventh-grader)

Was it the right move? If the child feels it was the right move, is that right enough? If he looks back from age forty and thinks it was the wrong move, does that make it wrong? This is not a story about public versus private school, nor is it a story about the importance of friends versus academics. It is a story about trusting children to tell us the undeniable, irrevocable truth about their lives in school. When a ninth-grade boy has not made friends for three years in a new setting, and he admits that it has been a more-or-less willful choice, that is for me the defining truth with which we must reckon. You may agree with me or not, but I believed my job at that point was to help his parents past all of their normal, thoughtful, expectable parental anxieties to see that their child's journey through school belonged to him.

I hope to persuade you that, when it comes to school, children are smarter than we think. Whatever it is we hope to teach them, as parents, as teachers, and as communities invested in creating good schools, for it to be of value we have to value the truth of a child's experience. We have to listen and be open to what they have to teach us.

I am not an educator, nor by temperament a policy maker or reformer. I cannot write a book about creating the perfect school environment to fix all the difficulties I have observed, so I'm not going to

try. What my students have taught me is that school can be an exciting and even joyful experience, as well as a difficult, painful, and
sometimes humiliating one. The information that children give me is
invariably helpful. It is often somewhat different from what their
teachers report, and it is almost always at variance with what the students' parents believe about their children's school life.

If you believe what these children say to me and accept my con-
tention that there is something about the parental role that obscures
what a mom or dad can see about her or his child's experience and
strategy in school, you may feel challenged to get back in touch with
what school is really like. The only way to remember what you have
forgotten is to return to school and view it through the eyes of a child
or listen to children who are describing exactly what it is like to go to
school. I think every parent, at one time or another, has had the impulse to follow their children into school. Even if school personnel
would allow you to do so, your own children would be horribly embarrassed if you trailed after them into the building. Instead, I am
inviting you to go with me while I shadow some children through
their school days. Since your own children probably won't tell you
exactly what is going on for them—even if you ask them—I offer to
serve as your guide.

To write this book, I felt a need to shadow students. The students
sent to a psychologist are, by some criteria, unhappier than other
kids. I could not be sure that my patients represented the broader
community of their peers. I had to follow and interview students who
might never end up in a therapist's office, students who were well ad-
justed and successful, to test the validity of my premise that even the
best school is difficult for all children, that even the best students find
the challenge of school difficult and at times overwhelming, and that
any child's *success or failure* at school are windows into that child's
unique and complex strategy for psychological survival. Children
possess the knowledge—the "facts on the ground," as they are called
in wartime—and the wisdom to react to the realities of school. A
critical part of our job as educators and parents is to understand a
child's daily experience in school and the unseen strategies that shape
the child's destiny there.

Let's go back to school.

2

A Place of Truth

A Day in the (School) Life of Helena

———

For everybody, between September and June school
is the main part of their life. It may not be for learning,
but you spend most of the day there with the same
people, and we're all in this together.
—*Ben, sixteen*

The memory pictures of the first fifteen years of life
that drift back to me now are a medley of all sorts
of things, mainly play and school. . . . I am not
at all sure about the lessons I learned in school,
but I do know that we got a great deal of fun
between the study hours, and I have always been
glad that I took all the play I could as it came along. ✳
—*Clarence Darrow,* The Story of My Life

It is early December. A light snow is falling as I approach Kensington High School, an elongated brick building set back from Main Street by a sloping stretch of lawn. I park my car in the lot, driving past the rows of numbered parking spaces to the few reserved for visitors. I am here to go to school, not as I usually do (as a consultant or speaker), but to shadow one student and learn from all of them.

My first decision of the day is whether to cut across the wet, snowy grass and go straight to the entrance of the school or to walk through the paved lot, twenty yards up to the driveway, and enter alongside the line of cars stopping and starting their way up to the front door. My dress shoes have seen better days and I am worried about being late to meet Helena. I cut across the grass, recognizing that I am probably breaking a rule, but also knowing that no one is going to enforce it. Isn't school where you learn to calculate and weigh the difference between meaningful and not-so-meaningful rules? They are both still there inside me: "Use the path" and "What the hell."

The history of Kensington High School is on view in the amalgam of its many renovations. Numerous architects have taken a crack at this building, adding yet another redbrick section, so that from the street it now looks something like a freight train with single-story and multistory segments. There are two clearly marked entrances—one a 1920s three-story façade, the other a slightly more modern fifties version with white Greek pillars—both monuments to conventional architecture. They both have formal letterings, KENSINGTON HIGH SCHOOL, above the doors. I head for the older entrance—it looks grander to me—only to find that the kids are streaming into the other one. They know the way.

> "I would like it if they were in my shoes and knew what i was going through."
>
> (Eighth-grader)

It is 7:54 A.M. as I enter the principal's office, concerned that Helena, a junior and an unusually conscientious student, might have arrived there before me and is waiting. She has not yet arrived. She appears at the office door at 7:59, calls out my name, greets me, and confidently sweeps me into her schedule.

We head for her eight o'clock class through the crowded front lobby filled with students in parkas, conversations converging into a dull roar filling the halls. We take the glass-enclosed stairway, proceed down a long corridor with off-white walls, past banks of gray lockers, around a corner, through some brown fire doors, and down another long corridor with more gray lockers. It is a rapid trip through a world that an early-twentieth-century photographer could have captured quite accurately in black-and-white or sepia tones. Slightly anxious about making her late for class, I ask Helena whether her homeroom teacher cares about the eight A.M. starting time because there is no doubt that we will be three or four minutes late. She dismisses my concern.

"The teachers don't get mad about homeroom," she says.

We stop briefly at Helena's locker, her designated island in this monochromatic sea. Hers is on the lower tier of a block of forty lockers. She bends down to open it and spins the dial with her left hand, expertly managing the three turns with her thumb. When the lock flops open she hooks it over the locker door. I am struck by how small a space it is, perhaps only eight inches wide. Unlike lockers I have seen in many other schools, Helena's is bare. It contains no photos, no magazine clippings, no makeup or deodorant, no keepsakes. Is there a ban on locker decoration? "No, just not much interest in it," she says. "We do it sometimes for people's birthdays."

Unless a student makes a connection with a teacher who allows her to feel ownership over part of a laboratory, a classroom, or a theater backstage room—and some teachers do share their territory in that way—the locker is the only place in a school that a student can call her own. It is the only personal space to which a student is entitled.

I once consulted to a school where a boy, an only child, had been killed in a car crash in the fall of his tenth-grade year. In the hours following the accident, his classmates spontaneously scratched appreciations and good-byes into the metal door and interior of his locker. Other than the crash site itself, where else could his classmates express their feelings of loss? Late in the spring, the administrators asked me what they should do about the locker. They did not feel that it was appropriate for it to become a permanent memorial, but they didn't just want to destroy the inscriptions, especially since this informal memorial meant so much to his parents. Should they have a welder cut out the locker and give it to the parents? Should they cut it out and leave it outside to rust away naturally, in a sort of Himalayan bones-on-the-mountainside burial? I suggested that they give several art classes the job of transcribing the inscriptions and creating a piece of communal artwork. One of the pieces of art could be given to the parents; the other could be framed and hung in the corridor. The locker could then be sanded down, repainted, and given the next year to a friend of the boy who had been killed. He could be the custodian of the locker on its journey back to anonymity for different students in the years to come.

Helena makes quick work of her locker stop. She hangs her jacket on the hook and kneels on one knee to find the books and notebooks she will need for the day, choosing from two rows of books, one row propped on the top of the other. She needs different books this morning than she will need any other morning of the week. Kensington High School is on a rotating block schedule, as are many high schools, in an attempt to combat the monotony of the classic sequenced schedule that places the same classes in the same order every day of the week. The rotating block schedule allows some variety and flexibility: longer science labs and double periods become possible, and neither kids nor teachers get stuck with the same class during the last period every day. Block scheduling isn't everybody's first choice. Some complain about the longer periods spent at a desk and prefer the shorter classes and the opportunity to move around and socialize in the more numerous periods in a day. Either way requires logistical planning, and Helena will make three trips today to her locker, each time trading one set of books for another, taking only what she needs for the next block of time, to avoid having to haul more than necessary in her backpack up and down the long hallways.

We arrive at Helena's homeroom around 8:07. I don't see a teacher immediately—perhaps there is one here, but not at the desk. This is the staging area for the day, a warm-up period held in a physical sciences classroom decorated with blue and red plastic plates hanging from the pipes, representing the planets. Perhaps on some days there are announcements or discussions. Not today. The students sit at their desks, Helena across from a boy in a gray sweatshirt and a baseball hat and on the diagonal from two girls, Bridget and Jennifer. Like all the students in the room, they are engaged in quiet conversation. Helena later reports that she was learning upsetting news from Jennifer, who works part-time at Pesto, a new upscale eatery. She found the nutritional information for Helena's favorite sandwich, smoked turkey and cheese, and notified her that it was 830 calories. Bad news for Helena. She is tall, about five feet eight inches, trim and lovely, but, like virtually every girl her age, and despite her good looks, she worries about her weight.

* * *

"We're going to discuss the whole of *The Scarlet Letter,*" begins Mrs. Lord, the English teacher. "If you get cold, let me know and you can go get your coat, but the heat may come up."

The room is quite chilly. Mrs. Lord is clearly recovering from a cold herself. There are speaking gaps in her voice, she is sniffling, and there is a bottle of water on the edge of the desk, close at hand. She speaks with authority, in spite of her illness: an admirable effort. We're in an honors English class, the highest level available to an eleventh-grader at Kensington. It is the wrap-up day for the great American novel by Nathaniel Hawthorne. Most adults who recall having read the book in high school do not remember it fondly. Mrs. Lord takes us back to the final scene of the book, when the Reverend Dimsdale mounts the pillory to finally tell the truth about his adulterous relationship with Hester.

"What does Dimsdale do when he comes out of the church?" she asks.

Long pause.

A blond girl to Helena's right says, "He looks at Hester."

"What does Chillingworth think of that?"

Long pause.

"He doesn't want Dimsdale to do that," answers Helena.

"The pillory is a place of truth," says Mrs. Lord. "So Dimsdale tells the truth, finally. He tears open his shirt." She looks directly at the students, a look of respect, if not curiosity. "What's on his chest?"

Long pause.

"The letter *A,*" replies a dark-haired boy in the row to our left.

"So Dimsdale tears open his shirt and then conveniently dies, which has always bugged me," Mrs. Lord says, injecting the first personal note into the discussion. I wish she would tell us why she teaches this book year after year if she thinks Hawthorne is manipulating us with Dimsdale's death. I wish she would go a little further and tell us about her reaction to this book, or ask ours. She doesn't. She plows ahead, reminding us that Pearl cries at the death of Dimsdale, proving she isn't a witch, because real witches cannot cry.

She continues to ask questions, which are answered, after the mandatory pause, by the same four students. The hesitation, the two-count, between her questions and the student responses has a deliberate, almost ritualized quality that conveys some message. I don't understand it, but sitting there, I try to interpret it. Are they telling the teacher that the questions are too simple and the answers are obvious? Are they letting her know that they hate the book? Is it because it is Monday? Is it simply too early in the morning to work up a head of steam about some hypocritical minister long ago in Massachusetts? I cannot read the answer in their faces. The rows of silent adolescents, including Helena, are sitting upright and staring ahead as if they are engaged, but they are on automatic pilot.

At lunchtime I mention to Helena that in her English class few students answered Mrs. Lord's questions. "Is it always like that?" I ask.

"Yes. Not many kids answer questions in that class."

I ask her why and she doesn't exactly tell me. Instead, she gives me a surprising response. "I answer her questions because I feel bad for her," Helena tells me. "I feel guilty that no one answers."

Once she says it I remember the feeling clearly from my own days in school. I remember trying to prop up some teachers because it made me feel miserable that they were dying up there, like bad stand-up comedians. Today I hadn't experienced Mrs. Lord quite that way. Though her class wasn't riveting, I respected her for being a well-meaning adult, courageously tackling one of the hardest jobs on earth: facing a group of twenty teenagers at 8:40 in the morning and trying to get them interested in Nathaniel Hawthorne. However, mine is the adult point of view. What does Helena think? I remind her that she had told me as we went into class that Mrs. Lord was a good teacher. I inquire again. "Is she an effective teacher?"

"Yes," Helena says with conviction, "but she's absent about one day a week."

"Why is she out so often?"

Helena shrugs. "She must have a lot of sick days saved up," she says. "She's close to retirement." Then Helena defends her: "She doesn't take it off because she doesn't want to teach us. It's not that she doesn't like us. She just doesn't want to come."

"How old is she?"

"She was born in 1949," reports Helena, a fact she picked up from some class discussion.

I calculate. "That makes her fifty-three, a long way from retirement."

"She's been teaching thirty years," Helena informs me. "Most teachers retire as soon as they can after fifty-six, I think."

And how does Helena feel about the fact that her teacher exercises her union-given right to use up her sick days?

"The only thing that bothers me," Helena says, "is that students can't do the same thing."

In their book about schools and the "moral contract," entitled *The Students Are Watching,* Ted and Nancy Sizer remind us that the most important thing teachers provide for students are models of behavior:

> By means of their design, all high schools teach. Their rules and routines are lessons of substance and value. Thoughtfully or unthinkingly students and teachers ingest these values, thereby learning to live by them. These lessons may promote optimism or cynicism, hard work or shortcuts. Most often . . . they promote different attitudes in different classes, so the student herself is left with the job of sorting it all out.

That is exactly what Helena has done every day she has been in school: sorted it out. Her psychological strategy for managing school has been profoundly optimistic: to work hard, trust the environment, see the good in her teachers, and try to bring out the best in her classmates by helping them succeed. She is, by any definition, a great student. Therefore, it was somewhat surprising that at the beginning of my very first conversation with her, in response to my question about the difference between her view of school and that of her parents, she told me, "My parents think it is so great. They would be surprised to hear it, but I can't wait till school is over."

Besides the normal wish to grow older and become more autonomous, what is it that makes her want to leave school? In small part, it is teachers like Mrs. Lord, whom she likes, but who are a psychological burden for her. Helena struggles to retain her optimism in the face of her English teacher's intermittent commitment. I can see that she does not want to say anything critical of her English teacher.

"I like Mrs. Lord," I say, while looking directly at Helena. "I think she's a good person, but I wonder whether she's a bit burned out as a teacher."

Helena glances away. "Yeah, I imagine she is."

This lunch conversation occurred three hours after the class, but knowing a little bit more about Helena's perspective allows us to return to Mrs. Lord's classroom for the remainder of the discussion of *The Scarlet Letter* better equipped to view the experience through Helena's eyes. (Besides, I'm not going to let the reader skip out on English!) Mrs. Lord is now up at the board, writing things in chalk.

"It feels like the heat is coming up, or maybe it's because I'm up and moving around," says Mrs. Lord. The two blackboards are so old it appears they can never be fully cleaned. They've absorbed too much white chalk to ever be black again. There is a string of white Christmas lights strung along the bottom of the blackboard, attached to the shelf that holds the erasers. That festive touch helps to liven up the place, but the truth is that the entire room, and the lesson itself, feels timeworn. There are file cabinets against the wall with pieces of blue duct tape holding the drawers shut. The faded blue *Peanuts* poster of Snoopy lying on top of a dog house reading a book feels vaguely poignant, like a relic from an elementary school classroom. Perhaps it refers to the last time many of these students spontaneously read for pleasure. I hope that's not true. To the left of Mrs. Lord is a desk piled with manila folders that look as if they have been there for years. I search for any modern touch, and there it is, right in front of me. To the right of her classic wooden teacher's desk, decorated with a NO WHINING sign, is a more modern steel desk with a computer, monitor, and printer on it. I am glad to see it, glad that the teacher has a computer, but am reminded of how quickly and obviously technology ages. Most of the students in the room—this is an affluent suburb—probably have a better computer at home. I know Helena does.

I am reminded of a student a few years ago who attended a state education technology conference. In the open-mike forum following the keynote address by the state superintendent of Education, the student urged him to devote more money to computers and technology training—for teachers. "We want to be able to learn *from* our teachers," he said, "but right now it's mostly *us* teaching *them*." For most students in America, technologically speaking, their teacher is their poor relative.

None of this would matter if the sources of life in this English classroom, Mrs. Lord and the kids, were producing some heat. It isn't happening. No sparks. From time to time there is a little smoke, but no moment of excitement when the discussion ignites. It isn't that Mrs. Lord doesn't try. She is moving back and forth among the points of the lesson she writes on the board—"symbols," "romanticism," and "plot structure"—and attempts to share real-life experiences with which the teenagers might identify. After telling us that every time Dimsdale goes to the pillory it is a high point in the drama, she draws three mountaintops and labels them chapters 2, 12, and 23. She then draws stick figures standing on a pillory and round faces looking up at them. I find the visual display engaging. She goes on to tell us that a fifteen-year-old girl on her street got pregnant—people right near our homes are having illicit sex—and her large Catholic family did not shun or hide or abandon her. "They were very open about it. They did not hide it the way they would have in my day," declares Mrs. Lord.

She then asks the class to discuss aspects of human nature: hypocrisy, ostracism, and adultery. Gritty stuff. Although she tries to generate some sympathy for Hester—"she was so isolated"—and again offers a personal observation—"I know from friends of mine that adultery can really mess up a relationship"—she cannot get a discussion going. I imagine the response if she were to ask the class, "Have any of you suffered because of adultery in your families? Have any of you ever known a hypocritical adult who reminds you of Dimsdale?" but I am aware that I am just entertaining myself. Teachers cannot ask these things in class. Yet, the hooks for a lively discussion are there, right under the surface. Adultery, divorce, and community hypocrisy have surely touched the lives of students in this class. Is there any way to harness the energy pent up in the collective life experience of these twenty sixteen- and seventeen-year-olds? I have seen a few teachers who can do it, but that's not going to help Helena and her classmates right now.

I'm here to try to see it through Helena's eyes. And what does she see next? Mrs. Lord, having touched on some of the juiciest topics in human life, is now sitting in a chair starting to free-associate about

Dimsdale's final assertion, "Of penitence, I have known." The phrase has power for Mrs. Lord. Apparently, there was a principal, a bad man, who headed Kensington High twenty-two years ago. In her estimation, many faculty members behaved hypocritically in their relationship with this educator. She implies that her colleagues should long since have climbed the pillory and repented, like Dimsdale. Dressed professionally in gray slacks, a blue blazer decorated with a gold pen, and gray shirt, she tells the class: "I still won't have a cup of coffee with some teachers here. They were so—and I hate to insult you—adolescent. They sucked up to him."

This surprising revelation apparently produces no reaction whatsoever in her students. Something interesting does happen, however, in the next few moments. Having finished the lesson three or four minutes before the end of the period, Mrs. Lord relaxes and starts to speak in a more casual, less teacherly manner. She is at ease with the kids. She commiserates with a girl about the deteriorating binding on her paperback copy of *The Scarlet Letter*. "These only last about two years," she says. "The hardback editions"—she points to a few lying in reserve on the desk with the manila folders—"some of them have lasted thirty years."

Helena is sitting in the second row, only a couple of feet from Mrs. Lord. She turns to me and says in a voice easily loud enough for her teacher to hear, "Now we're going to math. You'll see what an idiot my math teacher is. This is the most horrible experience."

Mrs. Lord asks the name of the math teacher. Having heard it, she says to me, "I don't know her." Then she explains, "We're having trouble keeping math teachers. Many of them haven't taught before."

Walking to math class, I ask Helena what she likes about Mrs. Lord. "She's connected to the kids and she seems to know what high school is like." That might sound like faint praise. It is not, especially in light of what I am about to witness: Helena's math teacher's complete emotional disconnection from her class.

We arrive at a side door. Helena bangs on it, two quick knocks that are quite aggressive. "We hate going around to the front door," she says. Another student opens it for her. It is the first time I have seen any strong emotion from Helena. She is girding her loins for this period. The math class has to finish a test that they began on Friday, Helena tells me. Though the radiators in the building are clanking, this room is also cold. At the beginning of class, all the students are grouped and talking in knots of three or four. The teacher, Mrs. Williams, is walking among the students, conferring with a few of them. It doesn't quiet down quickly and a few kids are calling out, "Mrs. Williams . . . Mrs. Williams," in a tone that has an edgy quality. I recognize it as the same tone that small children use when they are calling their mom, not really for help but to be slightly irritating. I had an elementary school friend who kept asking his mother, "Do you love me? Do you love me?" over and over until she blew up in annoyance. "Of course I love you," she shouted furiously. "Now, don't ask me again!" My friend was quite triumphant that he had probed his mother's anger by asking her a love question that she was compelled to answer. I think there is a subtle attempt by several students to needle Mrs. Williams, but on this day, no one is going to get a display of anything like anger from her. She is completely psychologically inaccessible.

> "I felt hopeless when I didn't finish my social studies, and then I found out we had to color it too. I wish I could've gotten out of that one."
>
> (Fifth-grader)

The sound level is higher than at any point in Mrs. Lord's class, but by no means is this class out of control or near to it. These are serious students in an advanced math class. Helena is giving help with equations to some classmates gathered around her. Mrs. Williams hands out what I assume to be the tests, but which turn out to be worksheets. She doesn't have enough for everyone. After a huddled conversation, she hands some sheets of paper to a gregarious girl in very low-rise jeans and a short shirt showing a lot of midriff, who takes them and flounces out of the room.

Some students begin working on their papers; others stare at them. One boy, in a handsome blue-and-green sweatshirt, is lying, head on arm, on his desk. The boy behind him in a gray sweatshirt is staring straight ahead, immobile, as if hearing voices, or attempting to hold his breath for the entire period.

Mrs. Williams turns on the overhead projector, and fifteen equations in tiny, tiny handwriting are cast up onto the screen. Originally written with a light pencil, even at this level of magnification they are barely legible. Moreover, they are jammed together very tightly.

There is something spectacularly passive-aggressive about this suffo-cating visual display; the teacher has made these equations manda-tory to study, but also virtually impossible to read. It is as if the equations themselves are taunting the class, daring anyone to read them. As Mrs. Williams launches into the lesson on negative expo-nents, most of the boys have their arms folded and are staring, with the exception of the boy lying with his head down on his desk. I now understand that I am watching a full-fledged stealth war between teacher and students, each using any weapons at their disposal.

"Are there any problems you want to discuss?" Mrs. Williams asks, glancing up at the square of light filled with her tiny hieroglyph-ics. No response. The room is dead and hopeless.

"There's one I want to go over with you," says the teacher. "It is addition x to the 3 plus x to the 3."

The girl comes back from photocopying the papers for the teacher. Mrs. Williams examines them unhappily and questions the way they have been copied. The girl, posturing for effect, counters, "You *said* double-sided," in an exasperated tone of voice, looking not at her teacher but to the faces of her classmates. Her contemptuous tone of voice, her attire, and her posture are a declaration to her peers: "I'm no suck-up. I didn't do a favor for this teacher because I wanted to." I am struck by the fact that at no point in Mrs. Lord's class did I hear this tone of voice—commonly known as "attitude"—from a student.

I look around the classroom, taking in the blue venetian blinds bowed at the bottom and pulled halfway up the windows. Outside, a beautiful snow falls. It startles me and gives me a pang of longing. I want to be out of school walking in the snow, even though walking in the snow is not something I generally enjoy doing. At the moment anything but this math class would be a relief. It is now 9:42.

Mrs. Williams runs through several problems on the board, sev-eral times asking, "Any questions?" No one answers. It is close to im-possible to pay attention to this teacher. She seems smart, she's not mean, her voice isn't inherently boring, and as far as I can tell she isn't going too fast. She just makes no contact whatsoever. She has withdrawn so far back inside herself that she isn't ever going to take a risk in front of kids, beyond showing up for class. No personal obser-vations or disclosure. No banter about math or about anything.

"Enough of negative exponents," she says. "You have a work-sheet. Get some practice. The rest of the class, you can finish the test you started on Friday. Others can do the worksheets." She starts handing out the tests. The disconnect is complete. The period is not over but class might as well be. At least the intense, silent power struggle that characterized the first twenty minutes is now done. There is no more need for guerrilla warfare on either side. Three boys are now playing around with their calculators. Two boys are talking, and the boy in the green-and-blue shirt who had sat with his head down for most of the period is up and smiling now, staring at his cal-culator. Helena later tells me that all the boys have games pro-grammed into their calculators. The teacher either is clueless or doesn't care.

Now that all the tests are handed out, the class focuses on their papers. This counts: tests = grades. The boy in the green-and-blue sweatshirt sits up, calculator out, focused on his paper. His leg bounces constantly. He leans forward, hands at the sides of his neck holding up his head, fingers stroking his hair. Mrs. Williams walks among the students. The boy in the gray sweatshirt in the back of the room is now jackknifed forward, his chest on the desk, staring right at the floor. He has been in an unhappy posture during the entire class. I don't know why he isn't working on either paper, but it is clear that he is on strike. The three girls who had been social are now focused, no longer talking. Another student gets up to take a Kleenex from a box at the front of the room. Mrs. Williams circles over and talks to the boy in gray for a considerable length of time. After she leaves him, he is noticeably more relaxed. He still does no work for the re-mainder of the period, but it was clearly a relief for him to talk with her. He has come out of his stricken, miserable place. After Mrs. Williams leaves him, he leans forward and jokes with the boys in front of him. Because I am shadowing Helena, I do not learn his story. No doubt he has one.

The students pass in their test papers. Advanced math ends on a classic note. One girl asks, "Are all these problems worth the same number of points?"

Walking down the hall together, Helena gives me a wither-ing commentary, saying that the math teacher doesn't know how to explain anything. She cannot make herself understood. It has been like that since the third week of school, when the kids realized that she couldn't teach.

Says Helena, with resignation: "I try to pay attention. I actually want to learn." Her voice conveys the futility of trying to listen to this teacher. Was she listening to the lesson on negative exponents? "No," says Helena, "I was doing the worksheet."

At lunch, Helena informs me that her father had called the school to complain about the math teacher. He wasn't the only one. The father of her friend did as well. Both parents were told that the school was lucky to have found a math teacher of her experience. She had worked for ten years at the high school in another highly rated district, one with some of the highest scores in the state. She is glad that I have been able to witness the math class: "I wanted you to see my math teacher because I wanted you to understand how hellish the week is. Why we dread it. There's just no enjoyment."

> "In eighth grade everybody gets distracted. It's like if you've been in jail for eight years and you can see you're gonna get out."
>
> (Tenth-grader)

We head to Spanish class. At the door of the room Helena announces, in front of the teacher: "This is my best class." The teacher, Mrs. Arboleda, greets us warmly. A small, dark-haired woman in an attractive black sweater outfit with a striped jacket, she has a big smile. Energy radiates from her. Music plays on an old tape recorder: a green thing with a black plastic handle that looks as if it were manufactured in 1973. There is a bouncy tune underscored by an accordion. The class, Spanish 3, is conducted completely in Spanish. I am lost from the beginning, but it is obvious the teacher wants the students to listen to the words of the song. She asks them questions about the lyrics and they reply.

The conversation shifts. There is only one boy in this class, a dark-haired, golden-tan boy who might be Latino himself. At first, only Helena speaks, but soon other girls are speaking up and the boy chimes in. They are clearly having a conversation about everyday events. We are fifteen minutes into the period before the kids take out their books to do a lesson, *Primer Paso*. The teacher brings me a text-

book and asks whether I speak Spanish. I say no, and she is clearly
sad that she cannot include me in the fun.

A colorful page lists the vocabulary words: "*A la vaz* . . . at the
same time"; "*la autopista* . . . freeway, highway"; "*el rascacielos* . . .
skyscraper." After some discussion, the teacher leads the students
through a verbal recitation of the words. It is 10:45 and I am tired at
this point. It already feels like a long school day. However, the students cannot take their eyes off the Spanish teacher. She moves constantly, asking questions in a constant stream, always in connection
with her writing on the board. The pace is faster than English class
and there is a spontaneous feel to it. Mrs. Arboleda is the embodiment of natural authority and the Spanish language itself.

After giving instructions, five students, including Helena, head
for the blackboard, writing sentences that use the vocabulary words.
Helena writes, "*Adaptarse: cambiarse para vivir mejor en situa-
ciones nuevas.*" When Mrs. Arboleda calls on Helena, she reads her
answer with the confidence of the best language student in the class.
"*Mucho gusto,*" the teacher declares, with emphasis, while moving
immediately to call on the next student.

The room, like the teacher, is cheerful. It doesn't have the ancient
feel of the English teacher's room or the sterile feeling of the math
teacher's. Once again, Snoopy lies on top of a dog house. Here, however, the poster colors are vibrant and he is asking, "*¿Cuánto falta
para el fin de semana?*" There is a map of South America, a Picasso
drawing of a bullfight, and a classic black sketch of Don Quixote and
Sancho Panza on their horses, the sun in the background. Most of all,
there are student projects everywhere, tacked to the walls or mounted
on poster-board triptychs: Galicia, Andalusia, Aragon, Castilla la
Mancha, featuring bullfights, cheeses, rock formations, and literary
figures from the different regions.

After a different set of instructions, Helena is up again in front of
the class, reading a poem written on a large cutout snowflake with a
photo of a winter scene on it. After she has finished her recitation, she
goes to the teacher's desk to get tape and adds her snowflake to the
wall, as do two girls who follow her. When she returns to her desk,
she tells me that she wrote the poem she recited. Was it difficult?
"No, I just don't like it very much." Mrs. Arboleda is showing us
someone's project: a living room, a tree, and a Christmas scene. She

says, *"Muy bueno,"* and she's right. It is lovely. I cannot see which student made it, but she is relying on the teacher to show it off for her.

The teacher makes another change, the fourth shift in emphasis in the period. Mrs. Arboleda hands out white paper. Helena returns to her desk and explains that they have to make snowflakes and put wishes on them for the New Year. She folds the paper over and tries to make a snowflake, cutting down the middle. Two girls watch her and she says, "Don't watch me." She is dissatisfied, because she cut on the fold and the diamond-cut shapes go down the middle of the page. She gets up to get a new piece of paper. As the kids cut out their snowflakes, the teacher encourages them.

The bell rings and the teacher shouts, *"Ay caramba,"* in disappointment that the time is over. She stands at the door and bids her students good-bye: *"¡Adios!"*

"We have to go up a lot of stairs," Helena informs me. Indeed we do: three flights, kids streaming by in all directions. I feel like an ant might in an ant farm, squeezing through narrow passageways. The central staircase enclosed in glass starts in the middle of the cafeteria. Creating a common gathering point is probably what the architect intended. However, it turns the cafeteria into a subway station. We arrive at the chemistry lab on the third floor, the coldest classroom so far, disproving the scientific point (at least in this building) that heat rises.

Ms. Holland, a young teacher with cascading curly hair, glasses, and a broad face, wears a wool jacket, blue sweater, and long, tan skirt. It seems surprising that she is not wearing a parka; some of the kids in the class do. One girl is wearing a Bates sweatshirt. A boy wears a Red Sox baseball hat backward and a New England Patriots jersey number 54 with BRUSCHI on the back. Glancing around the class, you'd have to say that in general the local sports teams are well represented by the boys, colleges by the girls. An Asian-American boy with a shaved head wears only a red T-shirt. Isn't he freezing?

Ms. Holland has a high tolerance for noise and works quickly. She hands out a worksheet on moles and mole ratios, which helps explain the presence of a sticker on the metal flue over a lab table that declares, "A chemist's best friend is a mole." You may wonder, what are moles and mole ratios in chemistry? If you don't know, then you have a sense of how most of the students in this class felt a few days earlier when the concept was introduced, and how some of the students clearly still feel today despite Ms. Holland's instruction and homework assignments. Regardless, copies of the worksheet are being passed around and Ms. Holland expects the students to get to work on it. They do, but there is a lot of noise and discussion going on, particularly from a boy up front in a baseball hat. He is entertaining a group of girls. The number of boys in the class creates a chemistry of its own in the room. More boys = more physical energy, more restlessness, more noise.

Ms. Holland says, "Well, if everyone is finished or no one is working on this, we should do it as a class. Get out your calculators." She then goes quickly across the columns she has written on the board, asking for values. "How many moles of oxygen do I have?" The boys jump in to answer.

"We're going to turn this into mole ratios. We want a nice whole number." She writes "1,1,4" on the board. "So what is our final formula?" Pause. "Amy?"

"$FeCrO_4$."

"And what is that?"

"Iron II chromate," Amy says.

"So this is iron II?" asks a boy.

"Iron II chromate," emphasizes the teacher.

Helena is seated in the middle of the class of twenty-two students, ten boys and twelve girls crowded in a small central space surrounded by lab tables.

"There is always a relationship between the empirical formula and the true formula. We've spent the last two days solving empirical formulas," the teacher reminds the class. Many of the kids are talking now. I hear a lot of boy voices. The early sleepiness of the first three periods is lifting: Kids want to talk.

"Let's get this empirical formula worked out," the teacher says. "You can all do these problems," she calls out, and repeats, a little more loudly, *"You can all do these problems."* She picks a girl to work out the problem on the board. "Way too many people talking," observes the teacher, and then repeats it: *"Way too many people talking."* The sound level slightly drops and she races along. It is tough to keep up with the pace of this class. You have to be on your toes.

In the midst of all this, Helena is a calm island, wearing silver reading glasses and working her problems. She smiles and talks a bit with Corey, the girl next to her. At one point, the two girls go up to the teacher's desk. The teacher writes Corey a pink slip, and Helena waits patiently as Corey leaves the room holding the slip in her hand. A student may be sixteen years old, but she still needs to get a permission slip to go to the bathroom—and only one at a time.

"May I have everyone's attention?" says Ms. Holland. "I've been looking over everyone's shoulders and most people have this, but you *need* to know it."

We do the formula for nylon, and then for urea, the main component of urine. There is a bit of giggling at the mention of urine.

Ms. Holland breaks the class into small groups. "Get together with your base groups and work on number seven," she instructs. "Can everyone find their base groups?"

"No," says one girl, though everyone begins to move. Helena switches from one side of the room to another. A group of four boys stand two-and-two across a lab table tossing humorous jibes back and forth. The social boy in the baseball hat surrounded by girls hasn't moved: His base group and his all-girl social group appear to be one and the same.

Two boys and a girl stand at the lab table right beside me. Initially, the boys don't seem at ease working with the girl. Tall and athletic-looking, in a crimson sweatshirt embroidered with KENSINGTON ICE HOCKEY in gold thread, she takes the initiative and starts to read the problem out loud. Their small work group comes together. The room is filled with good spirit.

"We do have a test coming up on Thursday," says Ms. Holland, her voice rising. No one is paying much attention now, or at least they are not looking. Everyone knows that the bell is about to ring for lunch. "Tomorrow is the seventeenth. I want three references on your chemical-company project." The noise level is growing. "You guys did very well today," she shouts over the rising din. It is difficult to tell how industrious the students are, but clearly the teacher enjoys being with the kids. And it's clear that she trusts them, because she allows them to be kids in her classroom.

Indeed, the sense of trust between teachers and students turns out to be an excellent measure of the quality of the day's experience for

"The things about school that I absolutely hate aren't very important. I hate the bathroom monitors who are so vigilant. . . . They interrogate you and will even reach under the stall for your pass. I also wish we had longer than 3 minutes to get from class to class because I have some classes that are on the other side of the school. The most important thing I hate is probably teachers who treat their students as inferiors." (Eleventh-grader)

Helena—from the distant and hostile environment of the math class to the warm and trustworthy Spanish class. Chemistry clearly falls on the trustworthy side of the line. Ms. Holland informs me that after earning her Ph.D., she worked for several years as a chemist in a corporate lab. "It took me a few years to realize that it wasn't for me," she said. "Teaching is."

We head for the cafeteria and are joined by Helena's friend Paula. Helena takes her lunch out of her backpack. She *never* buys lunch in the cafeteria, pronouncing the school's food "disgusting." Her father makes lunch for her every day. It is not an economic matter for her family; it is an issue of nutrition, personal pride, and family style. Our twenty-minute lunch break feels like a quick ten; then Helena stands up and stuffs the remainders of her lunch into a brown bag and then into her backpack. We're off to class again.

I confess that I was tired at the beginning of Spanish, around 10:40 A.M. I glanced at my watch several times and felt a bit of a headache coming on in chemistry class. True, that was the coldest classroom of all, but I think the biggest factor was the loss of my autonomy. I'm not accustomed to conforming to someone else's schedule unless I am being paid to do it. At the end of lunch, I am grateful that we have only two more classes to go to. I check with Helena about the dismissal hour for school and am disappointed to learn that it is 2:30, not 2:15, as I had believed. Fifteen minutes have never seemed longer.

We expect that kids will be good-natured about the school schedule because going to school is, in a sense, all they have known since kindergarten. Our educational system operates on the assumption that students *should be* compliant to the demands of school. From the point of view of child psychology, and especially adolescent psychology, that is an extraordinary assumption. Quite the contrary is true. Research on adolescent mental health suggests that the most powerful variable in determining the mood state of a teenager is the role she is occupying at that moment—daughter, friend, student, girlfriend, employee, etc.—and, in particular, whether she has a sense of control over her own life.

From a psychological standpoint, going to school becomes more and more difficult as children grow older, even more so in later adolescence. One would predict that the more time they spend in school, the worse their mood would be. That is why I was getting a headache in Helena's chemistry class. As adults, too, we don't like being in a subordinate role. Perhaps the most important thing we need to remember is that it is a remarkable daily act of discipline, love, faith, and moral commitment for teenagers—indeed for all children—to go to school at all.

This reservoir of unquestioned compliance drops when children feel misunderstood or misused. A compliant attitude fades even more when they have passed the age of sixteen, at which point they are no longer legally required to attend: a factor in the psychology of dropouts that we'll explore in a later chapter.

At this moment in my day shadowing Helena it is *for me* an act of personal discipline to stand up from this brief respite and launch myself back to class for two more hours. Helena, too, would welcome the opportunity to end her school day now. Her staying is an act of love. She does this to honor her family and their hopes for her. It is also an act of faith: She has to believe that her attendance at school, her attendance in a class, and her listening to a teacher and doing the homework are going to lead to a better life, even when she cannot feel the connection between the present boring or difficult moment and the more exciting, satisfying future she imagines.

Finally, going to school is a voluntary moral commitment because kids outnumber adults. If they wanted to, the children could get up as a group and walk out of school and the adults could not physically stop them. This is as true in an elementary school as it is in a high school. Ted and Nancy Sizer, addressing the problem of the "voluntary moral order in schools," write that in order to operate successfully, schools have to have "a collective culture, a 'moral order,' but one which is in balance with individual autonomy. . . . There is a strain in all this, but the end does justify the means. A community's functioning rests on trust, and trust comes from the understanding that emerges from dialogue."

Even Helena, a highly successful student who is fully prepared to go to college for four more years, told me that it would surprise her parents to know how anxious she is to get out of high school. When she told me this she was in the early days of her junior year. She had met all of her teachers and was embarking on a year of "dialogue" with them. She found it difficult to trust her math teacher from the first class. She found the very first assignment insincere. This is what she wrote to me at the time:

> I met all of my teachers today. My math teacher assigned us a two-paragraph paper about our interests and our "relationship" with math. I have had similar assignments in the beginnings of previous years and though it may sound cynical, I don't believe that most of these teachers care very much about our interests and/or our relationships with the subjects they teach. Over the past several years, I have noticed that teachers try to make an effort to become more personal, but often it doesn't go very far, except with a select few.

By contrast, on that very first day, Helena loved her psychology teacher:

> She was very nice and honest about herself and straightforward when she told us about the class. When she was talking to us this afternoon, she made her speech sound more like she was having a casual conversation with us rather than a lecture. She also treated us like equals rather than looking down at us.

I had been looking forward to meeting this psychology teacher for several months based on e-mails from Helena. It was not to be. Sadly, the psychology teacher had left the school for medical reasons related to a difficult pregnancy and complicating illness. There would be a substitute in the psychology class today. It will be a waste of time, Helena tells me.

Does she feel that much of her time in school is wasted? No, she says, but she feels that way in Italian and Spanish because she cares so much about language and other kids don't seem to. She doesn't mind in the other courses, she says, because she doesn't care about them. That is, she has at some level given up on getting much out of English, math, chemistry, and psychology. Her hopes are fully engaged only in her language courses.

The Italian teacher meets us at the door and greets us warmly but defensively. The class is "heterogeneity in spades," she says. There aren't enough students, or enough money in the district budget, to justify having two separate Italian classes. The class I'm about to see is a combined group: seven students in third-year Italian and three in fourth-year Italian. What becomes clear quickly is that only six really care about Italian or have mastered enough to be comfortable answering the teacher's questions. Four students behave as if the language were an embarrassing surprise that had just been sprung on them. Helena had warned me that some students "don't remember anything from last year," and that "the teacher has to keep reminding them."

Signora Cognati guides the entire class through an exercise on the use of the conditional tense. The students all have a worksheet and are supposed to fill in the blanks with the conditional forms of the verb. She then calls on them to read their answers out loud. Helena silently mouths every sentence before one of her classmates says it. She is intensely focused. By contrast, Kevin, the boy in the baseball hat who had been the center of attention in a social group in chemistry class, is doing his best to celebrate his own incompetence with the language: smiling, mugging, hesitating, and, finally, answering. The classic clown, he entertains the two girls sitting beside him, forcing his teacher to slow down the pace of the lesson in order to adapt to him. Though she is temporarily his hostage, Signora Cognati perseveres with remarkable grace. She looks him in the eye, meets him at his level of ability, and challenges him to speak Italian. She is never sarcastic or angry.

Signora Cognati knows that to get into a power struggle with

Kevin would only alienate him further from the class and the language. That would defeat her purpose. Signora Cognati obviously wants her students to love Italian and she is a remarkable ambassador for the language. She is hostage not only to Kevin but to the small enrollment for Italian—any fewer students and she would be out of a job—and the profound disinterest that so many American teenagers have in learning foreign languages. Unlike European students, whose daily experience includes adults who are competent in many languages, American students have difficulty feeling the relevance of learning foreign languages. Forty percent of the members of the United States Congress do not have passports and have never been abroad. These students are not so different from adult Americans. Helena is the exception here.

The girl behind Kevin is Melanie, one of the most—if not *the* most—gifted athletes in the high school. She is moving constantly within the confines of her desk, sometimes sitting up, sometimes lounging with her head back and legs outstretched, sometimes lying with her face on her arm. Being pinned in a desk is obviously tough for her. Furthermore, her identity rests on her athletic ability, not her performance in academics. When Signora Cognati changes the exercise and asks a girl named Rita to use the conditional in the sentence "If I could be any animal, I would be a . . ." the designated student hesitates, and Melanie shouts out, "A cheetah!" in English. Signora Cognati corrects her pronunciation of *cheetah* until it conforms to the Italian, but then says, "Let Rita choose her own animal." Melanie cannot be held back. "No, cheetah, they're so fast!" When Signora changes the sentence to "If I could change one thing about school . . ." Helena answers, "I would have all of the classes be language classes," and receives a contemptuous snort from Melanie, as if Helena's wish were beyond belief.

Melanie continues to interrupt and talk throughout the rest of the class, joking around with Kevin and two other students. Helena stares forward angrily. She tells me later, "I want to strangle them every day." She resents the behavior of the four Italian 3 students who have such a different level of motivation than her own. She attributes the problems in the class to the fact that it is not an honors section. In her mind the unmotivated students want only the appearance of a third-year language to impress the colleges to which they will apply. She believes that Signora Cognati is every bit as good as her Spanish teacher, and that her Italian class could be as good as Spanish 3 if it were an honors section.

Later she confides how it felt in the first days of the class: "When that whole group walked into Italian during the first week, I said, 'No!'" Dramatically, she holds her hands to her face. "They're lost. They know what we're doing now, but they don't remember anything. And by the end of the year they won't know anything."

Helena is experiencing the tensions produced by having students of radically different ability levels and motivation in the same classroom. She wishes to be with students who share her dedication to Italian, and thinks that if the school were tracked more effectively, her time—at least in her beloved subjects—would not be wasted.

The debate about tracking is one of the most ferocious in all of American education. The majority of the research evidence on tracking convincingly demonstrates that it doesn't necessarily improve learning for able students and can create a self-fulfilling prophecy of low expectations and low achievement for others. Viewing the class through Helena's eyes, however, it is hard not to share her wish to have equally motivated classmates.

As we leave Italian class, Signora Cognati seeks me out to tell me something surprising. She wants me to know that Helena took a national test at the end of Italian 1 and was the top-scoring student in the nation. She repeated the feat at the end of Italian 2, so she is a two-time national champion. (At no point in our August interview or in any of the e-mails she has been sending me over the course of four months has she ever mentioned this achievement.) Signora expresses her pride in Helena and says, "Maybe she will spend a year abroad in Italy, and then a year in Spain, and, who knows, a year in China," implying that Helena is so gifted in language that there is no language

---

"I do my work, but then my teachers are on my case if they think I'm not paying attention every minute. I'm not like daydreaming. I'm worried about my friends and their problems, and my mom has cancer and I'm thinking she's going to die. There's just no time to yourself and it's a long day." (Eighth-grader)

she could not master, given the opportunity. At the end of the school day, when I recall Signora Cognati's comment, Helena says, "It is really encouraging that she thinks I'm that good."

Our day at Kensington High School ends with a whimper, not a bang. Helena's beloved psychology teacher remains absent indefinitely, due to her serious illness. There is a substitute named George Habib, whose heavy Middle Eastern accent makes him difficult to understand. He lacks confidence. A human resources manager at a water-pumping plant in Jerusalem who moved when his wife became pregnant because "things were difficult," he has been a permanent substitute for two years while he has considered going for teacher certification, but he has decided that "teaching does not fit [his] talents." He is embarrassed to be substituting in a psychology class because he doesn't have any knowledge of the material. He makes it clear that other members of the faculty have helped him think up things to do in the class.

A majority of classes led by substitutes are a waste of students' time. When I had stopped by Kensington High School early on the previous Friday, the principal, Mr. Goodlad, groused that he had fifteen teachers out of work that day and was struggling to arrange coverage for the classes. He was bitter about having so many teachers out of work. Were they suffering from the flu? "They're suffering from the pre-Christmas flu," he commented ironically. "They need a long weekend to shop."

In the previous psychology class, Helena tells me, the class watched part of an inspiring film, *Stand and Deliver,* about an inner-city high school math teacher who believes in his students' innate ability and challenges them to enter a high-level math contest. Mr. Habib starts the class by declaring, "We're not going to discuss the movie. The one thing we won't do is reflect on the movie."

He then hands out copies of an outdated IQ test, linking it to the fact that the students in *Stand and Deliver* took an IQ test. The questions are both difficult and outdated. One girl says, "This makes me feel stupid." Most of the students take a stab at it, but don't make a real attempt to complete it. Mr. Habib has the answer sheet and he goes through the test with those who are interested, but everyone recognizes that this class is baby-sitting. Everyone waits for the final bell. Though the students are kind to Mr. Habib and generally well behaved, they are obviously disengaged. They talk among themselves. A few tease Helena, suggesting that she ended up being shadowed by an author because she is such a good student.

"Of course it would be you," one girl tells her. Helena's defense that she had come to my attention as the result of a coincidence (she baby-sits for my administrative assistant) is regarded as implausible. Her friendly critics prefer their theory, that she is a high-profile goody-goody. Later, Helena tells me that she has learned to ignore the teasing that comes her way as a result of her being an outstanding student. "It doesn't bother me. It is something I should be proud of and they shouldn't try to make me feel bad about being a good student. They don't do as well as me." Then, with compassion, she suggests, "Maybe their parents put too much pressure on them."

We have followed a high school junior on a typical Monday in December. There were no school shootings, no fights, no extraordinary assemblies, no principal roaming the halls with a megaphone confronting bullies and exhorting students to achieve. Nothing here would qualify as a plot for an episode of *Boston Public*. Kensington High School felt both safe and calm. Indeed, at the end of the day, Helena told me that she had wanted to show me a "nice school." She succeeded. However, it wasn't the school I was there to see, it was her school day, and Helena's school day was more than "nice." It was complex, full of tension and feeling. I had been witness to a meaningful slice of her life.

School has an enormous influence in the lives of young people, not just in terms of the academic preparation it provides them but also in terms of the moral and social lessons it teaches, and in the sense of identity they craft for themselves there. What happens to Helena in school contributes to who she is as a person. She is not, however, a passive recipient of these influences. She is absolutely aware of what she is learning about herself, about her abilities, about the motivation and hypocrisy of some adults, and the strengths and limitations of others. Nothing in the school environment is lost on her. Nor are the lessons she learns there necessarily the ones intended by the adults who crafted the curriculum or who present the material. The deeper lessons are those that emerge from her experience of the place, of herself in the place. No adult can know or understand all that she experiences. Her English teacher does not know her math teacher. Her parents probably have never had an extended conversation with any of her teachers. And none of them know—or know much—about how Helena feels about herself in the context of school and in the context of her inner life of dreams, desires, and disappointments. Helena is the only person with her brain, her motivation, her friends, and her experience. Helena's day belongs uniquely to her, and it is incredibly rich.

When I was young there was a television program called *The Naked City*. Each episode told a dramatic, unexpected story based in New York. At the beginning of the show the narrator would always intone: "There are eight million stories in the Naked City." Throughout the day with Helena, looking at the diversity of students in each class and in the halls, I thought how different the school day must certainly look through each one's eyes. What if I had been following Kevin, the socially magnetic boy in the baseball hat? What if I had been following the gifted girl athlete who was physically uncomfortable in Italian class?

Each student lives a different version of the day. Each student is growing up in school, meeting challenges, discovering strengths, confronting weaknesses and vulnerabilities, tolerating some aspects of the experience, and reaching his or her limits on others. Much as educators create the place for the day to unfold, and much as parents are familiar with the shape of the day and the curriculum presented there, it is only the child who knows the real story.

3

Children in Charge

The Miracle of Development

———

The only person who can really make me do my best,
do everything up to what it's supposed to be is me.
—*Erik, fifteen*

The things we know best are the things
we haven't been taught.
—*Vauvenargues,* Reflections and Maxims *(1746)*

A couple of weeks ago a boy, Reggie, came to see me in my office. We had a warm meeting, like two old friends. We had last spoken when he was an eighth-grader. For two years he had desperately wanted to leave the school and go anywhere else. He had no friends—at least not in the school—he was failing one course and had a D in another. He was feeling a great deal of despair, and was furious with a couple of his teachers. He fought them at every turn. From where he stood in eighth grade there seemed no way to make a success of himself in school.

It was four years later when he walked into my office, a senior, at six feet two, weighing 215 pounds, a varsity basketball player and track star. He came because he found that he was anxious and upset with himself a good deal of the time. He had fallen two points short of the honor roll last semester and was afraid he might not make the honor roll during the current marking period. Because I remembered him as a middle-school boy who struggled academically, I congratulated him on being such a strong student, but the admiration I expressed didn't assuage his concerns. Now his goal was to go to the college that his grandfather and uncle and aunt had gone to, and he was afraid that if he didn't make the honor roll for the whole of his junior year, he wouldn't be accepted there. He was frantic that he would not realize the goals he had set for himself.

How did this boy move from seventh-grade failure and despair to junior-year honor roll and its accompanying anxiety? It was certainly not something anyone would have predicted. The ability had always been there, but it had never been clear that he'd pull himself together to pass seventh grade. Indeed, he had to go to summer school between seventh and eighth grades just to avoid repeating. What factors might have contributed to his turnaround? Teachers who cared about him? Sure. Athletic success and the recognition that brought him? Without a doubt. Parental pressure? That almost certainly helped. Yet, all of those factors were in place in his life when he was in seventh grade and failing.

What had changed? He had matured. Though he was the same boy—still somewhat socially isolated—his development had delivered him to a different place psychologically than he had been as a middle-schooler. Not only had puberty turned him into a formidable physical specimen, his psychology had dramatically changed. He wasn't totally transformed, but in some fundamental ways, he was profoundly different.

DEVELOPMENT IS A MIRACLE AND SCHOOLS ARE THE STAGE

The reason I have stayed connected to schools my entire adult life is because they are the Broadway stage of development, and classrooms are the front-row seats. If you want to see the miracle of development played out on a grand scale, if you want to see all the dramas and the hit musicals, schools are the place to be. Children are always onstage there, showing us what's new. I never tire of seeing the story of growth played out in the life of a child.

The school year is a continuing backdrop against which children's growth and development stand out clearly for us—and to the children themselves, too. The third-grader who has learned cursive writing laughs when looking back at the block lettering she had used to write her name and fill out her worksheets when the year began. The incoming fifth-grader who found the labyrinth of hallways confusing that first week of school in September knows all the shortcuts by Thanksgiving. The boy who cringed at girl cooties in the fall of seventh grade sees girls in a different light by the time the spring dance rolls around.

Maturity happens. In retrospect, it generally happens in the right way, consistent with a child's identity. It can also be the case that a child's development is bafflingly slow, or different from others, or seriously delayed in a way that requires intervention. For the moment, however, I am going to stick to the course of normal development. Even when parents are confident that their children are on a normal path, they worry. American parents, in particular, do not trust development. They want to make it happen; they want to push it or feel they're controlling it. I've had the same impulse with my own children, when their childish ways became a burden to their mother and me. However, there is a useful distinction to be made here between being impatient with development sometimes and believing that development is something you can engineer like a new hybrid soybean. You can create a good growing space for a child—a family and home life, a school, and a community that support growth and development— but you can't *make* development happen.

Development is the fundamental engine of a growing child, and, to the extent that anyone is in control, the child is in charge. The mystery is how nature and nurture merge, and what person comes out of that ongoing process. Whatever else he is doing in math, science, English, and social studies, every child is also immersed in his own uniquely internal curriculum. Each must find a way to manage the opportunities and expectations of school and the deeper desires and demands of his own development. It is a huge job, an arduous and often painful one. For the most part, a child does it alone and unappreciated.

ALL CHILDREN ARE PINOCCHIO

Remember Gepetto, the puppeteer who carved Pinocchio? As much as he wished for a son, he couldn't turn Pinocchio into a real boy. Divine intervention did that, and bitter experience made Pinocchio a good and worthy boy. The story of Pinocchio illustrates how a young person has to follow his or her own developmental destiny, has to make mistakes, sometimes has to fall in with the wrong friends, tell lies, and get caught. The story of Pinocchio is a story of development. Its moral is that we cannot make kids out of wood; they create their own selves out of their own growth. The story is as much a reminder to parents about the limits of their power as it is a reminder to children to develop a conscience.

Throughout the story, Gepetto tries to find and save Pinocchio, but he cannot save either of them from anything. Indeed, he himself ends up in the belly of the whale. I like to think of this as a metaphor for parental helplessness and powerlessness in relation to the process of growth. Pinocchio ultimately helps to save his own father, just as all young people grow up to care for their parents and take over the world in their turn. Pinocchio's awakening arises within the context of his loving relationship with Gepetto, but it is not Gepetto's saving or doing that brings the wooden boy to life.

Kevin, who was clowning around in Helena's Italian class, is eventually going to have to grow up, whether or not he ever starts to love Italian. Being immature will eventually mean his peers will avoid him (Helena already does) and he will end up as an embarrassment to himself. Most likely, he will find his own behavior an obstacle to achieving something he wants. When he cannot get the jobs he wants or the respect of the boss who has the power to promote him, he will change his behavior.

Children get embarrassed by their own immature and childish behavior. They want to grow up. That, too, is the miracle of development.

BACK TO BASICS—EIGHT LINES OF DEVELOPMENT

Whoever summarized school learning as three basics—"reading, 'riting, and 'rithmetic"—grossly underestimated the task that confronts a child at school, and failed to include the most critical coursework of all: the developmental curriculum a child manages in school all day every day. Moving smoothly through the day, mastering physical skills and factual material, integrating socially into a new classroom, managing frustration, anger, and disappointment: These are all part of the developmental agenda of each day.

Great psychologists—Jean Piaget and Erik Erikson among them—have described child development in a number of ways: as a series of stages, each building on the achievements of the previous one; as different threads or lines; or as developmental "tasks," or growth homework, that a child must complete before he or she can move to the next life stage. We generally identify eight lines of development along which all children travel toward maturity and adulthood: (1) physical development; (2) the development of attachment; (3) social development; (4) cognitive development; (5) academic development; (6) emotional self-regulation; (7) moral and spiritual development; and (8) identity development.

Though it is extraordinarily clarifying for adults to think of development in this way—that's why I am going to rely on the "lines" paradigm—it is important to remember that a child doesn't see or experience things in this well-defined, linear way.

Children know they are in third grade and will be in fourth grade the next year, but they don't have any sense that they are in the "concrete-operational stage" and will move to the "preoperational" stage of cognitive thought. There are no yellow double lines, red lights, and orange cones outlining development. For the child, it is all one seamless enterprise. It is her life and it is all happening at once.

There are times when experiences feel separate from one another. If a student is playing volleyball she is aware that she is working on her athletic skills and not studying her math or socializing at the mall with her friends. For us, however, it is possible to see that when she is playing volleyball, she is also simultaneously developing her friendships, her sense of identity, and her close relationship with her coach.

Every child is simultaneously dealing with different challenges and must respond concurrently to each. Picture a Super Mario video game where the little Mario figure is climbing a ladder at top speed and suddenly runs out of rungs and has to leap sideways to another ladder in order to continue his journey, and you will have a sense of the pace and the threats that attend the developmental process.

"I have to get there," your child thinks. "I have to get there soon—oh, no—I died!" he exclaims when the fireballs drop on him or he encounters a hostile alien being quicker than he is. Then he picks himself up and continues upward again.

It would, however, be more accurate to say that every child has eight little Marios inside, making progress up eight different ladders of development, all at different rates. In no child does development proceed in a completely even way. It is typical for children to be at different places on all eight ladders at any given moment, and, inevitably, the gaps can make life uncomfortable or even emotionally harrowing.

Obvious examples come to mind: the early reader who is shy and frightened in the social arena; the gifted athlete who has learning differences and cannot organize himself; the child who is academically gifted but who struggles with poor small-motor coordination and can't write legibly.

When there is some significant discrepancy in a child's progress among the various ladders or lines of development, the child feels it. Children hate to fall behind. It's frightening. They also hate to be repeatedly rescued by their parents. It confirms their worst fears about themselves. In the developmental breach between where they are and where they want to be, it is their parents' faith in the developmental process (supported by parental memories of their own uneven growth) that will sustain a child's confidence. If parents can't summon that confidence, their responses become expressions of their own fears, only adding to their child's burden.

THE CHALLENGE: EIGHT LINES, EIGHT LADDERS

Do parents play some greater part in this intense drama than having faith in development and trying *not* to become a burden? Are they more than just spectators, standing on the sidelines watching their child negotiate these eight lines of development, watching them jump from ladder to ladder, sometimes missing and falling, sometimes hanging on for dear life? Do parents have any meaningful role here? Yes.

Parents, both explicitly and intuitively, help their children's development all the time. Not always aware of the ways in which their children are growing, however, at moments they unwittingly become obstacles to the process. It has been my experience that if parents have some understanding of the nature of development, it may help them trust the process and may prevent them from making clumsy, ill-conceived, or ill-timed interventions. As a prelude to our tour of school and the lives of some children there, I offer this short guide to the eight lines of development, as children experience them in the school realm.

Physical-Athletic Development

Children are, first and foremost, physical beings. Every child has to become accustomed to the body that nature gave her and wants to continually practice new physical abilities as they emerge. Throughout childhood, every child is working unself-consciously on mastering hundreds of physical tasks, learning to control her large movements and small ones. The child seeks to have control over her body. She wants to enjoy a confident relationship with her own physical being.

Children rush out the door to recess, running and skipping, then shooting hoops, kicking a ball around or practicing batting, climbing jungle gyms and skipping rope. All that exercise is tiring work—or would be for an adult. Children consider it play. For most of them, being outside is fun and, even though their activity may require intense concentration and exertion, they do it because nature impels them to do it. They want to practice and get better at the physical task, both for the intrinsic satisfaction of being skillful and because they see other boys and girls, and men and women, do it. Whatever the child chooses to do, he thinks that succeeding at it will solidify his identity and win recognition among peers. He is right. The same child who struggles desperately with handwriting in class may be the kickball star because gross motor skills and fine motor skills develop independently of one another.

All children are physical beings, but not all children are born athletic. Some do not have, on a physiological basis, the muscle strength or coordination that other children do have. For such children, structured PE classes and organized athletics are a nightmare. They may need more support to keep up their willingness to try things that are athletic, or they may need exposure to many things that allow them to use their bodies but are not overtly athletic at all. If you want to see happy children, visit a summer camp that offers a wide variety of choices, from competitive water sports to an art barn and a nature center. A boy or girl who isn't interested in a competitive swim race may spend hours walking around the woods trying to find luna moth pupae.

Because the physical-developmental needs of children are so diverse, schools are rarely able to devise a physical education program that pleases all the children all the time. Over the years that I have been a school consultant, I have talked with many children about their physical opportunities in school. Elementary school children, boys especially, tell me that PE and recess are the best parts of their day. They feel terribly confined in the classroom and being able to exercise is the highlight of the day.

Other children report that PE period is a waste of time, that they don't really get any meaningful exercise or that they are forced to engage in activities for which they have no aptitude and therefore find humiliating.

Exhilaration, joy, dread, and humiliation: There is a lot of emotional energy tied up in physical development.

The Development of Attachment

If the first experiences of a baby are physical, they are also interpersonal. A young child knows she is safe in the world when that has been her experience from the beginning with her mother or primary caregiver and trusted others. Children who have a secure attachment pattern bring that expectation to school and the adults they find there, from the principal and teachers to the school secretary and custodian. Children who have insecure attachment patterns will constantly seek reassurance from the teacher and the school, and, because they are not so easily reassured, they may become withdrawn, anxious, or avoidant.

The American Psychological Association, in summing up the fourteen most important contributions that psychology has made to an understanding of the learning process, states in formal language what we should all remember from school: "Quality personal relationships that provide stability, trust, and caring can increase learners' sense of belonging, self-respect and self-acceptance, and provide a positive climate for learning."

We have already seen this in the life of Helena, who lights up in the presence of her beloved Spanish teacher and partially closes down in the presence of her "horrible" math teacher.

The drama of trusting or not trusting the teachers and the school—in loco parentis—plays out in the lives of children throughout their years in school. The teachers they trust they describe as "nice," "fair," "funny," "strict, but good," or even just "okay."

Untrustworthy teachers?

"The teacher hates me."

"She never calls on me when I'm ready."

"You can tell she likes some kids, but not me."

"He never said that stuff would be on the test."

"No matter what I do, she'll find something wrong with it."

School, and teachers in particular, make some anxious children less anxious, and frighten others. A third-grade child reported to her mother that she was frightened of her teacher. Her teacher, who was extraordinarily effective for boys and robust girls, did not believe that it was possible for a student to experience her in that way.

"I'm not scary. Children don't find me scary," claimed the teacher. But the child found her very scary indeed, and it was my job to persuade the teacher that the child was entitled to her viewpoint, even if it didn't conform to her teacher's self-image.

Educators believe themselves to be trustworthy, but it is only in the experience of the child that a teacher proves trustworthy or not. When a child does not trust a teacher or the school environment, it is not open to argument; they are not trustworthy and the ground is prepared for an unhappy relationship.

Social Development

A seventh-grade girl remarked to me that on a recent day when her school received a bomb threat, she preferred to stay at school with her friends than call her parents to pick her up and go home. Why?

"If I stayed home and there was a bomb and they all got killed . . . I'd be alive, but they wouldn't be in my life anymore and I'd have to live knowing they were dead and I'd never see them again. I'd rather go to school and then if we're all blown up, well, at least we'd all be together. If something bad is going to happen, I'd rather be with them when it happens than be without them when it's over."

A sixth-grade girl in Texas wrote me the following e-mail after I had visited her school and invited correspondence:

> The other day at gym we were jogging (what we have to do every day. . . . yikes) and I guess they are my friends but a couple of "i guess my friends" came up to me and told me specifically to NOT hang out with a friend of mine. . . . Of course they are popular, so i said okay—so i wouldnt be known as a loser. . . . . but i cant do that because shes my friend. . . . so, what should i do or say to the "i guess my friends"???? and are they my friends if they ask me questions like that????

In the months that followed, almost every one of the more than twenty e-mails she sent me about school were about her social life. Unless I asked explicitly, she barely mentioned teachers, never touched on the curriculum, and didn't report her grades. For her, school was a social experience.

"Academics and social life, they go together a little more than people think," Ben, sixteen, explains. "We're all in this together, and if we all have to go through this, put up with it, experience it, it makes that bond that much stronger. For example, in American lit we had a huge research paper and it really was a rite of passage—twenty pages—so the next day everybody's saying, 'Yeah, I stayed up till two in the morning.' Everybody's going through that and it helps you bond."

Human beings are social animals, and we spend an enormous amount of time developing and cultivating our interpersonal relationships. For most children, friends are indeed the reason they get out of bed in the morning, brush their teeth, get dressed, and head for the bus. The only excuse for school in the minds of children is that there are a lot of other children there. School is the central arena of social development.

Of course, it is not full of true friends. It is full of children, some of whom are potential friends and some of whom are potential tormentors. Every child spends a great deal of the school day trying to develop a social life with his or her peers that is: (1) safe and comforting; and (2) independent of his or her family (and parental—usually, maternal—control). The child who develops fully in the social arena will make solid friendships and find a strategy for negotiating the sometimes treacherous jungle of competing groups, cliques, teasing, and harassment that is part of every child's social universe.

> **"As well as an intellectual playground, school is also a training course for social skills."**
>
> (Twelfth-grader)

Figuring out all the rules of group life—who's cool, who's up and who's down, who's in and who's out, who's a leader and who's a loser—takes up an enormous amount of any child's focus and energy. Learning the ABC's of social interaction dominates the day for young children. It seems to every middle-school teacher as if they are competing for children's attention with the compelling social agenda. By the end of high school, students grow more sure of their friends, and relaxed or resigned about their group affiliations.

Whether a child is a social butterfly or a social snail, every child has a strategic view of the social milieu, an intuitive sense of what he or she brings to it and wants most from it, and an accurate idea of how it's going.

At any age, the child who struggles with this developmental challenge and cannot devise an effective strategy will either withdraw from the world of peers and find himself marginalized in the social life of school, or crash aggressively through the school world and ultimately be rejected by his peers. It is children without friends or groups who are seriously at risk, as are kids who are so desperate for friends that they join deviant groups and begin to drink or take drugs to solidify their group membership.

If, from an adult perspective, the social lives of children seem an interference with the business of school, it is important to remember Howard Gardner's seven "frames of mind." He believes that two of the most important types of human intelligence are *inter*personal intelligence (the ability to read the moods, temperaments, motives, and intentions of others) and *intra*personal intelligence (access to one's own moods and thoughts, and the ability to discriminate among them in order to direct one's own behavior). When children congregate in the front lobby of the school, talking, gossiping, touching, and reassuring one another, they are practicing their social skills with as much intensity as an orchestra practices a piece by Bach. Social development amounts to a kind of symphony of its own, and if you want to play with the orchestra, you've got to know how to read music.

Cognitive Development

It is not just the future scientist who takes a watch apart to see the mechanism work. The engine of children's learning is their own biologically driven desire to master every mystery they encounter, to understand its underlying forces. Intellectual curiosity exists in every child. Every child has the intense desire to disassemble, to study, to dissect (if not frogs, then watches or computer games or musical or visual images), to experiment, and ultimately to understand. Children aren't taught how to think in school. Children think and solve problems from the moment they come into the world. Development of the ability to master language, to understand symbols, and to master the physical world is what we call cognitive development. The capacity to think and solve problems is an innate ability that emerges in the course of childhood. Ideally, school provides the right environment for children to develop as thinkers.

The hardest thing for adults to understand is that children think differently than adults do, and the younger the child, the bigger those differences will be. A child's failure to see or understand things that her parents see and understand is not simply a matter of her lacking the relevant facts or experience, though lack of experience is part of the picture. We do not teach algebra to kindergartners because their minds are not yet ready to understand the underlying principles of physics. Cognitive child psychology has demonstrated that children perceive the world differently than adults do. Their memories do not work as quickly or as reliably. Their reasoning is based on different assumptions than adult reasoning is. Children's thinking does not change simply as the result of experience, practice, the right kind of lessons, or excellent teaching. It is a combination of intrinsic ability, the child's maturation, the context of learning, motivation, and relationships that propels development.

Children's ability to think, know, and understand moves through a set of stages. These stages are not as clearly defined as the great Swiss psychologist Jean Piaget originally described, but over time a child moves from the unreflective and practical experiments of the nine-month-old to the playful and symbolic communication of the two-year-old, from the wishful and often illogical thinking of the three-year-old to the hard-headed critical views of the six-year-old. Children who are gullible at four are no longer so gullible at six. Young children of four who cannot understand things from another person's point of view develop the ability to take another person's perspective. That is why an eight-year-old is a more reliable friend than he was when he was four. He is able to empathize with another child. It isn't that young children are mean or uncaring. They lack the cognitive ability to take another child's perspective.

How do we see cognitive development at work in the school setting? When second-graders study Pilgrims they take everything they are taught as fact. They cannot imagine that competing theories about the Pilgrims could exist. That is because they haven't developed the critical abilities to question what adults tell them. By middle school, however, children's thinking begins to change. They become more challenging and questioning. The romantic, heroic story of Pocahontas and John Smith thrills young children, while high school seniors prefer to debunk the myth and examine the story of love and betrayal under the harsher light of historical accuracy.

At each advancing grade level, the curriculum is typically designed to engage a higher level of cognitive development. Content becomes richer, explorations deeper, analysis more critical. How does a child experience that?

Typically, before the age of six or seven, children are not capable of thinking about their own thinking (this ability is called metacognition). They cannot analyze their own thinking, for example, and figure out whether the teacher has given them complete or incomplete instructions. They simply attack the task with the lousy instructions and become discouraged and upset when they cannot complete it. Older kids are able to perceive that they have not been told all they need to know. For that reason, it is essential that teachers understand the average developmental level of the children with whom they are working.

In every class, however, there is a range of cognitive developmental levels. Not all of the kids are at the same point in their development. In a typical fifth-grade social studies class, for instance, there are students who can think abstractly, who write essays in which they hypothesize about cause and effect and competing theories of history. They want to move the discussion much further into "what-if" territory than is comfortable for classmates whose thinking is, at least for now, at a less abstract, more concrete stage.

These cognitive developmental differences have profound social implications. The abstract thinkers are considered weird by the concrete thinkers, and the concrete thinkers are considered dense or slow by the abstract thinkers. Depending on who is setting the tone for the class, and to whom the teacher is directing the lesson, a child may feel exhilarated by the conversation and companionship or feel discouraged and isolated, even alienated, by the lack of it.

The gap affects interactions between adults and teens, too. A large minority of teens have attained a level of cognitive development that allows them to reason as well as or better than many adults. Teenagers may not yet know everything they will eventually know and they are not yet wise, but they may have adult analytic capacity. Adolescents who have reached this stage can tell that their thinking is deeper and more analytic than that of many of the adults who have power over them. That is why some teenagers—and even younger children—delight in catching teachers in mistaken logic or superficial conclusions. Those students may have a more highly developed and powerful mind. As we will see in the case of David in chapter 6, his ability to pick apart the concrete and bureaucratic aspects of schooling led him into a state of profound disgust with the school. Though all children can learn something from adults, even adults who think in concrete terms, it is a problem in schools when teachers are not as cognitively capable as many of the students.

"It would just be nice if somebody got my jokes," a particularly bright and cognitively capable seventh-grade girl (with a subtle dry wit) told me. "It would be nice if somebody 'got' me." She expresses a sentiment that might be echoed by any child who doesn't feel that her classmates or teachers are meeting her at her developmental level. And here's the toughest part of cognitive development for teachers and parents: If a teacher says something to a class of twenty-five children, she is understood at twenty-five different cognitive developmental levels!

Academic Development

Students learn two sets of skills in school: One is essential to their growing up as educated adults, the other is specific only in the context of school. They learn the vital academic skills and content of the curriculum: reading, writing, math, and all of the scientific and historical knowledge that makes for an informed citizen. They also learn the rules of the game of school. Though someone could well object to my doing so, I am going to lump the two together under the category "academic development," not because I see them as the same thing— indeed, they are and should be different—but because children often experience them as closely related.

For children, the distinction between the meaning and importance of mathematics and the importance of math *tests* is lost. There is no distinction. For perhaps most kids, the importance of learning math is so that you can pass the math test and not be in trouble with the teacher and not have your parents get angry about your report card. When asked by an American sociologist why he did so well in school, a French boy did not reply, "So I can learn to read and write and understand the history of France." He actually said, "So people leave me alone."

Most teachers, and even some children, wish that the focus of class conversation were on the deeper aspects of the subject matter, but are resigned to the fact that more often everyone is focused on how the system works. How much does an assignment count? Will this one be graded? How many tests this quarter? Does the teacher count off for spelling errors? What if I turn it in a day late? Students have to be focused on the rules of the game if they want to make good grades—if they want to win at this school game.

This latter kind of learning calls for the acquisition of all the skills that enable a child to manage the demands of the school environment. On the positive side, these include time management, organization, listening, note taking, and the ability to focus, study, organize information, and attack problems. On the negative side, they include test taking and focusing on a narrow range of material that is likely to be on the test, anticipation of the teacher's wishes and efforts to please, hiding out in the class so that the teacher does not call on him, copying from others, compliance, resignation, manipulation, and other kinds of game-playing.

If you want to understand the difference between the two academic skill sets, answer these questions: How much have you used your ability to read since you became an adult? How often have you taken tests since you left school? I trust the answer to the first question is "constantly," and I imagine the answer to the second is "never." However, when they are inside the walls of the school, children have to learn it all: the skills they will need all of their lives, and the skills they need to be able to survive and achieve in school.

I know a young mathematical genius who came very close to failing math year after year in school, from first grade on. His superior mathematical brain enabled him to absorb the material quickly from a text or conversation and then see in his mind's eye the solutions to the most challenging math problems. He also had attention deficit disorder. That made it extremely difficult for him to focus on material and tasks that did not engage him. In high school, his SAT math scores were over the top, and he consistently aced every quiz and every exam in his honors-level math courses. He did not, however, do his nightly math homework, and the resulting accumulation of zeros and incompletes significantly brought his grade down. His problem wasn't with math, but with the demands of math class—or, more specifically, the demands of a teacher who insisted on compliance. Her view: He needed to comply with the homework policy, if not to learn the material then to "learn self-discipline." As it turned out, her homework policy succeeded only in turning math—his most beloved subject—into a chronic battle over meaningless busywork. Judging from year-end grades, he never learned self-discipline in her class (though one might argue that it took considerable self-discipline to come to class at all). However,

> "I wish people knew I am a hard worker. And that I don't have a mother."
>
> (Third-grader)

when he graduated and moved on to adult life, he developed sufficient self-discipline and strategies necessary to succeed at things that
mattered to him.

The Development of Emotional Self-regulation

Human emotions are always powerful, but they are experienced as
especially raw and strong by the young. Every human feeling that is
well known to a middle-aged person—yearning, love, neediness,
greediness, envy, anger, anxiety, competitiveness, perfectionism, despair, and fears of abandonment—is new to a child. In the emotional
realm, children are living and dying and living again. That is what life
feels like for them.

If you ever saw a second-grade boy flip out in school, suddenly
begin to shout at another boy in the class, verbally struggle with the
teacher who intervenes, then—once he is out in the hall—break
down in tears so intense it takes him a half hour to recover, you might
find the before-and-after contrast confusing. If you ever saw two
teenagers savagely fight in the halls of a school, you would, naturally,
think of school as a place of intense emotions. Later, you might reflect on the fact that such a display of explosive feeling is the exception to the rule; most children go through the school day in a state of
relative emotional calm. Just because they appear peaceful does not
mean children are not full of feeling. Most students control their feelings most of the time when they are inside the school building because they do not want to attract attention, the censure of teachers, or
the disapproval of the group.

The technical term for that control is emotional self-regulation,
and it takes years for children to experience their feelings, practice
managing them, and ultimately bring them under control.

If a child never becomes able to regulate her feelings, if she
blows up constantly, takes offense at everything, or is constantly
weepy or endlessly demanding, we begin to give her a diagnosis: oppositional defiant disorder, personality disorder, bipolar disorder, or
depression. In other words, being able to control your emotions and
behavior is emotional health. Failing to develop self-control is the beginning of mental illness. That they are able to manage their feelings

is a tremendous developmental achievement for children, and an essential building block for a civil human society.

The child who practices self-control in school is not necessarily that calm and collected through and through, but he will save the turmoil of his real self to share when he is in the emotional safety of his parents' presence. We have all witnessed our children's emotional meltdowns when they climb into the family car or return home at the end of the school day. At that point, all that day's suppressed frustrations, disappointments, and neediness bubble to the surface. A first-grader is suddenly starving and furious that his mother won't take him to McDonald's. A ten-year-old girl may start to cry about the up-and-down social roller coaster of fourth grade. A fifteen-year-old is apt to get in the car and swear about his coach or the hypocrisy of the "damn" administrators at the high school, or, having waved a cheerful good-bye to his friends, brood in stubborn silence all the way home.

Moral and Spiritual Development

I was part of a school community after the Columbine shootings and the terrorist attacks of September 11. At such times, children's questions go far beyond their own safety; they are interested in the moral basis of behavior. They ask the direct questions that need to be answered: "How could they kill other kids?" "Were they bad men?" "How could God let this happen?"

In the day-to-day business of school, it doesn't appear that children often look up to the sky and ponder the meaning of life and the origin of the universe, but looks are deceiving. Children are naturally spiritual and naturally moral. They are always searching for fairness and honesty and meaning. They are extraordinarily sensitive to adult hypocrisy and cruelty. Children are intensely curious about the major spiritual questions that confront all human beings: the meaning of good and evil, the mystery of death, and their own relationship to God. They just don't need to look skyward to ponder. They find all the material they need right there in the classroom and around the lunch table.

In addition to being spiritual explorers, children are also natural moral thinkers. Among all the words used in school, *fair* may be the one used most often. "That's not fair," kindergartners say to one another when they are fighting over who gets to stand in line or use the block corner. "That's not fair. We already have a math test on Friday," students say to their high school teachers. "That's too many tests in one day."

If you watch a game of four square on a school playground, it is as much a game of moral accountability as it is of bouncing a ball. Children are certainly calling whether the ball lands inside the square or on the line, but they are also watching the thrower's intentions. How hard is she trying to get someone out of the game? Why? Is it mean-spirited or is it fair?

Throughout childhood, children develop a sense of moral conscience. The capacity to think about moral issues is part of the larger unfolding in the development of cognitive ability that grows from simplistic and self-centered to an orientation that includes respect for others and the need for a social order for its own sake. In high school, students who develop into abstract thinkers go on to embrace a set of self-accepted moral principles that they will adhere to even without any authority present, or at times in opposition to authority they believe is wrong-minded.

A high school senior once told me that he did not participate in the hazing of younger boys, even though everyone in his group had done so. He simply said that hazing was wrong and he did not believe, as his compatriots did, that it was the right of upperclassmen to haze lowerclassmen. When I asked him why he was willing to stand up to the behavior of the group, he shrugged and gave credit to his Catholic upbringing. However, there were other Catholic boys involved in the hazing. He had a more sophisticated understanding of moral principle than the other boys in the group had. The reason for his maturity was not simply religious training. It was the combination of religious training, strong moral feeling, and moral development on a cognitive basis.

Students sometimes find themselves at odds with school policy or curriculum, or with teachers and administrators whose demands present a moral conflict. It may be a requirement to dissect animals, read books with offensive language or content, or sing religious music that contradicts their spiritual identity and commitment. However the adults justify their requirements, a child experiences both the internal and the external conflicts. The lesson the child learns goes beyond any curriculum rationale, to the deeper questions of right and wrong, and how adults with power use it.

Identity

By the time most children walk into preschool they are fluent in the language of identity development. "No, I won't!" they'll say. "Leave me alone," or, "I don't want that!" That ability to be negative—the terrible twos—is a child's first proclamation of selfhood, of a separate identity from parents. It hardly involves a sophisticated insight into oneself, but it is one of the first signs of an independent identity. The child is verbally breaking the world down into "me" and "not me" experiences, and announcing them to everyone. Such are the early signs of identity. Most parents smile when they see these indications of a child's individuality because they know that an independent identity—though it will take many, many years to fully develop—is at the core of a child's mental health.

Elementary-age children, even though they spend most of the day away from their parents, love them deeply and are still very dependent on them. They are profoundly identified with their parents. They know who they themselves are precisely because they are part of a family. Their identity is almost completely wrapped up in their relationship with others. Without their parents to provide it, elementary-age children do not have the basic sense of identity as Erikson defined it: "a sense of continuity" and "historical sameness."

As children grow older they become more psychologically differentiated from their parents and begin to celebrate those aspects of their personality that make them unique. This declaration of identity is an unstoppable aspect of development. A teacher once said to me, while observing how some children were dressed on that day, "They're all making a statement all the time." It is a statement of identity. Clothes are easiest to point to, but everything is a statement of identity: "I'm good at Italian and not at math," or "I hate PE." That's who I am!

Here is a ninth-grade girl at a large public high school, introducing herself to me via e-mail:

Me, well i'm not really anything special on the outside, frizzy
curly dark brown hair which only calms down under a straighten-
ing iron, fairly dark tan skin, big lower lip, pretty eyes, sort of yellow at some times, greenish at others. other than huge hands and
enormous feet, that pretty much covers the outside. I am your
basic teenage girl in terms of shopping, but I do have other hob-
bies as well. One is that I'm starting to teach myself acoustic and
electric guitar. I have a sort of passion for music, maybe because
it can calm me down or forget about everything else after a bad
day or when my life is chaotic. I also really enjoy reading, but my
love for tv kind of overpowers that hobby.

After describing some of her classes and writing that she had
made the sophomore tennis team as a freshman, though she qualifies
the accomplishment by noting that two freshmen made the junior
varsity team, she wraps up her introduction:

That pretty much covers me as a person! I am your average
teenager in most other fields; sarcasm, relationship with family,
friends, etc. Basically I'm just trying to find somewhere to fit in in
this huge high school.

Throughout, there is the presumption that she is who she is, that
her likes and dislikes are established and not going to change easily,
and that she has to find a place for herself in the world.

Teenagers are—in Michael Meade's phrase—"works in progress." That is obviously true of their physical development, but, more
than anything, it is true of their identity development. They constantly work to create a unique identity for themselves. So much of
what we see among middle school and high school students is about
identity experimentation and formation: swapping clothes with a best
friend in eighth grade; being a member of a clique of people who are
"just like me"; joining an interest group in high school such as debate
or the yearbook or the gay-straight alliance.

Anything that runs against the views of parents is typically an
effort to declare two things: "I'm growing up," and "I'm different
than you are." We see the most extreme declarations of identity in
the kids with purple hair, all-black Goth clothing, or multiple body-

piercings. These manifestations may appear in children who are frightened that there isn't enough about them that is unique. However, even in children who are not wearing their psyche on the outside, the inner experience may be one of constant differentiation. Here is a fifteen-year-old girl writing about herself in the social context of her high school:

> I like everyone I like mainly because they aren't all obsessed with their looks or how skinny/cool they are, I mean I was in the bathroom the other day and there were these girls putting on like powder or something all over their face with one of those brushes and everything, and this morning before we went on the power program which is basically running around in the woods and doing a ropes course all day, this girl was putting on like eyeliner, eyeshadow, and lipstick!

In other words, this girl is saying, "I know who I am because *I'm not like that.*"

Other students define themselves in detailed contrast to classmates:

> I have a lot of friends, but my closest friends are exactly like me, they have the same grades, same kind of parents—annoying—we all pretty much play sports. I know that one of my friends struggles with school. He's just as smart as me but I do better. He's not in honors classes, and he still struggles with school. He's just as smart as me, but he's just the kind of guy who takes the easy way out.
>
> My friends are really cool. We're not, I don't know how to explain this. We're not wicked popular, but we are popular. We're kind of in the middle. But we could hang out with anybody. We try not to hang around with the wrong crowd too much. [*What's the wrong crowd?*] Um, basically the jerky kids. I don't know how to explain it. The ones who will sit outside and do weed or get into fights all the time. We'll associate, but we won't get in too much to those kids.

Erik Erikson said that if you boiled it down to its essence, all adolescent conversation and relationships are about identity: "I know who I am because I'm like you in some ways, and I'm different from you in other ways." Kids are endlessly fascinated by difference because it throws their own identities into a new light. Much of the gossip that preoccupies girls in groups is all about contrast and compare.

By the end of adolescence, a young adult should have a clear idea of his skills and weaknesses, his likes and dislikes, and his values. He should know what he has gotten from his parents and community, and have some sense of what is uniquely his own creation. He should be productive, and have some understanding of and confidence in the connection between his work and the attainment of a goal.

All of a child's experiences in the eight realms of development—of being a friend, a good (or not-so-good) athlete, artist, or student, a beloved child of her parents, an empathic and spiritual person; of controlling her quick temper; of surmounting her laziness—will be woven together into a sense of identity.

A child with a sense of identity will be able to go into different situations and experience herself as having a continuous, recognizable existence no matter what the circumstances. Though it sounds like something everyone should have, it is, in fact, an extraordinary achievement. People without a firm sense of identity are vulnerable to mental illness. They may be plunged into the feeling that they don't know who they are or why they are doing what they do. We describe such feelings as anomie or futility, and they can be the central-component parts of depression and suicide. Alternatively, people with no identity may remain childlike, needy, or immature. An individual pays a serious price for not developing a separate and unique identity, and every child is striving for it in their school journey.

> "My dad and mom are divorced and I get very upset! And sometimes I even cry!!!"
>
> (Fifth-grader)

Some years ago a boy was sent to my office because he was "underachieving." He wasn't living up to the expectations of his hard-driving and successful attorney father. The boy said to me, "I don't want a life like my father's. All he does is work." What the father perceived as laziness on the boy's part was his son's attempt to develop a separate identity. The young man eventually found the identity he sought by mastering Arabic and becoming a journalist in the Middle East.

The search for identity is ultimately an artistic process, during which a child creates a new kind of adult, one who goes beyond his parents' ambitions and limitations.

SUCCESS: THE EIGHT-DIMENSIONAL MODEL

Twenty years ago, I sat next to the mother of a graduating senior at the commencement ceremony of an academically excellent school. For the first half of the ceremony, she and I watched a small number of seniors go up to the podium—sometimes for repeat visits—to receive prizes in all of the academic subjects and in a few nonacademic areas, such as citizenship and athletic leadership. Her son was a wonderful boy who had overcome serious struggles in ninth and tenth grade and was now finishing with a decent but not outstanding academic record. He was not among any of the students who had been called up to the dais to receive a book or have their hand shaken by the school's principal. This woman turned to me at one point and whispered, in a very matter-of-fact way: "This ceremony exists for the glorification of the top fifteen percent of the class."

Though eventually the entire senior class—including her son—did file up onto the podium, receive their diplomas, and have their pictures taken by their proud parents, she was right about the ceremony's message. By celebrating the academic superstars—we also listened to the valedictorian give the graduation speech—the school was suggesting at this final symbolic moment that what mattered was academic achievement. Ironically, the school had a thoughtful, beautifully crafted mission statement emphasizing community, curiosity, integrity, and lifelong learning. Yet, the final ceremony brought to mind the Olympics, with only the top academic athletes mounting the podium. I have subsequently never been able to attend a graduation ceremony without remembering her remark, and wondering, Who is successful in school? Who is being celebrated here?

Ceremonies like these do not capture the experiences, heroic and tragic, of so many of the seniors walking across the stage.

In more recent years, I have been asked to deliver graduation speeches myself. Facing the same difficult problem that these institutions have faced, my solution has been to celebrate the experience of every child in the class in overcoming the agonies of school. I told one graduating class:

> Everyone who graduates from high school, whether he or she has been a strong student or a weak one, whether she or he has been a good athlete or klutz, whether she has been an artist or musician— whatever you've been—you have experienced an extraordinary and harrowing psychological journey. Though I am impressed by those of you who have achieved high honors and won prizes here today, I actually want to congratulate all of you for just surviving, and especially those who had to hang on by their fingernails.

While my solution resolved the problem of graduation speeches, it sidestepped the reality that some children have a more successful school experience than others and that some children are leaving school traumatized and damaged. How can we see beyond the conventions of academic tradition to recognize the deeper dimensions of children's success and understand their failures? Unlike athletics, where the "thrill of victory and the agony of defeat" is on display for all to see, the psychological journey through school is mostly hidden.

Looking at the seniors in their caps and gowns, I have to imagine what happened to each of these young people during their thirteen years in school, and I wonder: Are they psychologically intact? Are they emotionally whole? Have they developed resilience during their time in school, or have they lost their resilience? Do they feel competent, or has their education been fraudulent? Are they curious and still eager to learn, or are they cynical game players? Do they feel like productive young adults, or do they feel useless? Do they trust adults and institutions, or are they alienated and bitter? How have they fared on their respective journeys?

CONNECTION, RECOGNITION, AND POWER

Grades can be a measure of underlying ability, though at times they obscure as much as they illuminate. Grades can be a measure of motivation and effort; sometimes they reflect growing focus and self-discipline. But even good grades are never a measure of overall development. We've all known brilliant people who were immature; or mediocre or poor students who became wonderful, mature adults. Ultimately, neither the promise of good grades nor the threat of bad grades drives development. Development shows up in students who get A's and students who earn C's. It happens to thoughtful, motivated kids and impulsive, angry kids. It occurs in students who are close to teachers as well as students who are not.

With little else to consult but test scores, report cards, and the occasional personal note from a teacher, parents are tutored by the system to focus on grades. Any memory of developmental complexities fades and they come to accept grades as the goal and measure of their child's school success.

Kids know better. Their lives are about more than grades. Sometimes they even tell us that in so many words, or in less articulate ways. More often, they remain silent, not wanting to invite scrutiny and judgment by adults, leaving parents to wonder or stew about performance and outcomes.

"I don't feel a need to let them know exactly how every class is going," says Ben, sixteen, explaining, "My strategy is to keep conflict with my parents to a minimum."

Children grade themselves. They experience themselves as successful or unsuccessful a thousand times each day, and they come to know whether they are developing in a strong and healthy way through their experience of three key feelings: connection, recognition, and power. No child can ever have a technical perspective on whether she is developing satisfactorily. What she knows is that when she correctly answers a teacher's question in class, not only does the teacher say it is right but several heads around her nod with recognition. Her classmates are indicating, "We thought that was right, too."

That's how she knows she is thinking along the same lines that others are thinking, or leading in a way respected by her peers. If a seventh-grade boy tells a joke and the others laugh, he may think he's just trying to be funny, but he is also learning that he is socially on target for his age. If they don't laugh, or never laugh when he tells a joke, he knows he is in trouble in his social development without ever understanding that there is such a thing as social development! An ordinary school day is packed with moments that tell a child whether he is succeeding or failing in his search for connection, recognition, and power.

MAKING THE GRADE

All children crave connection to parents, to their peers, and to a community or organization that has meaning for them. When they are connected to peers who share their hopes and secrets, they know they are developing. A child hearing the secret thoughts of her peers thinks, "I'm one of them. I'm okay." Children also know they are developing when their teachers acknowledge their effort and respect their progress, whatever the child's ability level.

Recognition is the ultimate feedback for the child that she is making progress. How could a child ever know that she was meant to be an artist unless someone hung her work on the wall? How could a sixteen-year-old boy who mastered the complex backstage lighting board in the school auditorium ever know he was competent unless he had a chance to show his skills by running the lights for the spring play? How could a future writer develop a voice unless she had a chance to read her work in class and hear her classmates' appreciative reaction? There are so many types of recognition, large and small, and so many areas in which a child seeks it. Grades are only a tiny part of what a child, *any child,* really cares about.

It is also vital for a developing child to feel a growing sense of power. I use *power* as an umbrella term to cover physical strength, social competence, intellectual mastery, and personal efficacy. Adults make the mistake of thinking it is possible for children to have high self-esteem all the time. They demand that their child's caretakers work to maintain his self-esteem at a high level at all times. This cannot be done. It is just not easy to feel powerful when you are a child. How can a child have high self-esteem when he is short, and has no independent source of income, no car, and no control over his own daily schedule? How would you feel? Small indeed, and powerless.

Only occasionally does life allow a child to feel powerful. Only rarely does the school environment allow a youngster to experience that feeling. When it happens, the student is incredibly excited, and she will try to reproduce that feeling again and again. She will try to re-create the conditions that were in place when she felt grown up and competent. If her school doesn't present that opportunity often enough, she will try to shape her school experience to *make* it happen again. This is the stuff of strategy.

Many children find a feeling of power in challenging the power structure, by breaking the rules or getting around the requirements. This is never just laziness or bad character, but is often done because it creates a feeling of power that the child may not be able to achieve any other way.

MAKING THE TREK:
MAP, STRATEGY, AND BOOTS THAT FIT

A competitive culture defines school for many children, parents, and educators. However, school is neither a race nor a competition. What is it, then? School more closely resembles a long-distance hike, like the Appalachian trail, which runs from Georgia to Maine, a long, arduous trip that can take an experienced, determined hiker months to complete. The school journey is even longer, lasting thirteen years, and it is not optional.

A ninth-grade boy said to me, "It's so long. It's so many years. I don't want to do it." But they have to. Given that discouraging days, hardship, and exhaustion are inevitable, what constitutes a successful journey for any particular child? What does a child need for the journey and what does he expect to get out of it, besides a diploma and, for some, an invitation to hit the trail for four more years of college?

Long-distance hikers feel they have succeeded if they have experienced a great challenge, learned something new, bonded with some interesting hiking companions, developed wisdom and character, avoided having a traumatic accident, had some amazing experiences, and finished the hike. Whatever else occurs, if you achieve all of that, it qualifies as a successful journey.

Long-distance hiking is a test of endurance, character, and—above all—perseverance. So it is with the school journey. Once children begin to understand what school is—and I believe they "get it" pretty quickly—they want what hikers want. They want to be challenged, they want to learn something new, they want to develop friendships, and they don't want to be emotionally hurt. More than anything, they want to finish.

Last year, a senior at the school where I serve as a psychologist was killed in a car crash. He was immensely talented, both academically and athletically; he had collected a pile of honors when he was at the school and was surely looking forward to many more successes. At the funeral there was plenty of talk about the lost promise of this boy. Yet the most poignant comments came from six or seven friends who all told me, "All he wanted to do was graduate from Belmont Hill." Forget the awards or the promise of college and future success. Like all students, he'd been on a long journey, and all he had wanted to do was finish!

> "I had a terrible time in seventh grade. Part of it was my parents were getting divorced, but also all the kids were focused on popularity and how they looked, and they just wouldn't let me in."
>
> (Tenth-grader)

On the trail, anyone who is able to walk can potentially hike the distance, though the speed and ease with which they do it will depend on many factors, including their physical and mental preparedness, their access to good-fitting boots and sufficient food, gear, and other supplies, and the luck of the draw in terms of weather and other unforeseeable events. Someone with a natural affinity for hiking, who is fit and trim, with good boots and gear and the experience and confidence to handle whatever nature throws her way, is likely to finish sooner and have a better time of it than someone unfit or ill-prepared. But anyone determined and resourceful enough can do it in their own way and at their own pace, and eventually complete it successfully.

Every child works every day to find a sense of "fit" in school—the feeling that she can grow and develop safely in school, that she can find enough of what she needs, physically, emotionally, socially, intellectually. A child's strategy represents her attempts to find that fit—to manage the demands of school, her personal learning style, the expectations of her parents, and the complex social requirements of her peers. Every child constantly refines a strategy for holding all of these intense and conflicting forces in place. The central work for every student in school is to develop a personal strategy that makes her psychologically comfortable, that enables her to feel, "I belong here. There is something trustworthy for me here."

Five things boost the odds of a child finding a good fit with school: a school brain and temperament, a strong feeling of connection to the community, ambition, a close and confiding relationship with an adult throughout the teenage years, and some philosophy or perspective on school. Children with school brains have an ease with reading, writing, and mathematical thinking—a good fit with the demands of the school curriculum. They are quicker, they finish their homework faster, and they receive higher grades. Children with learning differences and a lower frustration tolerance avoid the tasks, fight the process, and don't achieve the same academic honors. Yet, all children are capable of learning at their own pace and it is a fact that the majority of them complete the thirteen years of school.

Having defined successful students as the ones who develop an adaptive strategy that enables them to meet and surmount most of the challenges of school, I emphasize that there is no stock strategy. If there are fifty-three million schoolchildren in the United States, then there are fifty-three million formulas for getting through the school day. Most children find a fit for themselves in school that helps them survive its many indignities. Tragically, some do not.

No type of student is guaranteed success in school: not the genius, the football quarterback, the master violinist, or the social queen bee. Each child meets the challenges of school life on a day-to-day, moment-to-moment basis. For every one of them, there are times—days, weeks, or even months sometimes—when their lives don't look too good. In the chapters ahead, I will expand on the ideas of strategy, fit, and success by looking at the varying experiences of children in very different schools. Some of the children find school a reasonably good fit, and enjoy a lot of developmental and academic success. Others struggle to find their place in school, and continue to struggle throughout their school careers. And, for others, the fit between their needs and abilities and the school environment is so acutely uncomfortable that they either fall into despair or make the decision to discard school and everything it stands for. In the face of all advice to the contrary, they need to leave school in order to pursue their development outside. Every child has something to teach us about his journey. Every child has a strategy, a story, and wisdom to share.

4

Finding Success

Passion, Politics, and Perseverance

———

There's a strategy for everything. For instance, you find
out fairly quickly what each teacher expects. You may
have to sacrifice some of your own interests, which may
or may not be a good thing, but it may be necessary.
—*Ben, sixteen*

The person who makes a success of living is the one
who sees his goal steadily and aims for it
unswervingly. That is dedication.
—*Cecil B. DeMille*

No one has worked harder than Cameron to find a comfortable
fit in school. After another boy at his new Connecticut high
school drove a car onto the sidewalk in an attempt to kill Cameron (or
at least terrify him), finding safety in school became a matter of life
and death. Cameron was so frightened, he left that school and returned to his hometown in Florida, living with a friend's family for
the remainder of his sophomore year and attending his previous
school. After regaining his courage, he returned to Connecticut and
the high school he had fled. He came back as a political activist.

When I told Cameron that I was going to use him in the book as an
example of a successful student, he hesitated, then suggested that he

might better be described as a struggling student. Indeed, he has struggled heroically for many years, both in school and in his life, and has tasted a sense of peace and success only in the last year and a half of his high school career. Nevertheless, he has found it. He was finally able to turn school into the place he needs it to be, a place where, for the most part, he can be himself and feel safe. He did it by coming out as the first openly gay boy in his high school and forcing the adult world to protect him at last. Cameron's journey is an unconventional success story.

Cameron was originally from Miami. His father was Cuban, his mother biracial, half white and half African-American. His father was a drug dealer, his mother a drug dealer and user. When he was three years old, Cameron's mother was arrested, convicted, and jailed for drug trafficking. Cameron and his older brother, Roberto, were left in the care of his father.

"Yeah, I have a lot of memories of my dad. No, he wasn't a good guy, but I do remember my dad a lot," Cameron says. His father beat his brother regularly. For some reason he beat Cameron only once, when he was in kindergarten: "There was the one time I ever got hit and I got hit really bad. I was beat. Like I went to school the next day and I couldn't even sit down. I'll never forget because it was with this belt that had big circles in it, like metal circles. And I had these welts from those circles. That's the only time I ever got it. And that was a blessing, I guess, that it was only once." Cameron went to school and was in so much pain that he reported the beating to his kindergarten teacher. She sent him to the school nurse, who saw the welts on his legs and buttocks.

Perhaps because it was a small private school, perhaps because most of the staff spoke only Spanish, perhaps because they were afraid of Cameron's father, neither the teacher nor the nurse reported the beating to the state division of youth protective services. "They just sent me home and I got in trouble from my dad and my nanny. I got yelled at." What does Cameron think about the nurse who failed to report the physical abuse? "Oh, my God, I definitely think she needs to have her job reevaluated. It was my teacher as well 'cause I told my teacher first and she sent me to the nurse." When asked to speculate on what might have happened had someone reported the abuse, Cameron muses: "I don't know if I would have rather ended up in foster care . . . that's when my mom was in jail and I didn't have a connection with my family up here. So I don't know if I would have rather ended up in a foster home or just, I don't know. . . . It was a really difficult choice."

But of course, there was no choice. When I asked Cameron if he had any other memories of the teachers in his private school in Miami, he says he cannot remember much, just "traumatic experiences that stick out in my head and that was one of them."

When he was seven, his father did not come home one evening. He had disappeared. Cameron and his brother waited for a week in the care of the family nanny before learning that their father's body had been found by the side of a road. Cameron was told that his father had been killed in a car accident. It wasn't until he was eleven years old and, as he says, "started putting things together, asking questions," that Cameron discovered that his father had been killed in a drug deal. Because his mother was in jail and he had no other family, he was sent to Connecticut to live with his mother's sister. He lived with her from the age of seven until the age of ten.

> No one else offered to take me and my brother in. And really my aunt has the least amount of money out of anyone else in the family, which is kind of depressing. . . . I don't know why no one else wanted to take us, but, yeah, my aunt took us in. Like [it was] the first time in my life I had ever been around people that did normal things. . . . She's the most amazing person in the world. . . . I really never knew I was poor 'cause there was so much love in the house. You know what I mean? We were poor. I'd wear the same outfit every day . . . but it didn't bother me because my family was so close. . . . My aunt could make the best of everything. I had my first birthday party, and she was amazing. She would make everything instead of buying it . . . like a kid I can remember at the school named Maureen. I was so jealous of her. She had a birthday party. Her parents had clowns and they had, they actually had like a ride, a ride in her yard. And my parties are nothing like that. We still had the best parties and I'd invite all the kids in my class.

That taste of a normal family life would serve—and continues to serve—as a reminder to Cameron of what a family can be. Prior to moving to Connecticut he had become quite distrustful of adults, and was beginning to show symptoms of anger and poor mental health. He stole his nanny's credit card: "It was actually the summer going into the first grade, and I stole my nanny's credit card, just 'cause I wanted to get in trouble. My brother got beat for it."

When he moved to Connecticut a short time later, he went to an elementary school he loved and found adults in whom he could place his trust. "I loved my school up here. . . . It was a small school. I felt kind of awkward because it was all black kids. I was actually the only Latino kid in the school. But actually my mom is half black. So I loved the school up here. I started making friends. Like it was the first time I ever felt really loved." Unfortunately, it didn't last.

Cameron's mother was released from prison when he was a fourth-grader, and midway through that year he moved back to Orlando to live with her. She worked long hours in the restaurant business. Cameron describes her as self-absorbed and not the motherly type. He was left in the care of his mother's best friend, who served as baby-sitter to Cameron and his older brother. This man, Dwight, began to sexually molest him. Cameron reports, "at that point, after living in Connecticut, I had learned to respect my elders . . . and I didn't learn to question what they did. I just learned to be respectful and [the molestation] started right away, when I came down. I would cry the whole time . . . he would touch me anywhere."

In sixth grade, Cameron was saved from the ongoing abuse by an unlikely source. One afternoon he was watching *The Oprah Winfrey Show* when Oprah herself began talking about her history of sexual abuse at the hands of her uncles. Cameron told me, "Oprah cried on her show and I was like—wow, this is not right, I do not need to take this. You know, she gave out this number for this help line. I was going to call it, but damn, he was baby-sitting me. He was on the phone. . . . I just locked the door and I was like, this is never going to happen again." Cameron called his mother at the restaurant, but before he could explain why he had called, she said, "I'm busy, I can't talk to you right now." Hours later, locked in his room, through the bedroom window he told his older brother about the abuse. His brother spoke about it to his mother and several other people. Ulti-

> **"In every situation, there is a way to better yourself as an individual. You are too tired to finish your homework and have to go to class the next day without it. You face the consequences, and learn that you'd probably be better off doing it next time."** (Twelfth-grader)

mately, Dwight was convicted of child molestation and is currently serving an eight-year prison term.

This is a dramatic story with a somewhat happy ending. What does it have to do with a child's psychological journey through school, and with success? Remember that throughout his ordeal Cameron was a fourth- and fifth-grade boy. During this period of molestation and neglect, he went to school every day. He was trying to complete worksheets, learn material, take tests. What did his teachers know? What did they see?

In fact, his teacher, Mrs. Bettencourt, did notice that there was something wrong with him, partly because she taught him in both fourth and fifth grades. When he arrived at the school, she saw what a good student he was: He had gotten A's in Connecticut. She witnessed his decline in school. Homework and grades took a sudden dive.

"I didn't want to do my homework 'cause whenever I was alone he would come in," Cameron says. "So I always tried to be around people. That's when my grades started dropping. 'Cause I wouldn't read the books we were supposed to read because I didn't want to be alone, 'cause if I was alone he would come in."

Mrs. Bettencourt kept asking him, "Is everything all right?" She asked Cameron's mother whether anything was wrong at home and was told that everything was fine. Cameron knew his teacher was trying to find out why he was not performing up to his ability. She told him she believed he could qualify for gifted classes, but she couldn't get him into those classes if he didn't get his grades up. She kept encouraging him.

Some months after the "Oprah" day and the end of the molestation, he talked with Mrs. Bettencourt about having been molested. Unbeknownst to him, his teacher had been notified of the molestation from the school social worker, who had been notified by the state. "She asked me to stay after one day and she talked to me about it. . . .

She didn't want to make me uncomfortable, and said if I didn't want to talk about it with her that's fine, but that she was here for me." Cameron felt enormously relieved to have his teacher know what was going on in his life. At least now she understood why he was getting C's.

Cameron moved on to middle school the next year and landed in all honors classes. He told me that he did not think his grades really qualified him for those classes. If not, how did he get into them? "I think Mrs. Bettencourt helped me. I definitely think she tweaked my grades up a little bit, because I don't think there's any way it could have happened without that. I did do extra stuff. She made me test on the fifty states and I could name them all. I got extra credit for it. You know what I mean. . . . In everything, she definitely helped me out."

> "To understand the homework the teacher gives, you've got to understand the teacher. You've got to know which class needs the time, and how much time to put it."
>
> (Tenth-grader)

He finished sixth grade with all A's and B's. I asked him if he was a natural—the kind of kid who is just "born for school."

"Well, I don't think it all comes natural. I definitely study for it."

There is no doubt in my mind that Cameron is a bright boy, but that is not what makes his school career so remarkable. It is his ability to use the system to help him live his life, much of which, unfortunately, he has had to design on his own. His kindergarten teacher betrayed him. He remembers that betrayal bitterly. In elementary school, he began to take control of his own destiny, making friends and learning how to engage the interest of adults (a talent he possesses to this day—the very ability that brought him to my attention). In seventh grade, he informed his mother and brother that he was gay. In eighth grade, when he was fourteen years old, he began working a job at JCPenney and became, to a degree, financially independent. In ninth grade he told two friends that he was gay. Although they promised confidentiality, "it leaked out," and it became increasingly difficult for Cameron to feel comfortable in school. When, at the age of fifteen, he found a gun and some drugs in the glove compartment of his mother's car, he was deeply frightened. He was also embarrassed in front of the school friend who also saw them. Around the same time, his older brother became increasingly disturbed and began to beat him up for being gay. As a result he contacted his relatives in Connecticut and asked to move back with them so he could grow up away from his mother and brother.

Now an emancipated teenager—he went to court last year to end his mother's legal rights over him—he has chosen to live with Carrie, his first cousin, her husband, and their baby. Carrie is the twenty-three-year-old daughter of his beloved aunt with whom he lived for those three years from ages seven to ten. He adores his cousin and looks up to her. Cameron works in a restaurant, earns a small salary, pays rent to Carrie, and attends high school, or rather, he uses high school as his personal political stage. His days are now dedicated to changing the system to make the school safer for students like him. Here is his description of the second day of his senior year in high school:

> The day started off well since I'm the announcement guy. I feel like I have power sitting in the principal's chair and reading out announcements today. It was nice to direct students to stand for the pledge, and then direct them to sit down. I then had to go to physical education. I have my opinions about PE as it is and it gets me so frustrated. Last year my district had a budget cut and we had to fire a few teachers and drop a few of the best "extra" courses that we offered. Still, we had the money to put in an entirely new basketball court—rather than buy books or paint over the word *faggot* and *Sheila is a whore* that are painted all over the bathroom walls. Still, I went to PE and was reminded why I dislike the class. As we are going through attendance, three Latino boys start making fun of me in Spanish, calling me "faggot" and "dick sucker" in their native tongue. All the while, Ms. Cushman didn't say a word. The teacher then divided us into groups—the "better" athletes and the "intermediate" group. The real skill that divided the two groups was that one set of students participated, and the others were lazy and didn't dress or do anything in class. [Cameron is an excellent athlete. He was on a Junior Olympics swim team when he lived in Florida.]

As soon as the list was called and all three of them were in the "intermediate" group, they started on me again. "Faggots don't play sports. Faggots paint their nails and go shopping." Frustrated and annoyed, I walked out of class and went into the main office to fax something out. As soon as I got back to class I told Coach Cushman and of course nothing was done [but] I felt a little better. The day was blah after that. I read in our handbook—that was something I was working to change—that our harassment policy didn't include sexual orientation or gender identity. It will next year. I then went home with a mile of homework and realized that I had no clue how to do my probability and statistics homework—it also occurred to me that I hate math!

Oh, yes, math! We'd forgotten about math, hadn't we? When you hear about the traumas in Cameron's life, it is sometimes hard to remember that he is just a kid, that he has math homework to do. When I interviewed Cameron in the small living room of his house, it never occurred to me to ask him what his grades were. I'm sure he does reasonably well, but I doubt that he's giving his schoolwork his total attention. Actually, I know he's not giving his schoolwork his total attention. Still, I am certain he is a successful student. If I can say that Cameron is a successful student, am I giving him extra credit for having survived traumatic life circumstances? No, I think he is a successful student because he has found a place for school in his tough life, and because he has found a place for his life at his school.

The most important factor in a child's school life is the goodness of fit. Though all children aren't traveling at the same pace in school, they are all working equally hard to find some sense of fit in the environment. Indeed, I believe that all children are doing their best to make themselves comfortable and be successful in school at any given moment. I will expand on this idea later in the book, because I have what may seem an unconventional idea of what it means to "do your best." I don't need to know that Cameron is getting good grades to know that he is doing his best. If he were getting D's, it would be totally understandable, given the pressures on him. He is poor, he is gay, he was sexually abused, his father was murdered, and he cannot trust his mother, who cannot raise him, or his brother, who has beaten him. Many doors (and minds) are closed to him. One day he wrote this to me:

> Today on the bus everyone was talking about senior pictures and our senior trip—both things that I can't participate in. I wanted to cry knowing that I am missing out on so much. When everyone kept asking if I was going on the senior trip to Virginia, it is so embarrassing to be like "no" and then have to explain that I cannot afford it. I try to be optimistic, but sometimes having the lack of financial resources is so stressful. . . . I wanted to stand up and explain to this student that "no, I can't afford $300 because my mommy is not paying for me to go and I'm too busy paying rent and health insurance and trying to save to pay for college."

Cameron didn't even have the money to pay for a senior picture. He says, "It is sad to know that my picture won't be in the yearbook—but it could be worse!"

Cameron has succeeded in life by his exceptional optimism. He has succeeded in school by becoming a public figure and enlisting the adults to recognize him and protect him. He has become a champion of justice and civil rights for gay and lesbian students. He has an identity and he has a sense of power. He has done all of this in spite of being parentless and poor. It is not that he doesn't think about those painful facts of his life; he does and they are a source of pain. Despite his pain, and with the help of administrators and teachers who have rallied to him, Cameron has made a success of school.

A WATCHFUL EYE, COURSE CORRECTIONS ALONG THE WAY

Cameron is required to make sacrifices every day in order to remain in the school building. He has to put up with antigay slurs from other kids in PE and the acceptance of cultural homophobia from certain teachers. He manages the pain of those encounters by forcing the system to acknowledge him publicly, and by cultivating relationships with adults who share their power and the microphone with him.

Cameron has succeeded in school by being a politician, but his strategy is not one that could easily be transplanted to another child. Helena succeeded by focusing on her strengths in foreign languages and by being disciplined about meeting requirements for courses that interest her less, such as chemistry. She openly criticizes some of the people who annoy her, like Kevin, and she avoids the food in the cafeteria altogether. These strategies help her get through a day. Yes, she pays a social price for being thought a goody-goody. Does anybody care that she doesn't eat the school lunch? I don't know, but I do know she stays close to her father by having him make her lunch every day. These are but a few of the many maneuvers she employs. Every student has a strategy for surviving school and feeling comfortable. Success is when it works more often than not, and when the compromises or trade-offs are not so great that they rob a child of dignity and self-respect.

On the second day of school, I was asked to follow Alan, a seventh-grade boy new to his small private school. I knew from his file that he was bright and had been academically successful in his previous school. I watched him assess his new environment and witnessed him develop his strategy for success from the opening minutes of the day. In one class, the students were asked to write an essay, the point of which—as the teacher made clear—was to provide a writing sample so she could assess the strength of each student's writing skills. Alan glanced up several times during the exercise in order to see how much the other boys were writing. When he figured out that he was writing far more than many of them, he slowed down his rate of output. Once he was satisfied that most boys were close to being finished, he added a couple of sentences to his own essay, being careful, however, to confine it to one page. He stopped two lines from the bottom and then handed the paper to his teacher. The mental strategy was clear: I want the teacher to know I'm capable, but I don't want to write so much that I make myself socially unattractive by looking like a total suck-up or a complete nerd, so I'll write just a bit more than the other boys. Alan's actions were highly deliberate: He was balancing the social

> "My parents care about my report card. I worry about it because I want to pass and do good to get in college or just get a scholarship."
>
> (Fifth-grader)

and academic sides of his life. The boy next to him did not have the skills to make the same strategic choice at that moment. He struggled visibly to fill half a page with writing and finished later than all the boys in the class. Everyone noticed and everyone understood immediately that school, at least writing, is a struggle for him.

No one likes to have their weaknesses revealed. Students who are strong either are simply capable in the academic areas that school emphasizes or maneuver through the school environment in ways that maximize their strengths. I have known kids who have survived school by finding a niche in the drama department, in athletics, or in music. I can always understand why students choose a program or focus energy into their areas of strength. Certainly, it is a scandal when kids are allowed to do that to the detriment of their education, for instance when athletes are allowed to graduate from high school even though they are functionally illiterate. I do not blame these kids for trying to maximize their strengths. However, they have been made too comfortable and their lives are not real. The adults have become overinvested in one area of a child's life and forgotten their obligation to educate.

CHILDREN WITH A "SCHOOL BRAIN"

It is clear that some children come into school better equipped for the journey than others. They feel comfortable and confident in school from the outset, and their success in meeting challenges and surmounting obstacles steadily builds over time. Such children have what I call a school brain. In and of itself, a school brain doesn't guarantee that you will finish the journey successfully, though surely it helps. Why do I call it a school brain instead of IQ? When I was younger, and more interested in intelligence testing than I am today, I believed that intelligence testing predicted school success. Indeed, Frenchman Alfred Binet, who developed the first IQ test, was hired to do exactly that: to develop a test that would predict which youngsters would succeed and which would fail in the Paris public schools. To a considerable extent, IQ testing does predict academic success in school, and only academic success. It cannot predict healthy development or social success or an array of other important developmental variables.

My own experience as a student persuaded me that intelligence alone did not predict a happy school career. I witnessed brighter people than myself who did not thrive in school. I also went to class with boys who were not as quick as I, but who seemed more at ease in school. Students understand this by being in class with brilliant children who have striking social or athletic limitations. They admire the academic skills of "nerds" or "geeks," but they don't envy the lives they have to live in school.

Like many educators and psychologists, I possessed the intuitive feeling that intelligence was a far broader thing than academic ability—a sentiment hard to articulate and one that garnered precious little support in a traditional school. Howard Gardner's groundbreaking book in 1983, *Frames of Mind,* which proposed a theory of multiple intelligences, was a revelation and a huge relief to me. It put into words what everyone who works with children observes every day, namely that children who are not conventionally bright are amazingly smart and talented. It freed me from believing that intelligence alone—at least as measured by IQ—could account for all the marvelous things I was seeing in school. Gardner concluded that human beings possess seven discrete kinds of intelligence: (1) linguistic ability; (2) logical-mathematical ability; (3) spatial intelligence; (4) musical intelligence; (5) bodily-kinesthetic intelligence; (6) interpersonal intelligence; and (7) intrapersonal intelligence.

All of these intelligences, Gardner claims, "have an equal claim to priority," but our society has put linguistic and logical-mathematical intelligence "on a pedestal" (Gardner, *Multiple Intelligences: The Theory in Practice,* 1993). In other words, schools favor children with verbal and mathematical skills. That should not be a surprise to anyone who has ever struggled with either of those areas of learning in school, only to graduate and find that it was possible to do just fine in the work world in a job that favored one of the other intelligences: the muscle memory of the dancer, the coordination and speed of the chef, the interpersonal—and sometimes the intrapersonal—skills of the sales rep, or the spatial intelligence of the graphic designer.

Some administrators and teachers have worked diligently to incorporate Gardner's ideas into the curriculum and design of their schools. Athletic programs, dance programs, wood shop, and metal shop give students with intelligence in the kinesthetic and visual-spatial arenas a place to strut their stuff. Inevitably, however, school will always be a place where verbal and linguistic abilities are on a pedestal. The edge will always go to students who test well in both verbal and math ability, and for the most part these abilities are innate. Some people are born with greater cognitive power than others in these areas that school favors. That's what we call IQ. Though there are many things that affect IQ—nutrition, socioeconomic status, and parental education are three of them—ultimately you cannot train someone to have a significantly higher IQ than he was born to have, and people who have a higher IQ score tend to do better in school than those who do not.

Having a high IQ alone, however, cannot guarantee school success. I still believe that the school brain is made up of several different factors: innate intelligence, a learning style suited to the school environment, the inclination to love teachers and the ability to play the game of school, and patience and philosophy with the dross of school. The combination of all these factors makes students with a school brain well adapted to the rhythm and regimen of school. The school environment will provide much of what they need—connection, recognition, and a sense of power.

Helena recognizes that difference between her learning style and that of other students at Kensington High. She told me that early on in elementary school there were other students, usually boys, who refused to do the work. Helena has always found herself able to do her homework. Her brain is as close to a perfect fit for school as one could imagine. In other words, Helena is fit and trim and ready for the long-distance hike. She's physically and mentally prepared, she's got the boots that fit and they're well broken in, she's got a backpack with all the right supplies, not more or less than she needs, and she enjoys hiking. Loves sleeping on the hard ground under the stars; doesn't mind rain and bugs.

In the American Psychological Association's set of fourteen psychological principles that pertain to learning, among them was this sentence: "Successful learners are active, goal-directed, self-regulating and assume personal responsibility for contributing to their own learning." This describes Helena to a T. She has intellectual interests, particularly in foreign languages, and she tries to connect personally with the material. Some classmates tease her about being a goody-goody, but it is also clear that many of them describe her that way at the same time that they admire her attitude and how effortless she makes it look. Like a circus performer, Helena makes the tough look easy. Does the fact that she's a successful learner mean that school is in fact easy for her? Not always. She works hard—long hours—to achieve excellence.

Helena doesn't like conflict—even mild tension—to erupt between students and teachers. It does. She wants her classmates to do what is expected of them and keep the class moving forward. They don't always. She wants teachers who are smart, interesting, caring people. Some are. Many are not. She knows her own weaknesses and shortcomings, too, and works hard, struggling in her own way to accommodate the gaps between what she wants school to be and what it is.

Helena is a classic superachiever, the embodiment of what most people envision as a successful school journey. It would surprise the adults in her life to know how much any pleasure in her academic success is tempered, for her, by frustration in even her favorite classes, and a basic dislike of much of the school day. Further, that it is her after-school babysitting job, the adult responsibility and unconditional love she experiences with those children, that buoys her spirits to meet the demands of the school day.

A PASSIONATE PICKER AND CHOOSER

It is 8:12 A.M. and Adam has already finished one class, chamber orchestra, in which he plays clarinet. Now he is making his way down the long halls on his way to morning homeroom advisory, where he starts each day at Forest Hills High School. Adam walks with a jaunty, devil-may-care air. Though he is nervous about his upcoming vocal audition, and though he worked into the night on an English writing assignment, got only four and a half hours of sleep, and is hopped up on coffee and adrenaline, Adam is determined to keep his attitude upbeat. "There's a lot of stress around here," he informs me. "You have to keep it from getting to you."

Greta, a tall, graceful girl holding books in front of her, falls in step alongside Adam and matches his pace. With great goodwill and some concern she asks, "How's the song going? Have you learned all the words?"

"I'm not prepared," replies Adam.

"What's the song?" she persists.

" 'Smoke Gets in Your Eyes' by Jerome Kern," he informs her, practicing the words of his introduction—composer and all—that he is going to use at his upcoming audition. Then, with Greta as his instant audience, Adam starts to hum, and then to sing, the lyrics to the song: "They ask me how I knew . . . my true love was true. . . ." His strong tenor voice grows louder. He is the only boy singing in the halls of Forest Hills High School at 8:12 in the morning. Indeed, there is no one else even close to singing.

> "I like my self because I'm a real good dancer. But when I see all those people in front of me I get embarrassed."
>
> (Seventh-grader)

In the space of twenty-five yards, Adam has passed perhaps forty slow-moving teenagers getting books out of their lockers, talking quietly, pushing off to their advisory classes. Not many of them looked capable of singing, maybe not ever, but certainly not for several hours. School starts too early for the biorhythms of adolescents. You can see that when you walk around any high school in the early morning. Adam is an exception. He persists in impromptu concert and Greta takes in this gift of song with low-key grace. As they approach the hall where she must turn off to go her way, she calls out, "Good luck," and departs for her advisory.

"Thanks," says Adam. "See you later."

We head for advisory. Eighteen boys wander into the classroom of Mr. Moore, a handsome, well-dressed math and statistics teacher in his mid-thirties. This is no late-career, burned-out teacher. The embodiment of competence, intelligence, and focus, Mr. Moore greets each boy personally as he enters the classroom, all the while consulting over his shoulder with a boy sitting at a computer. As boys file in, they find seats and begin to talk quietly with a neighbor, read the paper, or take out homework that needs finishing. Adam sits among them, acknowledging the others with a friendly nod, but he is not available for conversation. Perhaps another day. Right now, his head is filled with music.

He continues to sing "Smoke Gets in Your Eyes" quietly, with his finger in his ear to amplify the sound for himself. Despite his best efforts to rehearse quietly, his singing can be heard around the room, but it doesn't seem to bother anybody and he is neither self-conscious nor apologetic. After a piped-in recitation of the Pledge of Allegiance in which all of the boys dutifully join, facing the flag near the door, Mr. Moore reads the announcements of the morning from a printout. He then allows the boys to talk or work during the remaining minutes of the period. On another day, he might initiate a conversation on some topic of importance to the world or to the school. That would fulfill the formal requirements of an advisory leader. Today, they are all doing their own thing, at ease in one another's company: completing homework, talking about sports, staring straight ahead, thinking about sleep, or—in one case—preparing for an audition.

One boy turns to me and introduces himself. His name is Harris. I explain to him that I am writing a book about the lives kids live in school and that I am shadowing Adam. Harris takes it upon himself to let me know what kind of school he and his classmates inhabit: "Oh . . . well, this is a very prestigious high school: very competitive, very large, and very prestigious."

"Oh, how do you like it?" I ask.

"It's okay, I guess," Harris answers honestly. "I don't have anything to compare it to."

Forest Hills High School is a serious place, a jewel in the crown of America's public schools. It is one of the most academically powerful high schools in the country. Because of its success, it has an extraordinary grip on the imaginations of the children who attend the school, on the parents who move into the district to send their children there, and on educators across the nation. Through a combination of extraordinary financial resources, a highly educated and supportive parent body, a teacher merit system, and a tradition of excellence, it stands with a small elite group of public schools that have transcended the problems that afflict so many schools in the nation. More than 95 percent of the senior class goes on to college (the students themselves say it is 98 or 99 percent, a small but revealing upward distortion of the actual figure); the average SAT score of graduates is high at 1242; and the average ACT score is 26.7, compared to the national average of 21.

Still, that afternoon at home Adam's mother says that a friend who is worried about sending her eighth-grader to the school next year has asked if Adam believes the benefits of the place outweigh the drawbacks of size and competitive pressure. Adam, who has arrived home accompanied by a friend, responds immediately: "To be able to go to school at Forest Hills is an incredible gift. You're surrounded by excellence—teachers who are at the top in their fields, and students who raise the standard in every class. Whether it's music, debate, history—whatever your interest area is—you're in one of the best programs in the country."

His friend offers a different perspective. "The programs are good," she says, "but it's way too competitive and elitist. And the kids here have too much money." Girls at lunch talk about their upcoming nose jobs and liposuction plans. It's not unusual for classmates to get sporty new cars for birthdays and graduation. The aura of excellence and the "perfect image" culture hides teen depression and drug and alcohol use that is no different from that in other schools, except perhaps that the kids can afford more, she says, describing how some bring vodka in water bottles or leave campus at lunchtime to drink beer or smoke dope (among other things).

Adam recalls a time in his freshman year shortly after they moved to the neighborhood when his mother expressed concern about the fact that he was choosing not to attend parties at some classmates' homes. She urged him to go and make new friends. Adam politely ignored her at first, but eventually he found it necessary to set her straight: He had plenty of friends at school, but he wasn't a "party kind of guy," and if she knew what went on at the parties, she wouldn't be pushing him to go, he told her bluntly. She dropped the lectures on social development, she says, and reminded herself to trust her son's judgment about the kids and places he chose for socializing, and to be grateful he was making wise choices.

She and Adam's father are less sanguine about other aspects of Adam's approach to school. He has always been a good student, earning A's and B's, but an early interest in music has grown over the years into a passion for it—both instrumental and vocal music—and they have perennial concerns about the way he manages his time and attention in regard to his music and academic course commitments. Their concerns come down to these: that he is investing excessive time and energy in music and not enough in his work in academic courses; that inadequate attention to those other courses is costing him, not only in grades but in the richer experience he might have if he were to invest himself more fully in the work; that the lower GPA and class rank will limit his options for college; and that the work and study habits he is developing now aren't going to serve him well in the more rigorous academic environment of college and later adult life.

Typical, they say, is his pattern of devoting himself fully to his music classes, rehearsals, and related interests, while delaying work on homework and long-term assignments in academic classes until the last possible minute—literally the middle of the night at times. As a result, the English essays aren't as well thought out as they might be, the history texts not as well read, the math concepts not as well reviewed going into tests, and his grades reflect that lesser attention. When his mother nags him about homework or the need to work harder, he reminds her that there is some flexibility in the assignments and the times they are due, and that he will, as always, get to it.

"Don't worry," he says. "I always get it done."

Predictably, if he is working past midnight to complete a long-standing assignment due the next day, she launches into one of her stock lectures on procrastination, responsibility, character, or college admissions. Sometimes she hits all four.

Such arguments are standard fare in most families. Children avoid homework; parents press them to complete it. There is nothing new about that. Adam's parents' concerns are typical, too. Is he learning all he should and *could* learn at Forest Hills? Is he developing self-discipline? Is he living up to his potential? Should they push harder?

His father says he is especially concerned that although Adam is earning A's in most of his music classes, because they are classified as "minors," they aren't counted in his GPA. His B's and C's in honors-level classes are an admirable accomplishment, but those "above-average" and "average" grades put him at the lower end of the class ranking. Never mind that his ACT composite score is significantly higher than the average achieved by students at Forest Hills. Indeed, his ACT scores are comparable to the top 10 percent of students in the school, but based on grades alone at this superachiever high school, he doesn't make it into the top half of his class. There are consequences for a class ranking that low. Certain kinds of colleges probably won't consider him. More significantly, Adam won't consider certain kinds of colleges for himself because he has accepted the message implicit in the class rank; he believes he is "not competitive enough."

As a psychologist, I am tempted to interpret Adam's intense focus on music as a defensive strategy, a method of deflecting the competitive pressure of Forest Hills, or perhaps his way of feeling more socially at ease. However, when I ask him about it, Adam will have none of my psychological interpretations. He explains his relationship to music to me this way:

> Music makes me relax. I am addicted. I use it as a drug. My habit is getting worse: In my freshman year I took two [music] classes, and clarinet lessons. In my sophomore year I took two classes, and clarinet and vocal lessons. In my junior year I took three classes, and clarinet and vocal lessons. Now in my senior year I take five music classes, clarinet lessons, vocal lessons, and vocal jazz lessons. And I go to an after-school improv class on Tuesdays. When I make music, I forget about everything else. It is my escape. I don't use it as a social bridge, I use it as a way to forget about all the presures that make up life. Music is my antidrug.

But it is not simply an escape. In a college essay, Adam describes what it feels like for him to sing in a chorus. He writes:

> I can hear the note ringing in my mind; air rushes back up my windpipe and passes through my vocal cords, which vibrate with the exact frequency to reproduce the sound that resonates inside my head. My tone mixes with the three others that are already flowing around me, mixing and blending, creating a smooth, almost creamy sensation. Yet even more wonderful than to listen to the chords and their tantalizing changes is to be an active participant, to be enveloped in the blissful sound, to feel yourself vibrate in concurrence with the environment.

If Adam were a more disciplined student in his academic classes, he most likely would have higher grades and a different class ranking.

But what about his feelings for music and his obvious talent and drive in that arena? Adam is what I call a passionate picker and chooser. He has chosen to do school his way, and his way is to make music for a large part of every day. Now, among parents, educators, and anyone who cares to think about "what colleges want," it is an unquestioned verity that a child with a passion is a wonderful thing—but only if the passion doesn't get in the way of the serious business of grades.

Adam's parents admire his devotion to music, but worry that he has followed an impulsive path, one placing the music he loves ahead of the academics that "count," without thought to the long-term consequences. Listening to his parents, knowing the premium for high grades in this particular school culture, and looking at his grades in academic courses, it would be easy to think of Adam as a stranger to strategic thinking about all this, oblivious to the consequences. He is not.

In our conversation regarding his choices in school life and his school career, Adam is thoughtful, introspective, and savvy about himself and his schooling. He sees it differently, lives it differently. He has made every choice and commitment with careful consideration of what matters most to him, weighed the costs and benefits of different choices, and made decisions that felt right and good to him. He doesn't think of it as a strategy. When I call it that, he concedes that if it was one, "it was an unconscious strategy," but in the next breath he describes the careful considerations he has given the issues. For instance, he points out, he could have dropped from the demanding honors-level courses to a level that is less demanding, where A's would be a sure bet, but he chose to remain in the honors classes "because they're more stimulating." Some people "are more focused on the actual achieving part because to achieve is to succeed, whereas some are into the learning more than others," he says. He identifies himself as one of those who values the learning experience more than scholastic achievement. He continues:

> To get A's requires a lot of work, especially in the classes I'm taking, so in this particular context I think I choose to do other things instead. I just don't feel the need to get A's as long as I'm enjoying myself. I haven't missed anything . . . it's always worked out well . . . I could easily drop down a level and get all A's. If I went

down one level I would be learning half the information a year as I do now. I probably shouldn't do the [honors] level, but I enjoy an intellectual environment . . . I like to challenge my mind. That's what it's all about. . . .

Adam acknowledges that his motivation differs depending on the class and his interest level. There are two kinds of classes, he says: the ones you have to take and the ones you want to take.

A lot of the academic subjects I'm not keyed into to learn because I'm not going to need them. . . . I always thought when you figure out what you really want to do you'll know, and I've known I'm not going to do math ellipses and equations. . . . Sometimes I do the classes—well, actually I do *all* the classes—but I do some and enjoy learning for the sake of learning. . . . The will to learn is important to the achieving. But in high school they toss this hodge-podge of stuff at you and make you do it. But if a class isn't what I'm going to be doing, then I'm not motivated. If I'm in music, then it doesn't matter to me where a pig's pancreas is. I do biology and get a grade, and the learning part is always important, but not always as important in one class as it is in another. . . . I just do what they want and get it in.

When did he first become aware that his strategy for making uniformly higher grades in school wasn't working for him anymore, and that to do it was going to require something different?

In junior high I didn't have to do too much to get the good grades. Then I got into high school and things started getting harder and it affects me in my life. I wasn't getting straight A's. The funny part is—it was a little odd—I don't think I felt overly bad after the initial shock wore off. The thing is I'm still me. It's not me to come home after school and work five hours to get an A. That's just not me.

Maybe not in his academic courses. But he was easily putting in that kind of time in those music courses he loved. On a day when he fell asleep at his desk in English class, he had rehearsed the night before till ten, stayed up until one-thirty A.M. completing other homework, and risen at six to get to school for his seven-fifteen orchestra class. Already that week he had learned four new vocal pieces and accompanying choreography for the upcoming school musical.

On the day I shadow Adam, his schedule includes AP statistics, AP psychology, honors-level English, and a PE class—one academic course fewer than the more academically ambitious of his colleagues at this school. At the same time, he is playing in two top orchestras, singing in the two top choirs, and playing in the top varsity wind ensemble. He spends three to four hours per day in school working on his singing or playing the clarinet. On this day, he will do it all knowing he has an audition to perform as well, along with the roughly one hundred other classmates in his vocal music class.

> "People think just because you're 'gifted' that makes school easy. Well, I have news. It's not."
>
> (Fourth-grader)

The audition itself is the kind of precision, demanding, high-risk, potentially humiliating test that most of us would never subject ourselves to in our own work arenas. Each student will sing solo in front of the others and their teacher—a sympathetic audience, but also a critical one, attuned to the slightest flaws. As I listen to the students perform, and see the nervousness, dread, and excitement in their faces, I wonder: How do these kids endure these risks in front of an audience? When his moment arrives, Adam may be nervous, he may say that he is underprepared, but he is very musical and he is appealing. Clearly talented, he is at ease in front of other people. Although Adam's self-assessment is withering—"I blew the lyrics, I didn't really know them, I sounded nervous"—he is clearly exhilarated by having completed his audition. He radiates self-confidence. I feel exhausted, as if I had held my breath while watching a tightrope walker cross a wire strung between two high buildings. After the nerve-wracking buildup to this audition, I cannot believe that Adam can simply plunge into the rest of the day, into AP statistics and AP psychology interspersed with three more music classes.

Is Adam undisciplined, underachieving, or failing to live up to his potential, as some adults looking at his IQ and ACT scores and then at his GPA might suggest?

The answer to the "failing to live up to his potential" question is yes, if you believe that it is a meaningful question. I do not. It is a meaningful question only if you believe broadly that all students with the IQ potential to make straight A's should make straight A's. It eliminates the human factors of motivation, personality, interpersonal chemistry, class dynamics, and—a significant factor in Adam's case—a consuming passion for a particular subject. Adam's experience of himself is as a bright, motivated, hardworking, responsible student doing well at one of the nation's toughest high schools, in addition to working part-time on weekends and after school. He is busy being a musician. Adam has turned Forest Hills High School into his own personal High School for the Performing Arts. He has designed a high school career for himself that emphasizes two things: enjoying music and protecting himself against the school's compulsive competitive climate.

I ask whether his parents, with their admonitions to work harder, might be trying to stoke the fires of his ambition, perhaps so that he achieves higher grades in these early autumn months of his senior year. He laughs. "It's not working. I'm doing my own thing here." For his own purposes, then, as he is beginning to focus on college choices and the inevitable attention to GPA and class rank, does he regret the choices he has made in high school?

> Actually, I feel as if I got the most out of my environment. I've taken three years and made advances in my academic abilities. Now, after I've surpassed the requirements to graduate, I can finally take the time to throw myself into what amounts to the top high school music programs in the country. . . . I feel as if I've had a good run at it, and will only have regrets if I can't manage to get into a college I wish to attend. . . . I do want to go to a school with a decent intellectual environment. If they don't accept me, that poses a problem. . . . I still consider myself intelligent. Unless I'm deceiving myself there's a definite separation between intelligence and knowledge. I'm not stupid. I don't get the A's anymore, but I still consider myself to be not that bad up top.

He concludes, "I'll know if I made the right choices when I see how it all turns out." He remains calm and philosophical about it, immersed each day in the demanding detail, yet adopting the long view, assuming the role of director for this evolving one-man play: the story of his life. In the end, you cannot argue with a passionate picker and chooser because he is an active participant involved in a blissful pursuit, and—above all—he has found a way to enjoy high school when so many other students do not. You can hope for consistency and discipline, you can wish for higher grades, but ultimately you cannot argue with passion.

A university professor once noted admiringly that a now-distinguished alum he had taught some years before had pursued an unconventional patchwork of studies that looked anything but distinguished at the time. "He manipulated the school to serve his own ends, which is how I determine a good student," the professor said.

In the psychological journey of school, the good journey is the one that leaves a child feeling mostly successful at the end of the day (or the semester) because he has managed to find a way to use school to serve his own ends.

We have accompanied three students—Helena, Cameron, and Adam—who have, through different strategies, found a way to adapt the school routines to their own purposes: Helena by following her linguistic talents; Cameron by becoming a political figure; Adam by investing himself passionately in what he loves, despite the academic cost. Theirs are only three of an infinite number of strategies that students use to find a successful fit in school.

The ability to forge a successful strategy for school depends on a huge number of factors, many out of the student's control. Most of them are out of her parents' control. Though it certainly helps a student to have parents who are themselves educated or who value education, in the end the student herself must find her own way to develop and survive in school. It may take years for a child to discover her individual strategy for getting what she needs from school, or to figure out how to protect herself, physically and emotionally, until she can get out and find a more hospitable environment that will support her growth. In the chapters ahead, we will meet students whose school experience has been not without hope but has been defined more by the struggle.

5

Devastation and Renaissance

Journeys Defined
by Struggle

———

I've thought a lot about what I went through.
I tried athletics—it wasn't meant to be. I tried art.
I never felt as if I truly fit in here.
—*Michael O., eighteen*

The best school in the world will scarcely save a boy
who hates the school and the purpose it serves
and the society that created it.
—*Gilbert Highet,* The Art of Teaching

"Dad, everybody hates school," my daughter, Joanna, tells me. "It is only you and Mom who don't know that." Joanna, a high school junior when she said that, has been a child who hit barriers in school almost from day one. Learning, at least school-based learning, has been punishing for her since first grade, ten long years ago. Her second-grade tutor said to us, "Every day in school is filled with mini-traumas for Joanna." That's strong language. Was it true? Why was school traumatic for my daughter and why weren't we able to make it stop being so?

Three of the basic building blocks of learning—receptive language, expressive language, and attention—have never come easily for her. In other words, her brain is not wired for three things that are at the heart of school-based learning: listening, expressing yourself, and paying attention. Joanna is officially a learning-disabled girl; her diagnoses are dyslexia and attention-deficit hyperactivity disorder.

Though Joanna's story illustrates what school is like for someone who struggles with these fundamental basics of school learning on an ongoing basis, I want to emphasize that it is not just learning-disabled children who experience school as if it were a constant uphill climb with rocks in their backpack. All children struggle to some degree, if not with the content of the curriculum then with the imposition of school, the infinite accommodations it requires of every child. *No one has an easy time of it in school.* It is designed to be a challenging upward ascent for the average, healthy child. If a program is intended to be challenging for mainstream kids, it is going to be that much more difficult for any student who is different. There are many ways to be different, but difference may hit a kid in an area where he cannot develop easily on one of the eight tracks of development. For a learning-disabled child, for instance, a neurological difficulty can hit him right in the center of the academic task of school.

For kids who aren't diagnosed as disabled, but who are unusual-looking, have neurological differences, cannot control their behavior, speak a language other than English, or learn in a different way from most of the kids around them, social development or athletic development may be extremely painful. The list goes on: School can be a struggle for children whose families cannot give them breakfast, or whose parents never come to school meetings because they are too uneducated or can't speak English, or whose parents cannot help them with their homework. My daughter is but one type of child who finds school to be a chronic struggle, and she has had to design her school survival strategy around that fact.

THE STRUGGLE OF GROWTH VERSUS THE STRUGGLE OF FAILURE

If you have ever watched a child learn to swim, especially your own, you may remember the sensation of watching her dog-paddle with her nose barely above the water. It is an uncomfortable feeling, both for the child to experience and for the parent to watch. You stand on your toes, biting your tongue, ready to jump in and help at any second. What makes that feeling tolerable for both parent and child is the knowledge that within a short amount of time, the child will be making progress; she will be up at the surface of the water, her arms swinging over her shoulders and carving into the water. She will gain speed quickly and soon you will be able to see her propel her own body through the water effectively. Maybe soon she'll even love swimming, but even if she doesn't, at least you'll know she's proficient enough to get by. All you have to do to cure your discomfort is to wait for her to practice enough. Spend enough time at the pool or at the beach and swimming takes care of itself. But does it always? What if a child continues to struggle?

Imagine for a moment that you had a child who started swimming class with everyone else, but for one reason or another never got the hang of it. He couldn't master the mechanics of swimming, and always looked awkward in the water. He hated the cold water or—if it was a lake or the ocean—imagined that there were eels or monsters beneath the surface. For such a child, any trip to the beach would be fraught with anxiety and ripe for failure. If he didn't get better at swimming the way other children did, or always lagged behind other children, or continued to harbor secret fears about the water, this most ordinary and pleasurable of human activities would then become a source of struggle, both physical and emotional.

I like to swim in the ocean, but even for an experienced swimmer there are uncomfortable moments. You can be swimming parallel to the beach, enjoying a good swim at what you think is a safe distance, and then be startled to discover that the current is carrying you slowly backward. You can use all your strength and still find you're drifting farther from shore. It is a disturbing feeling even if you are safely in touch with the shore. But imagine the moment you discover that you are too far from shore to get back easily, and the current is taking you out; in a rising panic, you realize that there is no one close enough to rescue you, and you have no choice but to begin stroking steadily back to shore. You arrive on firm ground—as most of us do—deeply relieved and exhausted by the adrenaline that your body has generated. Can you imagine experiencing that feeling every day? Children whose school journey is characterized by struggle have those moments of panic and recovery and ongoing struggle many, many days.

In a broad sense, all learning and growth require struggle, but there is a difference between the experience of struggle that leads to success and the experience of struggle that leads only to more struggle. At some point struggle becomes the defining element of a person's life. We may all briefly struggle in order to overcome an obstacle, to meet challenges, and we may struggle every time we come to an uncomfortable task, but the struggling student finds every day in school to be an ordeal. At the end of one particularly painful day, one discouraged fifth-grade boy with some learning disabilities complained:

> I just feel too overwhelmed from work. I never really know what to do. What should kids do? Should they go to their parents, their teacher, or . . . ? The teachers give kids an undoable amount of work. Some kids get overwhelmed and they need breaks. I get confused every day. That's why I have meltdowns. The day goes usually fine, but sometimes it's too overwhelming.

When does he become aware that his day is starting to fall apart? His answer: "By about the fifth thing you do. Sometimes it is right in the moment."

We can accept his definition. A struggling student is one for whom "the day goes usually fine, but sometimes it's too overwhelming." That is to say, there is a strong probability that in the course of every day, a student who struggles will hit some point overwhelming enough to send her tumbling in her feelings. A student who struggles is likely to feel intense panic, frustration, or deep discouragement—"that's why I have meltdowns"—every single day in school, some when they encounter academic tasks that are too hard or too frustratingly boring, others when they come up against the social or athletic demands of the school. The most important characteristic that distinguishes a struggling student from one whose journey is characterized more by success is the predictability and regularity of these frustrations, and the child's overwhelming feelings of helplessness.

Research confirms what common sense tells us: Children love the challenge of small, reachable goals ("Oh, let me try!"), and any child can lose motivation if the challenge is too huge ("Naw, I don't like that stuff"). A little anxiety is motivating; too much is immobilizing.

A little fear can focus a child's thoughts; too much destroys his concentration. One easy task can be a welcome relief; a chronic lack of challenge can be demoralizing for a child.

I have worked with children who start to cry before they have to take tests and not because they are unprepared; the testing experience makes them so anxious they cannot remember what they know. For a child to perform well, a number of things have to come together: her cognitive ability, her preparation, her ability to handle the task on an emotional basis, and the support she feels from her environment. In the end, it is a normal human response to walk away from any experience of chronic cognitive confusion, emotional overload, and failure. Just as no type of student is guaranteed success, no type is immune to chronic struggle. A fifth-grade girl who was an excellent student but hated school wrote this to me:

> Imagine going to school in the morning and dreading every second of it: not because you can't do the work, but because you *can.* Nothing is hard, or even slightly challenging. Nobody seems to care. All they ever do is say, "Feel lucky that you can do the work. There are so many children who struggle every day." *"Well, guess what?"* you think. *"So do I."*

Individual teachers are always trying to find that fine point between boredom—brought about by going over material the child already knows—and confusion—caused by confronting so much new material that the brain rebels. Piaget wrote that all developing human beings are constantly trying to balance between *assimilation,* integrating knowledge into structures that are already in place in the mind ("Oh, I had something like this last year"), and *accommodation,* the process by which you create new structures in order to hold the concept in mind ("Wow, this is totally new"). He believed that the minds of developing children are always trying to achieve *equilibration*—a balance between the two.

If this is true in the cognitive realm, it is equally true in the emotional realm. Children are always seeking new and stimulating emotional experiences, hence so many children's love for scary movies. However, they do not want to be chronically overwhelmed by novel feelings. The same principle holds true in all psychological arenas. Children do not, as parents sometimes believe, crave "doing nothing." They are always looking for a challenge of one kind or another that they can master.

The problem for a student who struggles is that he cannot find enough in school that he can regularly master in order to reach some subsistence level of competence and self-confidence, or he may be overwhelmed by his emotional reaction to some aspect of the work or the place. The journey of a struggling student is characterized by moments of panic and despair, interspersed—I hope—with successes in a different realm. Every educator prays that the student who struggles academically will find an area of competence in the social or extracurricular department for just that reason: to keep them in the game.

I once interviewed a man who had had a painful time in school, perhaps because he had an undiagnosed learning disability. He described elementary school in the following way: "I had friends and stuff like that, but I think that I was just, somehow, blanked. I just sat through the days, you know. I mean, I could look at the teacher and I don't think, sometimes, that I was really taking in anything she said." School was a constant struggle for him. He squeaked by academically, but found more satisfying experiences in extracurricular activities and friendships. For those parents who believe school is an accurate prediction of the future, it is worth noting that this man became an extraordinarily successful real estate broker. He earns more than four hundred thousand dollars annually, year after year, and is known and respected by everyone in his town. A struggling student does not necessarily grow into a struggling adult.

The students whom we got to know in the previous chapters are the good swimmers, consistently propelling themselves forward. They each use different strokes, they are all making an extraordinary effort, and at times they hit stretches that are a struggle, but they push through and rarely find themselves in serious waters that they can't navigate. Obviously, any one of them could be defeated by an overwhelming current, for example, a test for which she has not prepared, or a sports injury or relationship crisis that temporarily pulls him down. Each has faced more moments of frustration and boredom than they care to count, but each has also developed a strategy for dealing with "the worst" school life can throw at them.

Struggling students, on the other hand, end up treading water while looking frantically around for help or relief for part of every school day. For some reason, the mechanics of learning don't come easily to them, or the school environment makes them too anxious, or personal issues are weighing them down. We might call these students learning disabled, anxious, troubled, or disadvantaged. These labels, helpful for adults, provide no relief for a student. They do little to help a child get through a day. The subjective experience of a child is not "I am learning disabled," but rather "I am dumb. This stuff is too hard." As we will see, Joanna rejected the label of learning disabled for many years, resenting it, fighting it, or lashing out in anger at all attempts to help her. "Academic support is no help," she said, even though she has relied on it for years. On the other hand, school is not a completely desperate place for her. She has friends, she loves sports, and no matter how frustrating the school day, she is always glad to get out onto the field and see her coach. "I'm always in the mood for soccer," she declares.

Labels don't ease the discomfort for the anxious or school-phobic child who lives in the grip of fear. A sixth-grader wrote:

> School, for most people, or so I think, is just another thing. You go, learn a little, eat lunch with your friends, go home. For [me], however, school is another story. Picture a 3-D computer game. You are looking down a dark hall. You can't see anything, but you know what is there; you can hear the swords swinging and the gunmen ready to shoot. But you can see a small opening of light at the end of the hall. You have just seen a day at school for [me]. School can become so torturous that you start to feel physically ill when you anticipate it.

Many students become unable to function in school and are frightened to go in the mornings. With smaller children in elementary school, school phobia manifests itself as stomachaches, headaches, tantrums, and screaming. A small child who is phobic reaches desperately for any reason not to go to school, believing that his fear is reasonable and is really about school. Older children and adults know that their phobic fears are irrational, but they simply cannot control the dread they feel.

Let's think about dread of school for a moment. Don't you think it is fair to say that almost every student has dreaded school at one time or another? Can you remember the sick feeling of having a test the next day for which you hadn't adequately prepared? Do you remember being frightened because you knew—or imagined—that the teacher was going to be *very angry with* you for not doing your homework? Or perhaps you were the best at something and the pressure to never make a mistake was terrifying. Inside every child in school is the potential to be terrified on a given school day or frightened of school entirely. Considering the number of tasks that schools demand of children across a wide range of strengths and weaknesses, every child will experience fear in school and some will experience terrible fears. Add to these fears all the normal worries that children have about divorce, about the sickness or death of a parent, about lightning and thunder, and it is amazing that children are not overwhelmed by fear more often than they are. Most do not become school phobic, but they struggle with the mandate to attend school and struggle to manage their fears.

What keeps these kids in the game is the fact that they can find *some* things they like about school. The school day is not *completely* threatening or overwhelming for them, which differentiates these struggling students from others who have fallen in despair or fury. Struggling students find enough in school to keep them alive psychologically, to keep them hopeful, sometimes simply enough to keep them willing, at least, to come back each day.

It is my job to sit and talk with kids who are miserable in school. In my office, I have become acquainted with children who struggle daily because school is a mismatch for them. Despite the fact that I admire and respect educators and enjoy the school environment my-self, I have come to share the point of view of some children for whom school does not work very well. However, no matter how much I have been influenced by my patients, I doubt that I would have ever written this book were it not for my own children's difficulties in school. The chronic troubles that my daughter, Joanna, and my son, Will, encounter in school brought this topic home for me.

JOANNA

Joanna has been an athlete since the day she was born. She never liked to sleep a lot; energy emanated out of her all day and into the night. Though not a classic colicky baby, many nights my wife, Theresa, was up carrying and comforting our crying daughter, or Joanna was just wide awake, happy and excited, a true night owl. She continued to be extremely energetic throughout her babyhood. As soon as she could play with other children we experienced a phenomenon that persists to this day: She is always moving toward the next adventure. Typically, after a play date a friend would go home to nap and Joanna would go out the back door and across the lawn to find another neighborhood friend with whom to play.

Theresa and I had always imagined a classic bedtime reading ritual: our child asking for her favorite story over and over. Not Joanna. When we tried to read a book to her at bedtime, she didn't seem to like to listen to the content of the stories. She loved us to be with her and, like most children, she tried to prolong the ritual, but she also wanted to hang from the bars of her crib, and later, when she was three years old, to swing from the upper bunk of her bunk beds, always moving, testing her muscles. I could get her interested in *Where the Wild Things Are,* by substituting her name for that of the main character, Max. She would laugh with pleasure, but rarely would she stop what I began to refer to as her "nighttime gymnastics."

Looking back, Joanna recalls that when we started to read to her, she either felt "hyper" or would "just pass out right away."

"I couldn't listen to people read to me," she says.

Did she *ever* look forward to being read to as a child?

"Yes," she offers, " 'cause at least I didn't have to read it myself."

Now that she is seventeen, listening to people read—including teachers who read important passages from the text aloud—makes her tired. Being read to is an experience I have always cherished. Joanna dreads it and has an immediate physical response to it. Trapped in class, she wants to sleep.

Joanna lives in a different world than I do. We sit side by side at the same events, and absorb them in entirely different ways, often using different senses. We once went to the Broadway musical *Crazy for You,* which is based on the music and lyrics of George and Ira

Gershwin. While I was listening to the hero and heroine declare their love for each other through the lyrics of the great tunes, Joanna was sitting next to me whispering, "Dad, look at that . . . look at that person . . . look what she's doing." I was listening to the words being sung by the lead actors; she was watching the actions of every person in the chorus. What for me was a verbal experience was for Joanna a visual display. She lives in a world of visual experiences and of movement. You need only to watch her on a soccer field or an ice hockey rink to understand that immediately.

A friend whose child could carry on conversations at age two and read books at age three tells of the first psychological evaluation her daughter ever had—testing required by the school district to allow her to start junior kindergarten despite an "early" birthday—and the psychologist who remarked drily at the conclusion, "Well, it is clear your daughter is going to have a very interesting career in education, and it's probably *not* going to be in the public schools."

That was about ten years ago. As it happened, both our daughters have had "very interesting" careers in school: often frustrating and painful careers for vastly different reasons. Both have moved between public and private schools, struggling between hope and disappointment in both places.

There was a time when children like my daughter would have floundered, failed, and likely dropped out. Twenty-seven years ago, Congress passed a federal law requiring public schools to meet the needs of all children in this country. The special-education law, though never adequately funded by Congress, did make it mandatory for public schools to provide programs for *all* children. Following in the wake of the public sector, private and parochial schools have also responded to the need for more support services for special-needs children.

The law requires educators to attempt to meet the needs of all students—regardless of the severity of their disabilities. What it *cannot* do is make school an easy place for children. For many children with disabilities or differences, school can be a place of small humiliations and large disasters where they struggle every day. My daughter is such a student. That she has hung on and even thrived is partially due to the guiding support of many people, but mostly due to her courageous efforts.

> "I am so scared when my report card comes that like three weeks before i just study thru lunch—i am to worried to eat. If my report card is bad then my dad gets called and then he gets mad and yells." (Eighth-grader)

With an eye to Joanna's compelling need for physical movement, we found a small, progressive elementary school for her that would allow her maximal freedom of movement in the classroom. She seemed to love Clearview School from the beginning of pre-K. She made enduring relationships with her teachers, loved playing with her friends, admired the headmaster (whom she and the other children called "Dan"), and couldn't be pried out of the after-school program by her parents. At the end of the day, when many other children were wilting, she wanted to continue playing some board game or a card game. It would be hard to imagine any child liking pre-K and kindergarten more than Joanna. She didn't much care that some children were already beginning to read and she was not.

When she hit first grade, however, virtually every child in her class who hadn't learned to read in kindergarten mastered the skills necessary for decoding language that fall. They were all reading by Christmas. Joanna wasn't. She became sad. By January, she appeared genuinely depressed. For the first time in her life—but hardly the last—she didn't want to go to school in the morning. She complained of stomachaches and said she didn't like Clearview.

As a high school junior her most prominent memory of elementary school is, "Just that I always got in trouble for not sitting still."

Any other memories?

"Playing on the playground."

Nothing about learning?

"They tried to make you write letters in the sandbox. It was stupid. It didn't help you."

Joanna repeatedly describes school as a place where people didn't help. Our memory is different. We were trying to help, as were many other adults: administrators, teachers, psychologists, tutors, and psychiatrists. The problem was that all the help wasn't making school any easier for Joanna.

In spite of an understanding tutor, school became increasingly painful through first, second, and third grades. Constantly moving, Joanna had trouble sitting still under the best of circumstances. She just couldn't bear to sit and look at a page of writing that made no sense to her. Joanna learned to read in March of second grade, two weeks after she began taking Ritalin, a stimulant medication prescribed for attentional problems. Medicine helped her focus on the hated task of reading long enough to get a grip on it. It could not, however, take the daily sting out of school. She began to develop a repertoire of avoidant tactics. In the March conference with her third-grade teaching team, we were told that Joanna never finished tasks, was always sharpening a pencil or going to the bathroom, was behind in virtually all of her work, and was always looking for excuses to leave the classroom. (Learning-disabilities expert Priscilla Vail calls these "in-school field trips.")

The progressive open-plan classroom was not working for Joanna, but her teachers failed to discuss the possibility of a mismatch between setting and child. Rather, the focus of the conference was all about what Joanna couldn't or wouldn't do. Her teachers—both good human beings—had nothing to offer except a critique of our daughter's defects: her physicality and her strategies for avoiding school. Theresa and I walked into the hall, looked at each other, and made the decision to withdraw her from the school and find another where—we hoped—there would be teachers better trained to work with learning-disabled children.

Our decision did not come easily. Though Joanna had experienced a lot of failure in her classroom, Clearview had been her home since pre-K. She was furious at us for deciding to transfer her to a new school. While we were weighing the options between our public school and another, more structured independent school, Joanna made her choice known: If she had to change schools, she wanted to go to the public school in town. That wasn't an entirely easy decision for us. We assumed an independent school would be more likely to have smaller class sizes, closer relationships between students and teachers, and institutional flexibility to accommodate Joanna's special needs. It required a leap of faith to turn our child over to the town of Arlington, Massachusetts. However, we were reassured to learn that the schools had a highly respected special-education department and that other parents we knew rated it highly.

Because she was so far behind academically, we made the decision to have Joanna repeat the third grade. It turned out to be a great
decision. Her third-grade teacher was a gift from heaven. Joan Black
had waist-length gray hair and her arm was decorated with a silver
bracelet for every year she had been in teaching: twenty-four silver
bracelets, which Joanna remembers with great clarity (she must have
thirty-one bracelets by now). Perhaps more to the point, we learned
that Mrs. Black had a learning-disabled child of her own. Though we
never got a chance to meet with Mrs. Black at the start of the school
year, Joanna's reaction told us all we needed to know. One week into
her time at her new public school, Joanna said, "I like this school
much better than Clearview. That was the wrong school for me."

At our first parent-teacher conference, Mrs. Black opened the
meeting with the following observation: "Joanna is like a butterfly.
She alights on one thing, and then another, and another and another.
My job as her teacher is to try to persuade her that everything is going
to be all right. She can stick with something and finish it." Theresa
and I started to cry. We trusted Mrs. Black from that moment on.

Joanna's memory is simply, "She helped me more."

The school program was beautifully designed. Mainstream teachers worked so well with the special-education teachers that Joanna
was able to move at will from her mainstream classroom to a resource
room whenever she came up against a reading-comprehension task
that began to frustrate or overwhelm her. She could simply stand up
and walk out of one classroom and go to another. It seemed to us that
she had landed in academic heaven.

Joanna remembers it differently, however, the taste of frustration
still bitter. She remembers one of the resource-room teachers questioning whether she was dyslexic, as everyone seemed to think. It
was worse than insulting.

There is a major discrepancy here between what Joanna remembers experiencing at the school and what we, as her parents, were experiencing. For the first time in her life we felt we were speaking to
knowledgeable, trained people who understood learning disabilities
and had a handle on Joanna's difficulties. For two years we were generally satisfied and comforted by her education. It is distressing even
now to think that Joanna was not feeling helped, or that she believed
that her special-education teachers were discounting the depth of her

disability. From our point of view, a lot of adults were knocking themselves out to help her.

What is the explanation for the difference between the experiences she recalls and our memories of the same place and time? It is the same gap that exists between all parents and their children: Joanna was the one who was going to school, Joanna was the one who couldn't master reading, not her mother and me. Though we empathized profoundly, we didn't have to live the struggle the way she did. Joanna was the one who had to appear in her classroom every day and face the reality of not being able to read as well as the other children.

It is important to think about the time sense of children, because we often see them as "so young." By the time she was in fifth grade at the public school, Joanna had been struggling that way for *six* years. We thought of school as a tough but well-meaning place. Her experience was that it was punishing her every day and no one there was really helping.

I cannot emphasize this point enough and that's not because I want to create sympathy for my daughter or for her mother and myself. When it comes to schooling, there is a profound gap between the experience of children and the perception of parents. It is humbling to interview one's own learning-disabled child about her school history. Doing so made me grateful that she didn't walk away from the whole thing.

In fifth grade, it seemed Joanna might do just that. From the outset, things were rocky. Of the two fifth-grade classes, as it happened, her old friends were assigned to one and she was assigned to the other, where she had no friends and disliked the cliquish girls. Her teacher was in the final year of her career and was phoning in her effort. Also that year there were cuts in the district's special-education budget, Joanna's principal had a heart attack, and some of the key resource-room personnel in the school were reassigned to other schools. Gone was the high level of cooperation between mainstream teachers and resource-room teachers. The school that had been an academic heaven for learning-disabled children was starting to become just another school, and for Joanna a return to purgatory.

A new friend entered the picture and the situation worsened.

Angel came from a chaotic family, with a mother who appeared overwhelmed, both psychologically and economically. Angel had gotten her pubertal growth early and had a long, lanky body and a strong fashion sense. She began to wear sexy clothes and Joanna followed suit. Angel said increasingly disparaging things about school, and began to copy homework from other kids or simply failed to hand in her assignments. Joanna emulated Angel's attitude toward education.

Joanna recalls precisely how it felt and why she made questionable choices: "I started not caring about school because she didn't. She was a year above me and I thought she was cool. I thought I could follow in her footsteps."

After two satisfactory years in a school, Joanna was heading rapidly down and out of her educational career. She could not have been less interested or involved in a spring term-paper assignment. We were seriously worried. Theresa is also a psychologist, and we knew the research on what happens to learning-disabled students in middle school: They start to disengage from the academic side of school. They get tired of the struggle with their limitations in the school environment and they turn to activities that make them feel better, most of them social. The danger, of course, is that they will become involved in deviant activities: premature sexual behavior, drugs, and alcohol.

We could see Joanna losing interest in school. She no longer felt connected to her teachers. Most important, much of the time she was angry about school.

Did her resource-room teacher help her? Not according to Joanna. Once again, I want to differ with my own daughter's description of what was happening to her. I want to object and say, "There are two sides to this story." Our experience with Joanna was that she didn't ask for help from anyone because she never wanted to admit she was learning disabled. While she resented when a teacher said she was not as dyslexic as she thought, she did not yet fully accept that she was, in fact, learning disabled.

From an adult point of view, it seems irrational for a child to deny having a disability, for a child to consistently refuse to ask for help. From the child's vantage point, it makes perfect sense. A learning disability isn't physical. It isn't like the child is in a wheelchair or is unable to run. For the most part she looks and acts normal. Why would a child want to admit publicly that she struggles at something that other children around her find relatively easy to do? Why wouldn't a child hate school for rubbing her nose in the things she doesn't do well rather than admit it is her defect? To a child, it feels as if a disability is her fault.

For Joanna, the open admission of struggle would have been a confession of weakness, of difference, of something that—once admitted to—would become an undeniable fact. Why wouldn't a child hold out the hope that this difficulty would just go away? I have consulted with many parents of learning-disabled children who, in spite of the evidence and what they have been told by expert after expert, hold out the hope that their children will outgrow the problem that they never will outgrow.

For children whose school strategy is defined by struggle, the biggest psychological hurdle is to acknowledge to themselves that they are never going to be terribly successful in school in the area of their weakness. It is easy for me to state that for a learning-disabled child such an acknowledgment is the beginning of wisdom, that it is the start of his ability to use help and accommodations. However, to a child it seems like a defeat. To an adult, it would seem desirable for a learning-disabled child to embrace a diagnosis—to get him off the hook, so to speak. That certainly wasn't the case for Joanna, a proud girl, a competitive athlete, and someone who just wanted to be like all the other kids. That is perhaps the deepest wish that children have: just to be a regular kid, to be smart in the same way as other kids. As much as we assured her (accurately) that she was a bright thinker and learner, Joanna could not feel it when she was unable to read the way other children could.

Seriously worried about keeping her in school and determined to find a better fit for her, we examined our options again and decided to switch Joanna to a private school that specialized in learning-disabled children, particularly those with dyslexia. At least at the Eliot School all the other children would have a history of struggle with language as well. It was a momentous decision for all: for Theresa and me, because it put us on the road to paying the equivalent of a college tuition for our child's middle-school education (the town would not financially support such a move); and for Joanna, because it made it impossible for her to think of herself as just a mainstream kid anymore. She hated the idea of going to an LD school and repeatedly referred to it as a school for "dumb" kids.

I would like to be able to tell you that after a brief period of adjustment Joanna embraced being a part of a community of learning-disabled students and adults, that she was inspired by having teachers who themselves had suffered from dyslexia and had prevailed by finishing their educations. That was not exactly what happened.

Her retrospective assessment of the Eliot School: "I hated it. Right from when I walked into school I saw the cliques, I didn't like the people. The teachers thought it was the best LD helping school, but it didn't do anything for me . . . you know how I was always sick in sixth grade? Well, I faked being sick. I made myself sick just so I didn't have to go to school there."

Indeed, Joanna took to her bed with a variety of confusing symptoms in March of her sixth-grade year and slept close to twenty hours a day for the better part of three weeks. We certainly entertained the idea that she was depressed, avoidant, and malingering (we are psychologists, after all), but her exhaustion appeared genuine. Joanna complained of intense headaches. Theresa checked her room constantly and she was always asleep. We were baffled and so was her physician. Was it the residue from the flu? Was she depressed? We could not figure it out, and to this day it is hard to imagine that she could will herself to sleep like that. For a child so active, staying in bed to avoid school could not have been easy. That she was prepared to make herself sick is a measure of her misery.

What made school there tolerable for Joanna was the opportunity to play competitive sports and the love she felt for her two coaches, Mr. M. and Mr. K. There is still a picture on her bedroom wall of herself at her eighth-grade graduation with Mr. M., arms around each other's shoulders and huge smiles on their faces. Her "Coaches' Award," given to the best all-around graduating athlete at the school, hangs nearby.

"I loved them. They were like kids, kind of. They were so much fun," she says.

Does she have any memory of classroom teachers? Not really,

unless you count the teacher who also was a cheerleader for the New England Patriots football team on weekends, considered pretty cool by a seventh-grade girl athlete.

We saw a gain, even if Joanna did not. After three years at a school with other learning-disabled children, Joanna began to come to grips with the fact of her being permanently disabled with respect to reading. Though she might deny the Eliot School's impact on her, it helped her acknowledge her difficulties, even if it did not always motivate her to ask for help (that is still developing). And her Eliot School education prepared her to return to a mainstream school, which turned out to be the next stop on her journey.

Now it was time to start high school and we were faced with the familiar dilemma: public or private? There were some private schools in the Boston area with superb athletic programs that she would not be able to manage academically; there were three wonderful schools that supported learning differences and had relatively weak athletic programs that would have been disappointing for an athlete as skilled as our daughter; and there was our local high school, with its special-education services and classmates with whom she had played soccer and ice hockey for many years.

"It's embarrassing to get a test that you get a bad grade on hung up on the wall."

(Sixth-grader)

I said to Joanna, "You know, the high school is the natural place for you to go. You know so many kids there, you've played with them all, and you have a good shot at making the varsity teams."

Her reply was succinct: "Dad, if I go to the high school, I'll be in the lowest track and I'll hang out with all the kids who hate school."

The implication was that she was likely to get into trouble at the high school. When an adolescent says something so clear, you must act on her words. No teenager is likely to repeat that statement. Furthermore, it makes the point that kids know things about school that don't occur to their parents. Joanna was already anticipating the emotional impact of the tracking system in high school, something that we had not considered.

Our daughter had been saying since fourth grade that she never intended to go to college, that she couldn't bear for school to go on any longer than it had to, so it made sense for us to look for a private school, even a boarding school, that was a match for her abilities. If she did not thrive in high school, she might never get the basic education that we hoped our child would have. We wanted her to have a strong high school experience so that if she did choose not to go to college, she could at least approach the job market with confidence after her senior year.

Happily, we found the school of her dreams: Cushing Academy, a boarding school fifty miles from our home. It was a tough decision for us to send our daughter away to school. And yet, there we were, visiting a school and sitting across the dining hall watching Joanna talk excitedly with a group of girls who looked just like her: athletic, rugged, happy, and adolescent. Later, Joanna would say it was the best decision we—she would say *she*—ever made. She's right.

After eight more-or-less painful years in school since first grade, Joanna found a place that she loved. (She has said so publicly.) There are four hundred students in the school; she knows them all and they all know her. She has been captain of two varsity teams, soccer and tennis, and has been the captain of the junior varsity girls' ice hockey team, as well. She called home once during ninth grade and said, "Dad, this is the right school for me." Why? I asked. "Well, the girls here are just like me. We were outside the dining hall and the boys were throwing acorns at us. We didn't just scream and run away. We attacked them."

Because Cushing Academy is a mainstream school, where three-quarters of the kids do not have neurologically based learning problems, she struggles. Because one-quarter of the students have documented learning differences, she also has company and support. It is similar to the situation she experienced in public school when there was a strong sense of collaboration between the mainstream teachers and the academic support personnel. She and her roommate (also dyslexic) openly joke about their tortured efforts to spell. Joanna takes one scheduled extra-help class per day and has a twice-a-week tutor as well.

After more than thirty years in education, I come back time and again to the simple conclusion that one of the most important things that can happen between a child and a school is for the student to experience a sense of fit with the school. It puts a supportive floor under

a child's morale and sustains him in hard times, be they social or academic. Fit might seem like something that would be hard to come by
in the public sector, because children don't have a choice of schools.
Their families cannot switch, as we did, between a progressive and a
more structured, specialized program. Yet in my experience most students, even in a large high school, can find a niche where they really
feel that they fit.

Elementary school children often experience that sense of fit because of one homeroom teacher, and that's enough, even though they
might feel out of synch with the music, art, and gym teachers. Sometimes just one person, or a small group of friends, or a beautiful art
room, is enough to make a child feel, "I belong here."

Despite the additional factor of choice, fit isn't always that easy
to find in private or parochial schools. Many unhappy graduates of
these schools describe their sense of isolation and awkwardness in
their schools.

Fit is something that a majority of children can feel in any school
if the institution embodies five elements, all axiomatic to educators:
teachers who welcome children, trust them, and try to make them
comfortable; a challenging program that is a match for a child's
ability level; a program that is sufficiently broad-based that a child
can find a "hook" for her ability (a nonskier can never thrive in a
school for ski racers!); a safe climate and a sense of community purpose; and school leadership that focuses on the needs of the child, not
the needs of school-board members, unions, politicians, or education
critics.

The idea of fit is actually about mutual trust between teachers and
students, and a sense of confidence that the student experiences during the learning process. Like many struggling students, Joanna
stopped trusting teachers and the process of classroom learning at
some point in early elementary school. Her brain let her down, her
teachers couldn't seem to help, and she believed they didn't want to
help. Sadly, that trust was lost for years. Despite the best efforts of
teachers at subsequent schools, it took the better part of ten years for
her to regain it. She found it again, to a significant degree, at Cushing
Academy. For a child who chronically struggles with learning, who
can be blindsided by language at any moment, her sense of trust in
what goes on in classrooms remains fragile.

Here is Joanna's description of eleventh grade. Though she doesn't intend to tell us the story of trust rediscovered, that is, in fact, what she describes:

> Well, I sit there and I pay attention. I don't usually raise my hand because if I say something wrong I don't want to be laughed at or something. I mean, I know the people here won't do it, but just in my head. But I'm starting to ask questions more just because I'm getting older and I don't care anymore. And like now I can ask—in the middle of exams—I can ask Mrs. Lee like so many questions and she didn't get mad once. She didn't look annoyed, she was like always smiling. The teachers are helpful here. It's not like other schools where they'll just be like, "Ohmigod, not another question."

Joanna makes it sound as if there were a sudden turnaround. I remind her that she almost flunked out of Cushing in her ninth-grade year. She explains: "That's because there was a switch from Eliot where I never got help, and then to here, where I didn't know I could really get help. 'Cause you guys said that Eliot would help me so much and then I got there and it didn't help me. And then one of you said Cushing will help you, but *I didn't believe it*. Then after freshman year, in sophomore year, I started to believe it."

It was difficult for us as parents to hear that our child did not believe us telling her that people were going to be helpful to her, because she didn't trust them. I ask Joanna to think back to all the special-education teachers and support staff at her previous schools. Doesn't she remember their efforts? Perhaps she remembers them as unhelpful because it wasn't working yet. Her answer: "Probably that, but they didn't know how to help me."

Did she experience teachers as the enemy because the classroom experience was so inherently difficult for her? In fact, she experienced the room itself as overwhelming. In his important work on adolescence, *Identity: Youth and Crisis,* Erik Erikson describes how unhappy teenagers can distort time, so that it seems endless or unbearably fast. Here Joanna describes the class size just that way: "In Eliot, the classes were so big even though they didn't say they were. It seemed like there were so many people." I remind her that at Eliot the largest class she had was seven students. "I know," she replies, "but the rooms were so small. Once I came here it seemed [so large and roomy] it was like there was nobody in class."

Just as Erikson describes, Joanna is distorting the size of classes and of the rooms, based on her experience of isolation and helplessness in the face of the material. When she did not trust the learning experience, the class sizes seemed suffocatingly large, crammed into small rooms, when in truth there were only six other children in the room. When she trusts the process, it seems as if there are fewer children and bigger rooms, even when there are eighteen students in a room that is not, in fact, that large. The fact that Joanna loves sports and lives for sports makes Cushing Academy the right school for her: "I always wanted to be there. I've never felt that I didn't want to be there. I've always wanted to play."

At the end of her junior year, Joanna describes the psychological shift in her approach: "I used to feel like I *had* to be there [in class], and now I feel like I kind of want to be there. It's easier. It's a lot easier. I even had the guts . . . we had a PowerPoint presentation and I even had the guts to present in front of the whole class. And like I never . . . I told my group that I wasn't going to do it and then I got up there."

You can hope for a fit between your child and the school, between your child and a teacher, but you cannot make it happen. Even when we thought we knew what we were doing based on her identified learning disabilities, Joanna's experience of school was her own. Our most effective responses evolved when we could set aside our fears and assumptions and expectations, and let Joanna's experience inform us.

ALEXANDRA: TROUBLES WITHOUT A NAME

What would it be like to struggle in school and not understand *why* you struggle so severely? What would it be like to not have a name for the barriers that you keep hitting? For better and worse, our Joanna knew from an early age that she had a recognized learning disability that wouldn't go away. What if a student found herself repeatedly failing or unable to work, but did not know why? That is Alexandra's problem. Despite her intelligence, her optimism, and her generosity of spirit, Alexandra has experienced a lot of failure in school. She is still searching for the reason.

I met Alexandra at a mall in East Cambridge—*the* most popular hangout place for teenagers in the towns around Cambridge. It was a clear, sunny day in May, a month before the end of her sophomore year. Dark-haired and pretty, fifteen years old, she carried herself like an athlete and came across as willing to be tough if the occasion demanded. She didn't pull any punches in her description of her school performance: "Yeah, I'm going to fail chemistry . . . like I'm usually good in science but they had to go and mix it with math."

Do you remember the feeling, especially in a cumulative subject like math or science, that you missed some of the basic material and as the class moved on, you felt stranded and left behind? That's what Alexandra began feeling in her chemistry course sometime in the middle of the winter.

"It's got some math issues so that kind of confused me and when I started getting bad grades, like a series of bad grades, after I started studying and I didn't understand it, then basically I just gave up and you know you're going to fail," she says.

How did this happen? When did this downward slide start?

"At the beginning I was fine with it. And then I guess I have this thing where it's like, it's kinda way too easy, maybe, I won't pay attention, I'll read the book, and then I'll get through it. And then I decided to not pay attention. I kind of underestimated it and I totally, when we started to get to the hard stuff, I totally just like . . ."

Chemistry is not going to be Alexandra's only failure. She is also going to get an F in her math course. She is keenly aware that these failures are like slow-motion multiple-car collisions in her high school career. She has to have three lab sciences and four math courses to graduate from high school, and once she makes up these failures, she is going to come close to running out of time if she wants to graduate in four years. "I'm going to have to start cramming in two maths . . . and I can't stand math so it's going to be pretty difficult."

Throughout this description of academic unraveling, Alexandra is neither bitter nor blaming. Is there a personality clash? Does she hate her chemistry teacher? Not at all; she says her teachers are "all cool." Did she talk to her chemistry teacher when she was starting to get into trouble in the course? "No, not really." Had she talked to a guidance counselor? "If I had gone up to any of the teachers I knew, the guidance counselors, and asked them, like told them what was going on, like my grades or anything, they'd definitely talk about it. . . . I never really went to any guidance counselors or any of the teachers." Why not? I ask. "I don't know, I just never . . . I'm failing, what's the point of going to a counselor?" Alexandra is academically drowning and she isn't even shouting, "Help."

It is obvious that Alexandra needs assistance. Why isn't she seeking it out? When teenagers display this kind of resignation, this apparent lack of motivation, it makes adults feel intensely helpless. We tend to make suggestions, push them toward extra-help sessions, and exhort them. Alexandra's guidance counselor and teachers have done that in the past. Alexandra says, "I've had a lot of teachers actually get mad because they're like, 'Oh, you have a lot of potential. You are wicked, wicked smart, but why aren't you doing this?' And they actually get mad that I don't do the work, because if I had done it, I don't know, some say I'd be in honors or whatever."

A child with great potential who is failing makes everyone feel helpless. If telling a child she is smart and exhorting her to work harder doesn't work, we look for someone to blame. It has to be someone's fault. Guidance counselors blame teachers. Teachers blame the counselors for not discovering the mystery of the failure. Parents often blame the school and the teachers (They're out the door at three o'clock!). Teachers often blame the parents (They're never home to supervise homework). In the end, however, adults usually blame the child. You can imagine people saying the following about Alexandra: "She's fifteen. She's too old for us to force her to do her homework. She has to make more of an effort." That may be true, but rarely do educators say, "This child is failing and it is our fault."

The truth is that we don't know why she's failing chemistry, nor does she. No one seems to, or if someone does understand it, he or she is not connected enough to Alexandra to help her overcome her failures. Her parents, who emigrated to the United States from the Azores, speak Portuguese as their first language. Neither of them has a high school degree. Her father left school after sixth grade. It seems doubtful that either of her parents can diagnose her problems in high school chemistry or math. They both work long hours as janitors in a downtown office complex to support their family and maintain their small, attractive house just a short walk around the block from the high school.

Yet nothing about their circumstances explains Alexandra's struggle. They have four daughters, two still in high school and two in their twenties. Two daughters, the oldest and Alexandra, who is third in line, have struggled in school. The second and the fourth are superb students. Alexandra's older sister Louisa was an outstanding student and earned a full scholarship to college. She is now working on a Ph.D. and is the star of her department. The discrepancies in school performance among the children in this one family are striking, to say the least. It remains a mystery to them, a list of unanswered questions: What might psychological testing reveal? Could some tutoring help? Does she have the proper study skills? Did she miss some basic math facts in elementary school? Does she not have the underlying ability? Does she have difficulty concentrating? Is she spending too much time socializing? Is she too tough and proud to ask for help? Is she math phobic? Is she really unmotivated?

Alexandra certainly accepts that label: unmotivated. She wrote to me at the end of her sophomore year: "Well, since I had last spoke to you I failed two subjects: Chemistry and Geometry. My Chemistry teacher never stopped trying to make the unmotivated students motivated by giving us speeches and helping out by giving us some make-up work. It worked for a few students, because they passed, but for the ones that thought they had a snowball's chance in hell of passing it motivated us for about 2.5 seconds."

It is the repeated experience of failure—and failure with no way out—that makes so many children unmotivated. I tend not to label children as unmotivated and certainly never as lazy. I tend to view children in Alexandra's predicament as overwhelmed, underprepared, or immobilized. One thing is for certain: The word *unmotivated* certainly doesn't describe any other arena of Alexandra's life because her life is not all about chemistry and math.

Adults tend to define a child by his failures in school, as if those were the most important facts about him. The F becomes the center-piece of the child's life from an adult's point of view. Not so for Alexandra. She lives a life every day, whether she's passing chemistry or not. She cannot allow herself to be defined by her failure; she knows there is a lot more to her than that. It is clear that she works to have a philosophical attitude about school: "Sometimes you got goals you've got to set up, but once you achieve them, you are cool with that and then you've got your disappointments because you fail sometimes. You know. It's a balance. It all balances out. It's pretty cool though." Outside of school she has taken martial arts classes and developed skills to the point where she has participated in competitions. She has had to use those skills a couple of times in school when she was physically challenged to a fight by another girl. "I forgot what she said . . . something pretty violent: 'You're a slut, you're a whore' and she did the classic girls-go-after-you-with-their-nails. I got her down before she could touch me. Basically, I've learned how to put people down. . . . I don't need to punch people."

In addition to being able to drop another girl to the ground when challenged, Alexandra plays the flute in the orchestra, she enjoys history and English, and she holds on to her childhood love of dinosaurs and continues to read about them. She serves as a counselor to her friends and—more than anything—she dreams of being a writer. When I asked her how she passed the time in school and particularly in chemistry class, this was her answer: "Sometimes I'll just take out a paper, write a poem, or write a story or something. . . . I have like thirty-two poems at home, all written in chemistry class. They are small, so I can go and just do this, while he sat there talking about, I don't know, lab and stuff." What are her poems about? "Nothing really. They are just poems. Actually, they're metaphorical. They are not dark or creepy or anything. More like love. That's basically it. They are like love, or like fun . . ."

Martial arts, girl fights, the flute, dinosaurs, and love poetry: There is nothing unmotivated about this girl's embrace of life. When did she start getting interested in poetry? "It had to be in fourth grade. . . . I was in the hospital for an appendicitis and I was there for about a month. It was probably one of the worst times of my life because every day they'd come in, take all my blood. I had to go through a hundred different things. I used to be so scared of needles every day . . . like I had five IVs. It was horrible. So, I just started writing then."

Writing poetry helps Alexandra deal with anxiety. She also loves to write; I know that because after our interview Alexandra continued to send e-mails for the better part of a year. ("By the way," she wrote in one, "I won second place in the whole school my freshman year for a poem I had written on racial issues.") "Just a minute!" the adult mind protests. "Poetry and e-mails won't help her pass chemistry!" Fair enough. She needs to pass chemistry to graduate from high school and have any chance at college admission. Does she think about that? What does Alexandra plan to do about chemistry? Does she have a strategy or is she just going to sit there and wait silently for failure?

Actually, she does have a plan, though it is difficult for her to admit it. She holds herself, not her teachers, responsible for her failures and she is expecting, waiting—even wanting—to go to summer school. She will tell you that summer school is boring and no fun, but the pace and the personal accountability of the smaller summer-school classes works better for her than the crowded, socially intense classes of the regular school year. Here is Alexandra's extended description of summer school that she wrote at the beginning of the fall of her eleventh-grade year. (I have left the spellings just as she wrote them, some of them no doubt a matter of the hurried e-mail style and grammatical anarchy that characterizes most kids' e-mails. But whether they are carelessness, a gap in what she has been taught, or perhaps evidence of an underlying learning disability, her lousy spelling and sometimes difficult syntax in no way interfere with her gift as an insightful storyteller.)

My Chemistry teacher didn't really say anything to me about me failing the class, but my Geometry teacher gave me a chance to make it up in Summer school which surprised me greatly. He had always said that kids that don't do there work through the whole year shouldn't be sent to summer school to make it up because it would be simple and it would only take a month as opposed to the other that pass and had to go through the whole year working hard. I sort of agree with that, but the thing is kids that if you pass summer school, even with flying colors, you won't be put into any of the Honors groups and "summer school" on a college application doesn't look pretty itself. I feel as if he knew I tried at times and I knew my stuff enough to take the course over the summer and I really appreciate him seeing that. I think that like me

most kids really just apperichiate the teachers that know what a kid
goes through at our age and understand that sometimes we might
slip up. Most teachers do understand, but I know there is liable
(Not that I met any) to be a teacher out there who doesn't remember. Teachers are important cause there the ones that give you the
bricks to build knowledge. Without the bricks, there isn't anything to build on. So at times I might blame a teacher when I
know that I'm really the one at fault.

When it came time for me to go to summer school it was a
real drag. I didn't want to get up in the morning to spend four
hours everyday on two subjects. I mean who really wants to get
up and be like 'Ya!!! Time for Geometry and Chemistry class!'?
My teachers were great and once you get used to the fact that
learning something new is more useful than being in bed resting
up you find that it's not as bad as you think. I bearly knew any of
the kids there, but they weren't the trouble maker type as most
like to prejuidice. No one bearly made a word in class because we
didn't know one another and it was too hot and boring to waste
energy we were using to take notes from the board. Every three
weeks or so the teacher would look at our notebooks and make
sure we were doing alright and we'd continue on. Our chemistry
wouldn't do that but I found his method of teaching more effective and entertaining because he would make jokes (They were
funny because no one laughed) and show movies on the chemi-
cals as well as explain the uses and give us labs to do. That really
helped me because I only did horrible in one test and got a's and
b's in the others. I passed geometry with a c cause my test grades
were c's mostly but I have a few a's and b's absolutely no d's.
For me to get no d's in Math you know your teaching something
right . . . Summer school is different than regular school . . . The
pace in Geometry was fairly slow only because we did mcas
problems (for the state graduation test) to help us out on the side
and that usually involved much more advanced problems and it
took him more time to explain it and make sure everyone got the
point. I was almost thought I would die of boardom sometimes in
Geometry because all we mostly did was take notes and go over
them. It was almost like the movement of the pen was a sign
of life.

What is clear from her description is that Alexandra knows what kind of teaching works: the kind that holds her accountable and gives her "bricks" to build on. She is aware that, starting around sixth grade, she was able to take shortcuts in order to complete her work, without really learning. She would just pick out the highlighted parts of the book, skip to the answers page, and fill in the blanks on her homework. But she didn't learn what she was supposed to learn. "I still don't know my times tables, not all of them." Despite knowing that she has holes in her math background, at age fifteen she's not ready simply to go over the times tables. She briefly had a tutor in ninth grade who tried to make her do that and it didn't help. The day her tutor was absent, she got a different fellow. "I had another tutor, I learned the quadratic formula, flat, in one day." Was he a good teacher? "Yeah. The other guy, he just, I didn't learn anything from him, so I didn't go back to tutoring, 'cause, you know, what if I get someone like that again?"

Here is a point worth appreciating. Students, especially those who fail and struggle, know what works for them and what doesn't. Just because they aren't learning the material doesn't mean they don't recognize good teaching when they see it and lousy teaching when they are subjected to it. They are sensitive to failure and they develop allergies to teaching that is the wrong style for them. Adults often make the mistake of believing that because a child is failing, she is not serious about education or about the values of education, or cannot appreciate the aims of school. While it is the case that Alexandra often does not do her homework, it isn't because she is just blowing off school or trying to get away with being lazy. When I asked her what the worst thing she had ever seen happen to students was, she wrote me an unexpected reply, starting with an observation from a historical figure:

For that I turn to a quote said by Ben Franklin "Genius without education is like silver in a mine." I've seen extremely wise and intelligent people quite school for one reason or another without realizing what they're throwing away. A really close friend of mines had and I found it sad how I was the only one who seen the potential she had. I tried to speak to her but as wise she was she "slipped up" and did something stupid as not to listen. Anyone

who has a great amount of intelligence shouldn't throw it away or
make it useless because it's one of the more significant things you
have a hold on in life . . .

As she began her eleventh-grade year, Alexandra wrote me an
ominous note about her new math teacher, describing him as very
strict about "tardiness and candy," and really focused on homework:
"He's tough with homework and I can't miss too many because it will
make a huge impact on my final grade if I fall back with it. Seeing as
homework isn't my strongest suit and that this isn't my favorite subject, I kind of got nervous."

She also felt humiliated by the petty, bureaucratic demands of her
history teacher, who confiscated Alexandra's history book when she
arrived one day without the brown-paper cover on the book. It had
fallen off and Alexandra hadn't had time to put a new cover on. "Usually I manage things and get it done, but I couldn't, it was impossible." The teacher took the book away from Alexandra, saying, "No
book cover, no book." Alexandra writes about the exchange: ". . . so a
lil angry I say, 'what about hw?' She says you get no credit until you
get a cover. So this puzzles me cuz I'm sitting there figuring how I'm
going to cover the book when she has it."

She did manage to find a cover, get the book back from the
teacher, cover it, and do the homework. The teacher marked her down
because the homework was late. Alexandra was furious.

At that point in our frequent e-mail correspondence, Alexandra
simply disappeared. After writing long and informative e-mails for
months, I received nothing from her. I tried to renew our contact many
times, expressing my concern and prompting her with questions.
I couldn't get a peep out of her. She literally dropped off my screen. I
was worried about her, but other than driving to her house and knocking on her door, there was little else of a more casual checking-in that
I could do. I called her older sister and found out that she was alive,
but I did not feel that I could initiate contact when she was not returning my e-mails. Finally, months later, she wrote with an apology:

> I've been having great difficulty with school because I have de-
> veloped a bad Anxiety disorder. So I haven't written to you in
> awhile and I'm sorry but you can imagine this is greatly impact-

ing my school work. It's all stress related basically. I was having a
hard time dealing with it but I'm getting better with medicine and
therapy and all so I guess I'll be fine to go back and do my school
work again. I apologize for not writting back I truely am sorry.

Over the next few months, Alexandra described her experience of
being in a downward spiral through the fall of her eleventh-grade
year: feeling nervous in school, throwing herself into her social life,
being a "therapist" to all of her friends, feeling overwhelmed by their
problems, failing to do her homework, becoming frightened by the
prospect of failure again, and feeling nervous.

In doing so It's like Why should I care about my HW? I have a
friend that needs some serious help. Then my homework became
an issue and it was like a cycle. I thought I could handle it all and
it all jus fell up on top of me until I couldn't take it anymore.
Makes me feel like a weak person. But no matter what I know I
have to pull through this and that includes doing homework and
getting things back in perspective. I'm trying to.

Eventually, anxiety overwhelmed her. She couldn't leave the
house and go to school, or, if she went to school, she couldn't get herself to classes. She spent hours in the guidance counselor's office.
She couldn't attend psychology class because the content of the material so frightened her that she couldn't bear it. At that point, it was
her older sister, the Ph.D. student, who stepped into her life and
found help. Alexandra finally got to a psychiatrist and was put on
some antianxiety medications, one of which made her so sleepy that
she couldn't stay awake in class. During the two months she was out
of touch with me, she was struggling to get her medication levels
right, overcome her fear, and return to classes, and was making a relationship with her therapist. She finally received the help she needed.

There isn't one single factor that made Alexandra's life in school
so difficult. There were many—perhaps some secret in her life of
which I am not aware—but I want to address her difficulties in the
school context. An apparently successful student in elementary
school, she had slipped through without learning the basics of math.
(Shame on her school!) She found the transition to high school scary

and the pace of classes overwhelming. She never had someone who recognized that, after repeated failures and hidden personal shame about not knowing her times tables, she was becoming math phobic and eventually would become school phobic.

In order to manage her mounting anxiety, Alexandra developed a threefold strategy. First, she worked on subjects in which she felt capable and for which she had received recognition. As a prizewinning poet in ninth grade, she wrote poetry in chemistry class. It calmed her and made her feel competent. Second, she threw herself into her social life in school and became a therapist for many of her friends. Third, she made a decision to avoid homework after the school day was over. Alexandra sought experiences of recognition, connection, and power that would allow her to feel okay about herself and avoid the experience—homework—that would make her feel ashamed and anxious.

"But what about academics?" the adult mind screams. When children don't do their homework, adults often view them as willful, lazy, or defiant. The story is invariably more complicated than that. In Alexandra's case, I believe she didn't do her homework because she couldn't bear to sit down alone with math and chemistry and feel frightened and inadequate. Quite naturally, she threw herself into activities where she did feel competent: martial arts, band, and being a therapist to her friends.

From an adult perspective, it is easy to say that for Alexandra, avoiding homework was the wrong thing to do, but think again. What would you do if you were a struggling student? If you cannot do your homework on your own, if you don't want to admit that to your parents, if you know your parents cannot help you with your homework, if you are ashamed of the holes in your knowledge and you desperately want to feel like an independent young woman—even as you struggle with fifth-grade math—if, if, if, if . . . How many options did Alexandra have? There was no easy solution. Alexandra's strategy was to resign herself to failure during the school year and wait for summer school. If that doesn't feel like a conscious, deliberate plan to you, then ask yourself what you would have done if you were fifteen years old and trapped as Alexandra was? If you don't think Alexandra was doing her best, listen to her assessment of her summer-school courses again: "Geometry was like doing five miles

per hour on the highway with a old ford aerostar. You had to hang on
to the ride until it was finally over at the end of the class. Chemistry
was a lil better. It was like doing thirty on the highway, but none of
them fly by like regular school."

How did Alexandra experience the regular school year, at least in
math and chemistry? "It's like you have to buckle your seat belts and
just make sure you don't crash and have to repair da vechile in summer school."

Eventually, Alexandra crashed by developing an anxiety disorder. I don't believe for a second that she became so anxious as a
manipulation or to get out of something. Anyone who has ever experienced panic attacks knows that you don't choose that sort of terrifying experience. You become symptomatic because the conditions of
your life are such that you cannot do anything else. Finally, then,
Alexandra let down her guard, threw herself into the care of her older
sister and her guidance counselor, and, with the help of a psychiatrist and appropriate antianxiety medication, found a way to calm her
anxious experience of school. Her grades are up and she's doing her
homework.

> Previously I had a E in History now I have and A (I've been doing
> ALL my work) In math I have a c- from the previous E last quar-
> ter (My test grades are crap but I pass in all my hw) Phys ed is still
> like a D because I have to change for it more often, and I'm work-
> ing on it. Music Theory is a B and Portugese is a C. Culinary is an
> B This change is definetly about me being more focused in class.
> That's due to better control of my (You guessed it) anxiety, but
> it's also because I'm at that point where i realize I can't fool
> around with education because it's very important so I'm de-
> spretly trying to mend the great gash I had made.

When I asked Alexandra to reflect on what she'd learned about
herself from her breakdown into anxiety, this is what she wrote in an
e-mail:

> I have to say that psycologically I had to get my mind away from
> all that anxiety and even though I'm on like a very low dosage of
> medicine anything anxiety related is only to be solved by the

mind. Freud was out of his own mind because issues don't have anything to do with agression or sexual impulses.. It has to do with the way you think about things . . . I love learning and am very interested in it and that's schools greatest value. School was a hell because my grades, but looking at it from a different prospective it's not that bad at all. I think maybe failing was a good thing because that way I spend more time in school to change my decision about the future if I ever wish to do so, and because of all the encouragment of people around. I love learning and again school gives it to you, where else besides cruel reality can you be to learn? I know I'm going to be in school a long time, and that doesn't bother me at all.

She may be a god-awful speller, and her syntax and grammar are a little bit rough, but a writer she is. Alexandra may struggle always in school, she may never be a star in math, but her strategies for managing the pressure are improving and her capacity for learning despite adversity is impressive.

CALEB IN THE PROMISED LAND

Caleb was three years old when his father left Nigeria, yet he still remembers the sound of his father's suitcase bumping down the stairs. Caleb wrote about it in his writing workshop class for eighth-graders at Nativity Prep, a Jesuit all-boys middle school in Jamaica Plain, Massachusetts. He related his memories in an essay he read aloud in front of his teacher and fourteen classmates on a hot day in late fall:

> On a cold, windy night, I woke to the eerie sound of the wheels of luggage smacking against the staircase. *Clank, clank, clank.* Then silence. I rolled down from my race-car–shaped bed and jogged down the hall to Father's rooms. I opened the door and tiptoed in. . . . Where was my father? I was afraid. He wasn't anywhere upstairs.

Caleb was always the one to wake up his dad in the morning, and his father's departure was a painful wound for him. Caleb entitled his essay "Devastation and Renaissance." It wasn't until he was six that his father was able to bring Caleb, his mother, and four of his brothers and sisters to America. The family now lives in a town south of Boston, thirty miles from Caleb's school. There are six children in the family—one sister was born after the family's arrival in America. Sadly, they are not all healthy.

His younger brother, Jesus, age seven, suffers from the effects of lead poisoning. "He can't use his left hand at all," Caleb tells me. "My mother is starting to help him a lot. . . . He's seven, but if you saw him you would think he's three or five. He acts too young for his age." When did his brother start to get the symptoms of lead poisoning? "When he was young . . . his whole life," Caleb explains. And where did Jesus eat the lead-paint chips that led to his poisoning? "I think in school," he reports.

Caleb's parents work extremely hard—"all the time," he says—and they have only one car for the family. They are both health-care workers who care for mentally ill people confined to their homes. Sometimes they drive the same route, and sometimes not. Caleb did not explain how his parents get to their clients when they have different schedules. One senses that his father works late into the evening. One senses that nothing is easy for this family.

Caleb gets up at five A.M. to take the commuter train north to Boston. He has to be on the train at six in order to get to school by seven, where he gets a wonderful breakfast cooked by the parents of boys at Nativity. He also gets lunch there, and dinner, all prepared by the parents of Nativity boys. The school does an enormous amount with precious little money. In trade for the opportunity to send their children to this tuition-free school, parents volunteer to cook meals, clean the building, and help in other ways. There are many ways to serve the Nativity community. The Jesuit fathers who started the school believe that only by providing boys with maximum structure and maximum support can they make them ready to learn and achieve at a high level. They accept boys who they feel are ready to make that kind of commitment in return for high levels of attention and support. For Caleb, that means getting up at five A.M. and giving his entire day to Nativity. He often does not get home until after nine at night.

I first meet Caleb at about 7:45 in the morning. He has finished breakfast and played some basketball. He's a fine athlete. He is changing back into his shoes while talking to his math teacher, a young woman, who had come down to the basement to discuss his last test with him. They are having a focused conversation surrounded by the excited voices of boys sitting in front of their lockers putting on their dress shoes and ties. Eight or so boys are still playing happily in the gym, pushing things to the last minute. Like Caleb, they are all required to come off the court, change their shoes, and make it up to the second floor in time—that is, *on* time—for morning assembly. Many come from immigrant families, and being on time is not part of their culture. To make these boys successful, Nativity needs to make them care about punctuality. It does so in the person of Father William Campbell, who greets the boys at the door of the assembly room as they stream in. At the tick of eight A.M., he moves from the side of the door to the opening itself and bars the entrance. The three or four late-arriving boys collect unhappily in the hall, trying to hear the proceedings without pressing up against the glass and revealing themselves as latecomers.

There are no chairs in the assembly hall. The sixty-six boys who attend Nativity stand in lines, separated by spaces that informally demarcate the fifth, sixth, seventh, and eighth grades, each class rising in height and muscularity. They are almost all black or Hispanic, with an occasional eastern European or Asian face thrown into the mix. They are all poor and face serious obstacles in their lives. As one administrator said when I asked to shadow a boy who struggles, "All our boys struggle." You wouldn't know it to look at these neatly dressed, eager, handsome guys. The assembly begins with roll call. Each boy gets to call out "Present" when his name is called out by Mr. Harrington, the principal. All boys except, of course, the poor unfortunates out in the vestibule. When their names are called, Father Campbell responds, "In the hall."

The requirement that every boy stand for assembly is unusual. The idea that every child gets a chance to be heard by everyone in the school community is equally rare. I've attended many, many school assemblies and I've never before seen it. Of course, it wouldn't be possible with five hundred kids. However, it isn't even attempted in most small schools. Having to stand means that every boy is motivated to stand upright and look good; you cannot slouch in the same way that you can in a chair. They don't have to be told to sit up or put their feet down. It also means that boys can move constantly without causing much problem by shifting their weight from one foot to the other. The expectation that everyone speaks, or might be spoken to, means that every boy pays attention.

The eighth-grade boys appear grown up and sophisticated in comparison to their younger brethren. Many of them also care about their clothes in a way that fifth-graders don't. Caleb clearly does. Even though his tan-and-brown-checked shirt does not exactly match his blue tie with Easter eggs on it, he manages to look neat and fashionable. He has mastered the art of tucking in his shirt completely, like a Citadel cadet, whereas many of the other recent basketball players are looking disheveled. It is apparently his way. When the principal gets to Caleb's name he adds, "The best-dressed boy at the reception last night." Caleb tucks his thumbs under his arms and sticks out his chest, the classic boy-preening gesture.

> "I stopped paying attention in class so I could be seen as more of a 'cool' kid."
>
> (Eleventh-grader)

Though it is a Friday, the announcements make it clear that the faculty and students are going to be together over the weekend. One faculty member announces: "We will be attending the Grace Church Fair in Attleboro tomorrow. We leave at nine. We'll take the T into the city and then take the commuter rail. We're leaving at nine. That doesn't mean arrive at nine. That's when we're leaving."

Liz, the eighth-grade team teacher and soccer coach, announces the results of yesterday's soccer game. All of the eighth-grade boys exude pleasure when she announces the "glorious result": a 3–0 victory. Caleb beams. She goes on to announce another game this afternoon against an all-boys private school in a wealthy suburb. The boys tighten their fists, glance at one another; a few pump their arms. They're ready to do battle again. Mr. Harrington, the principal, steps back to the podium and congratulates the team for their win and their coach for "not running up the score on those poor unfortunates from Epiphany."

Mr. Harrington begins to discuss some sports events that will be going on in the lives of the boys over the weekend. Xavier will play a baseball game on Saturday and Cortland will play in a Pop Warner football game on Sunday. In a bit of sly humor, the principal looks at the boys, wishes them luck, and says, "We're with you, win or tie." His delivery is so deadpan that many boys miss it, or they're not familiar enough with the expression of support that ends "win or lose" to understand the adult joke. It does not matter to these boys. What matters is that someone in authority—their principal!—is taking the time to focus on them in a whole-school assembly. It doesn't matter that it isn't an assembly of four hundred or one thousand kids. They are famous in their own school. What a gift to them.

This sense that every boy is important suddenly deepens even further. After a short homily by Father Simon Smith, based on a phrase from a famous Jesuit that was adopted as a motto by a previous Nativity class, he asks, "Isn't this Alby's birthday?"

A voice calls out, "It's on Sunday."

"That's all right," Father Smith says. "Come on up."

When Alby appears before Father Smith, the priest wishes him a happy birthday and then places his hand on the boy's head. Everyone immediately bows their head in prayer, listening while Father Smith asks for God's blessing on Alby's birthday weekend. He then leads a final prayer. In the middle of the prayer he stops and solicits boys to include the names of family members. Many of the younger boys raise their hands and say things like "My family," "Father Hicks and the visitor," "My mother, who had surgery." After each boy names the people about whom he is concerned, the assembly intones the refrain "Lord, hear our prayer." The seventh- and eighth-grade boys let the younger ones go first and are respectful of the younger boys' yearnings. They understand the power of both prayer and individual attention and are respectful of both.

A boy like Caleb is at risk for many reasons. Educational research has shown time and time again, over many decades, that the single greatest predictor of educational achievement in the United States is socioeconomic status. Wealthier children outperform poorer children in schools all over the country. While no research identifies precisely why money is so powerful in pushing children up the educational ladder, it makes a kind of obvious sense. Indeed, the possible correlates of wealth are almost too numerous to mention. Family nutrition and health care are better. Children arrive at school fed and ready for the school day. They get what they need to study: glasses, a safe place, and family and community support for educational success. There are more books in the house because parents are employed and are themselves better educated. Neighborhoods are safe and schools are better equipped and staffed. There are so many socioeconomic factors that contribute to school success, it makes me angry to hear the debates about school reform. The one reform that would have the most influence over the fate of children in school would be for all families to have a stable, middle-class income. (The Scandinavian countries and the Netherlands make that point quite well.) If you were to predict the educational future for a Nigerian immigrant child from a family of six, with two overextended parents earning relatively low wages, it would be hard to be optimistic. Even before you knew whether Caleb is an able student, the cards are stacked against him.

Caleb is not, in fact, a great student, at least not in comparison to some of his classmates, and certainly not compared to some of the children against whom he will compete for scholarship money to elite private and parochial schools. His Secondary School Admissions Test scores put him in the bottom quarter of children applying to private schools. By all rights he should struggle. Yet, he has three critical factors going for him. First, he's motivated to succeed; second, his family deeply cares about education; and third, he has Nativity Prep in his corner. The school isn't going to let him fail if it can possibly help it.

That doesn't mean that school is easy for Caleb. When he arrived, he was not remotely prepared for the academic demands of the school: "I never saw the work before. . . . Yeah, I didn't understand what they were doing. . . . I was scared at first, I'd never gotten a C before." The experience of doing poorly made him angry, and he stayed that way for "pretty much half of sixth grade. My mother came in to talk to my teachers. She had me come with her and they started explaining it more to me, so that toward the end of the year, I started working harder."

One of the things that Nativity does best is to celebrate the lives of its boys. Even if they cannot get all get A's, they all get recognition for the lives they are living. That experience of being known must be what gets many boys through the day. In an eighth-grade English class, a gifted teacher, Curt Miller, conducts the writing workshop (Mr. Miller is on sabbatical from an elite private school in Brookline, Massachusetts, and is donating his teaching time to Nativity for a year). He has each boy write a memoir, and they read them aloud in class. These essays have evocative titles: "I Am Still Awake," "Change," "My Stealing Ways," and "The Tournament."

The day I visit, one boy describes how his parents forced him to choose between them. They were separating, one leaving Haiti, the other staying. With no advance notice and no psychological preparation, he had to step to his father's side or remain with his mother. His older brother chose their father. He immediately followed, only to turn around and see his mother's face. He realized he couldn't leave her, but was aware that he might never see his brother again if he stayed with his mother. As he read, he began to cry and then started to sob. Mr. Miller walked up to him and placed his hand on the boy's shoulder. "You're doing great," he said. The boy kept reading. Everyone in the class was riveted, wanting to know how the story had turned out. (He chose to stay with his mother, did not see his brother for years, but, finally, had been reunited with him the previous summer.)

It was Caleb's turn next. After describing the departure of his father, and the heart-wrenching disappearance of his dog, Jimmy—his "best friend"—he began to discuss the chaos of civil war in Nigeria.

> It was a time of undergoing vast destruction. People screaming up and down the streets, then from my house my family would hear "Pap!" and someone would probably be dead before they hit the ground. Some people had no place to go, and others had no place to hide. . . . This country was full of chaos. This country was full of no hope. . . . My mother tried her best to make us remember the good times . . . [but] she finally gave up. One morning she dressed my sisters and me, then put us in the van that was heading to the airport. She thought she was protecting us from all the pain and hurt that had been inflicted. She wanted to take me away from

the absence of my father and the loss of Jimmy. She closed the door to all our friends, family, and our home. But there was a bright side. We were heading for a new life. I would soon see my father.

If you have a child who struggles in school for whatever reason, you could not improve on what Nativity Prep offers its students: support, structure, a sense of mission, and the opportunity to celebrate their lives within the context of their school day. If, as I believe, all struggling students search for a fit with school, the best thing that can happen is for a school to reach out and try to fit them. Nativity is beautifully designed to do just that. Unfortunately, not all schools are.

6

Hell, No!

Journeys Defined by Defiance and Despair

I absolutely hate almost everything about school, the fact
that it is a waste of time, the fact that they make you take
classes that you have to waste more time studying a lot for
and its wasted time because you don't like the subject and
you're never going to use it so when you could be out
doing something you enjoy you have to stay home and
study trigonometry or something.
—*Kate W., fifteen*

Never give in—never, never, never, never, in nothing great
or small, large or petty, never give in except to convictions
of honor and good sense. Never yield to force; never yield
to the apparently overwhelming might of the enemy.
—*Sir Winston Churchill, 1941, Harrow School*

Some students become so discouraged in school that they can
bear it no longer. Their psychological struggle with the rules, the
demands, their peers, their anxiety, or academic failure—it all becomes intolerable. Leaving school is the almost natural endpoint of
this experience of chronic struggle. We call students who stop attending school dropouts. However, walking out of the building isn't the
only way to drop out of school. Many students who continue to at-

tend classes physically have actually left on a psychological basis. They take their souls out of the endeavor. They invest their time and energy elsewhere, sometimes in ways quite adult and understandable. They may slip almost invisibly from the educational scene. Though impoverished children of color are particularly at risk for dropping out of school, white middle-class children become profoundly disenchanted with school as well. Many of these departures from school are subtle and hard to categorize.

In this chapter, we will look at the lives of three students whose journeys through school gradually filled with despair. Their experiences there were so enraging, humiliating, depressing, or chronically disappointing that they withdrew from the process of their own education, either psychologically or physically. When saying they had painful journeys through school, I am not blaming teachers or schools. I am being descriptive. There were personal, familial, and cultural factors in all of these children's lives that were equally as powerful as the school factors. Despite the differences in these students' backgrounds, there are striking similarities in the course of their school careers' descent into fury and despair.

DAVID: ALLERGIC TO SCHOOL

David's education started in a promising way. As a little boy he was eager to learn. He remembers: "When I was four I looked around and I realized Mom could read, Dad could read, Maura could read, and I couldn't. I didn't like that so over the next year I basically taught myself to read. . . . In kindergarten I had a nice teacher and when they were teaching everybody else reading she let me go off and read by myself. . . . It was good for the first few years."

It is hard to say exactly what or exactly when something happened in early elementary school to make David feel that school was coercive, but there is no doubt that it happened. "After a while it became forced, and you had to read things you didn't want to read," he says. "They said, 'I'm sorry but you have to.' They said, 'You have to because I say so,' and I said, 'Well, why?' "

I am talking to an eighteen-year-old young man who has an uncanny resemblance to Paul Bunyan. He's not quite tall enough to fit the mythic character, but in other ways he resembles someone who could have an ax in his hand and be accompanied by an oversized blue ox. He is bearlike, probably close to 275 pounds. He has a full, untrimmed beard that gives him a just-been-camping look. On this mildly cold fall night he wears boots and a khaki-colored down vest that reaches almost to his knees. It has several pockets in the front, and if it weren't for the fact that we were sitting in a lovely home located in a highly domesticated suburb of Chicago, one might imagine that he had a knife, some shotgun shells, wire, and a forgotten fishing lure in his pockets. He could very well be carrying something that you might need to repair a motor. If you needed any of these items, I have no doubt he would offer them to you: David is polite and generous-hearted. Indeed, he is the classic gentle giant.

His polite demeanor makes his story of his long war with school so incongruous. One might have trouble believing that just eighteen months earlier, as a high school junior, this engaging young man was, by his own admission, "lashing out at everyone." When his younger sister started high school this past fall, he cautioned her not to tell the teachers that she was his sister. He said that if she told them, they might be scared. I questioned David. Had he ever done anything scary in school? Had he ever threatened to hit a teacher? The answer was an emphatic no. He qualifies his story: "I didn't mean scary so much as just a little hurt. Teachers weren't afraid of me, but they were a bit caught off guard. I wasn't the typical student, obviously. I was the one who questioned everything, and, you know, leads the whole class all the time."

David is "a polite and respectful boy," as his parents and personal friends describe him. He taught himself to read at age four. So how did this highly curious and bright boy end up just barely graduating with a D average from a program for emotionally disordered kids? How could it happen that the child of two well-educated parents ended up hating school so vehemently? How could it happen to a boy from a family that was willing to pay the tuition for private and parochial schools, willing to provide him with whatever support services he needed? How could David's experience have been so different from that of his three sisters, who all enjoyed varying degrees of success in school? His mother, Marianne, turns that question around and around in her mind. She advocated for him, battled with him, and moved him from one school to another in an attempt to make school life palatable for him. Nothing has worked. As she tells the story, she is by turns frustrated, angry, and, most of all, bewildered.

During a "mediocre" parochial preschool experience, David's teachers reported that they "couldn't figure him out." He had a wonderful kindergarten year in a "fun and loving environment" at the same school his older sister, Maura, had attended. At the end of that year, however, the teachers recommended that David stay for another year in kindergarten because he was young—he has a July birthday—and he had poor fine-motor skills. His parents, "mindful of David's gifts," decided to send him on to first grade. An enthusiastic young teacher in first grade really helped to nurture David and work with him on his organizational skills, which were noticeably behind those of his peers. Once again, the recommendation was made to keep David in first grade for another year. Marianne reports, "We looked at our bright boy and said, 'No, thank you.' "

His second-grade teacher joked pleasantly that David was the kind of guy who would always have a secretary. David enjoyed parts of second and third grade and tolerated others. However, we can infer that he was bored because he told his younger sister, fretting over her first day of school, "Don't worry, Amy, the first four years of school are all review!" His conceptual understanding of the material was superb. It was the mechanics of school—writing and organization—that were tough.

David and his mother both agree that fourth grade with Mrs. O'Connell at Notre Dame was the nightmare year. In retrospect, it was really the beginning of the end of his school career. That year with Mrs. O'Connell—even now he refers to her as "Ugly Old Ogre"—left him with extraordinarily bitter feelings about school. His mother remembers that at the beginning of the year they had David tested:

> David's struggles with handwriting and organization reached a peak. In math class, his invention of an alternative to borrowing was scorned. The increased written workload created absolute wars in our household. We wondered: Was it that David *could* not write, or *would* not write? We asked for testing, which revealed that David was a highly gifted child with poor fine-motor skills. As none of his scores fell within the range of needing help, it was suggested that we put David on Ritalin and buy him color-coded

folders. The ADD hat did not fit David, we were sure, but I did buy the folders.

Marianne walked into the classroom one day to deliver the colored folders and found a "teary-eyed David" standing at one end of the room and his "smoldering" teacher at the other:

> Between them was a desk, littered all around with crumpled papers. The teacher had left them, perhaps to shame David, but I saw a mountain of frustration. I went to David's desk, sat at it, and pulled up another seat for David. The teacher took this chair and pulled up another for David. She showed me a paper David had written that day. It was rather legible, with spaces between the words, some of his best work! But when the teacher told me that "It wasn't that hard," David lost control and yelled at her, telling her that she would not know how much work it had taken, she hadn't done it.

David's mother said about Mrs. O'Connell, "She is the first teacher I have ever wanted to strike. I was so angry and hurt that even though we were having these meetings and talking and talking, all she could see when she looked at my son was someone she could not put into a little box. You are either this thing or that, and she can work with types. David just didn't fit." What David remembers most about that year is having Mrs. O'Connell yell at him, and his fighting with his parents.

"Ugly Old Ogre was just awful. She would snap at people, yell at them. She yelled at me a good many times. At one point a teacher from across the hall came and asked us to keep the noise level down when no one had been speaking, except her, who had been shouting at me."

What was Mrs. O'Connell shouting about? Homework—David hadn't brought in his homework.

I asked him what she would say that would start the shouting matches. "Usually, 'You were supposed to have your homework in yesterday' or something like that."

His reply? "Usually I'd say, 'Well, I don't,' and she'd say, 'Well, you're supposed to.' I would say, 'Well, I don't.' 'You were supposed to have it in.' 'I don't have it. Give me the bad grade and move on.' I wouldn't say that, but close."

At eighteen, David is articulate about why fourth grade was so awful. "There was a big increase in the work and difficulty in things. . . . That came to be a problem because first grade, second grade, third grade, you get along a lot more easily by just doing the tests and neglecting your homework. That wasn't the case anymore in fourth grade." David's inability to keep up with the work, his anger at his teacher, and his teacher's frustration with him created a black hole that began to swallow up David and his family.

David remembers his fourth-grade report card: "I had gotten all C's and one or two D's. I had never done that badly before. My parents and I spent the next nine hours sitting at the dining room table arguing about it. Then eventually, I got exhausted and went up to my room and went to bed. Then I knew it got more and more intense. *It wasn't just school anymore.*"

David made a sad discovery that many children make; school has the ability to mess up your loving relationship with your parents. My guess is that David's parents stumbled into an equally unhappy insight: Your child's school performance can corrode your loving feelings about your own child. As protective and compassionate as you want to be, it is hard not to be both worried and angry when you look at your gifted son's report card covered with C's and D's. It is natural to think that the report card is an accurate reflection of your child. I hope by the time you finish reading this book you believe that a report card is only partly about a child. It is also an implicit evaluation of the teacher, the school, and the fit between child and school.

David's parents took him to a psychologist who recommended a new school, and they accepted the recommendation. They pulled him out of Notre Dame in February and moved him to the Sage School, a progressive environment specifically designed for gifted children. It had 198 children in grades pre-K through eight.

When David told me that his parents had pulled him in the middle of the year, I asked, "So, it was an emergency situation?"

David replied, "Pretty much." However, the emergency as he perceived it was the Sage School's need for him. "They needed another person in the fourth-grade class. They didn't have enough for the play. They were doing *A Midsummer Night's Dream*, which is Shakespeare, which is pretty complicated, but we were up for it." Even now, after so many years and so much failure, David lights up at the idea that a school needed him, that there was a place for him and there was a complex problem to tackle. He rallied from his terrible experience with Mrs. O'Connell: "I was even doing a little bit of my homework. I was even willing to compromise a little."

However, David, now highly vigilant, realized that this was a school, too. "But, unfortunately Sage, you know, just kind of minimized the problems that Notre Dame had. There was still a bit of authoritarian thing." He does favorably remember the discussions he had with teachers after problems occurred in gym class. The teachers took the time to actually talk and listen to children. This kind of respectful conversation was a "tremendously different thing" for David, who was used to what he calls "the Notre Dame mentality: You give the people who are causing problems detention and hope the problem will go away."

David liked his teacher in fifth grade. In fact, he liked a lot of teachers at the school. Unfortunately, the Sage School expanded to 250 kids in his fifth-grade year and to more than 400 in his sixth-grade year. With less individual attention and a bit more chaos, there were the inevitable efforts by adults to control the situation. David began to dig in against school once again. He stopped doing homework. His grades plummeted.

After two years of paying high tuitions and getting declining results, Marianne and Bob brought him back to Notre Dame, just to finish out middle school. He developed nosebleeds that took him to the nurse's office, typically on a Friday afternoon. While he held a Kleenex to his nose, he often overheard adults talking in the main office. The snippets of conversation confirmed all of his prejudices about school. It seemed to him that adults were saying stupid and hypocritical things on any and every occasion when he heard them.

His pubertal growth came early; he was tall and heavy. He found it hard to maneuver, socially and physically. As an overweight boy, the class intellectual, and the only student who regularly challenged teachers, David found himself unpopular with classmates. At Sage, some classmates had admired his revolutionary and oppositional approach; not at Notre Dame. I asked him if any teachers were talking

> "Whenever the teacher called me and I said something, they would all snicker in a little group because I didn't know the answer. They're just so mean. Everyone had something against me that year. This year, I'm not taking anyone's crap. If they say something to me, I'm just going to say something back." (Eleventh-grader)

to him during these years. He said yes, the usual things: "David, you're not doing your homework."

Both David and his parents hoped that things would be different in high school. David says about the large, respected community high school nearby: "It wasn't exactly like Notre Dame. It was like Notre Dame on crack and speed and several other narcotics. I knew a few weeks in that this is pretty much the same, only now no one even makes the illusion of caring. And again it was homework."

Marianne says, "I had such high hopes for high school. It was such a freeing experience for our older daughter. . . . By the end of his first semester, David was failing a few classes. He refused to do any work outside of school. The pattern was set for the next few years— each report card was followed by an argument. No matter how calmly we began, we dissolved into blobs of anger and frustration."

By high school, David had found the perfect weapon to rattle adults. He would simply state that *he had never agreed to be a student.* Then, in a spirit of compromise he would indicate a willingness to attend school, but he would do no homework. Homework, he felt, was an imposition on his time: an illegitimate extension of the school day that interfered with his life and his pleasure reading. I don't think there is an adult on earth who wouldn't react to a child's insistence that he's not going to do homework by saying, "But you have to! Homework is part of school." David had found a way to push the rigidity button in every grown-up by questioning the legitimacy of the homework demand. I'm sure that it amused him to see how easily adults fell into his trap. By attacking the entire premise of homework, David was attacking an aspect of school life that has grown steadily in the past fifteen years, at least at academically ambitious schools. Doing a lot of homework is regarded by many people as a marker of a good education, even though the rationale for it is shaky.

Teachers and parents often feel that a lot of homework is evidence of the quality of education being offered. However, there is much that is wrong with homework assignments, and anyone who is close to schools knows it—both teachers and students. Much of what is assigned for homework is uninspired drudgery. Worse yet, many teachers are requiring students to teach themselves concepts that have not been well taught in class. If you visit classrooms, much of the time is devoted to going over the homework, or correcting the homework, or handing in the homework.

To question homework is, however, to say that the emperor has no clothes. David not only kept saying the emperor had no clothes, he also refused to recognize the legitimacy of the emperor. The courtiers were outraged. David, however, went beyond just being the innocent child who pointed out that the emperor was naked. He read Ken Kesey's *One Flew Over the Cuckoo's Nest,* and began to experience school as an asylum to which he had been involuntarily confined.

At a certain point in high school, it became increasingly difficult for David's mother to support him. The many meetings she had attended on his behalf without any improvement in his school performance made her feel helpless. There were times when David's behavior had created tensions in her marriage; her husband suggested at times that she was overreacting to the situation, but he couldn't offer reasonable alternative strategies. Besides, the calls from school and confrontations with David landed on her watch. How could she not react? Most of all, she was consumed by worries about David's future. She thought to herself, "How can he know what he is choosing? He has never been an adult, responsible for all the details of daily living. How can he make that choice?"

Despite her feeling that David could not make informed choices, he continued to make them. Despite getting many in-house suspensions for not completing homework, he continued to boycott take-home assignments. He was supposed to use these suspension days to do homework; that's not how he used the time. He would sit in the small room with a window reading *Les Misérables* by Victor Hugo, presumably identifying with Jean Valjean. The next day, when his teachers asked him why he didn't have his homework done, he would say, "I was suspended yesterday and I didn't get the assignments."

Taking courses in art and photography were not the answer either. He liked these classes, but he wouldn't hand in assignments on principle. By the end of his sophomore year in high school, David would not keep any agreements. He was failing and clearly headed out the door.

It was at that point that he negotiated with his teachers to finish school in a pull-out program for emotionally disordered students. David describes it as a program "where they throw in most of the slower people, the people who are having problems with regular classes or they're beating up everyone or intimidating teachers." Neither he nor his parents considered him emotionally disordered, and certainly, even if he had been given a diagnosis of Oppositional Defiant Disorder, everyone would have had to acknowledge that David was one of the most polite defiant boys they had ever met.

He says: "I wound up there because the high school really didn't have anywhere to put me. I had been grating up against them for two and a half years at the time and the idea was basically move me over there, and you know I stopped failing because they stopped shoving homework down my throat."

He reached a compromise with his teachers: He would attend class if they allowed him to read in class. David got a sense of power from thinking that he had backed his prestigious high school into a corner because he was clearly prepared to drop out, and the administrators in his district are proud of their low dropout rate. He believes that the district finally compromised with him because they didn't want him to become a shameful statistic.

David did not hate all his teachers. He had a ninth-grade English teacher, Mr. Fast, who, David says appreciatively, conducted excellent class discussions and allowed David to lead the class into intellectual digressions. There was also Mrs. Mayo, administrator of the E.D. program, who finally had the power to negotiate a "no-homework" deal between David and all his remaining teachers. Her understanding of what homework had come to symbolize for David earned her a place of respect and affection in his heart. There is no doubt about his feelings of appreciation when he discusses her.

Even after all the negotiations, however, David still barely scraped through school with a D average. By that point, his mother was close to or beyond her limit. Unlike fourth grade, when she was absolutely on her son's side, by the end of David's senior year, she was profoundly discouraged by what she saw as his negativity and self-sabotaging choices. At the end of his school career, she wrote:

> Well, we are coming down to the wire now. After years of trying to get David to use his considerable gifts to "be a student"—bargaining, hoping, waiting, threatening, crying, fighting . . . in a few months he'll graduate high school. . . . We explored every alternative we could find . . . but I am still pushing him to school. . . . When we have meetings to evaluate the current term or plan the next one, we sit at a large conference table: David, parents, teachers, counselor, social worker, special ed. representative, vocational counselor, a very cordial group. I am grateful for their help. Sometimes I can sit there and plan and pretend that this is real—but lately my insides scream out that this is all about one boy's crappy attitude! He is not handicapped!

Neither David nor his mother had the appetite for graduation. I don't know whether his father or sisters wished that he had attended. The only ceremony he experienced was one of his own making: He knelt down on his knees and kissed the pavement across the street from the school. Free at last!

Within weeks after leaving high school, he began working the twilight shift for UPS and was enjoying it quite a bit when we talked. When I ask him how work compares to school, he says that physically he feels every hour that he works there, but "The immediate question that springs to mind is: is [work] what adults were complaining about? You know, I spent eight hours languishing at school and a good couple of more hours once I got home fighting with my parents, and everyone in the adult world was saying, 'Oh, enjoy those years, they're the best years of your life.'"

It is inconceivable to David that the school years could be the best years of anyone's life. What he is doing now, he reports, is "straightforward and clear and honest work. It is something I can do that's constructive after all those years of fighting. You really long to do something that is actually positive."

David portrays his school experience as a bruising fight for personal integrity, which he won—or at least survived. While I respect his experience, as an adult and a school psychologist, it is impossible for me not to regard his school career as sad. I wish for David and his family that it had been different. Why did this happen to him? I think of David as someone who had an allergic reaction to school. His psychological immune system caused him to break into an emotional rash when he realized that he wasn't going to be able to learn his own way.

The great American psychiatrist Harry Stack Sullivan brilliantly described infants as having two kinds of encounters with the world: "me" experiences and "not me" experiences. Even as adults, we still have moments when we walk into a situation or an institution and are overwhelmed by "not me" feelings. I would argue that every child—whether in math or PE or biology or sitting at a football game—has moments of "not me" feelings about school.

If so, then why don't more children become allergic to school in the way that David did? While school is a more or less difficult fit for all students, their allergic reactions are episodic, balanced by a majority of more affirming moments. We're not all *that* allergic to school! For David, the fit with school was terrible, and—psychologically speaking—by fourth grade he simply swelled up with painful hives that left him miserable and increasingly sensitized to the insult and imposition of school.

Let's stick with the allergic-reaction metaphor a bit longer. If you were to eat shellfish and experience an immunological reaction that caused you to itch all over, closed your throat, and made you think you were dying, would you voluntarily eat shellfish again soon? No, you wouldn't. How would you react if someone were to offer you some soft-shell crab for dinner, telling you it was good for you? You would refuse, politely at first and then with irritation if they kept insisting on the wonderful flavor. What would you do if you were trapped in prison and every morning a mammoth guard was preparing to shove some shrimp or lobster in your mouth? You would fight and battle and scream and you would consider it a triumph if you fought the authorities to a standstill every day. When they finally let you out of shellfish prison, you would kiss the pavement and sing, "Free at last." That was David's school experience.

David describes himself as having a "problem with authority." Actually, he had an allergy to authority, and all it brought him—to the very end of his high school career—was more authority.

But why was his reaction so extreme? Why did he experience school as a life-threatening experience? Didn't he come from a middle-class family that valued education? Wasn't he smart enough to do the work? Absolutely. However, there were cognitive obstacles in David's path from the beginning, and then the prolonged war with school exacted its own traumatic toll on David and his family. David suffered in school from three things: a learning disability, an assault on his identity, and his family's difficulty in seeing him as separate from the context of school.

David suffered throughout his school life from a nonverbal learning disability diagnosed in fourth grade. The school failed to address his special need along this line, and David never received the proper remediation for the disability. That is not surprising. Nonverbal learning disabilities are difficult to remediate and support, and too few teachers are trained to understand them.

> "I hate to sit at my desk. I just feel like running away."
>
> (Third-grader)

Marianne informed me that on the standard IQ test given to children in the United States, David had a twenty-nine-point gap between his verbal score and his performance score. In most states, an eleven-point discrepancy legally qualifies as disability. However, his family also learned that he was exceptionally bright according to testing standards, and his mother acknowledges that they felt he was smart enough to do the work and to recognize that it had to be done. David also considered himself gifted because some things came so easily to him. Therein lies a tale.

Twenty-nine points on the standard IQ test represents a huge discrepancy between the different areas of functioning of one's brain. David is almost certainly a verbal superstar, gifted in speech and reading. He is, at best, average in organization. Being average, however, is not a consolation for a boy to whom most conceptual matters come extremely easily. Nor does it *feel* average. What a boy like David experiences constantly is *the gap*. What he experiences is a daily roller-coaster ride: from the highs of class discussion to the lows of trying to keep track of his homework. The daily mechanics of school bedeviled David; writing legibly, keeping his papers organized, time management, and the sequencing of tasks were extraordinarily difficult. When he listened to his teachers talk, he understood everything. When he read material, he absorbed it all. However, when he had to produce writing in a timed situation or remember his homework, his processing was laborious and bewildering.

An internal discrepancy such as this is extremely confusing for a child. The effect is to feel extremely smart in some areas and extraordinarily dumb in other areas. The sensation would be like running a race swiftly and fluidly and suddenly tripping, getting up, and tripping again without any clue as to why you tripped in the first place. Since you cannot see the cause, you have to conclude that, at the very least, you are a klutz. Worse yet, an observer might conclude that you are tripping yourself on purpose to get out of running the race. In essence, that's what David's fourth-grade teacher did to him.

Remember when David and his teacher were having a furious fight over his handwriting and organizational problems? David's teacher proclaimed that his legible paper "wasn't that hard," and David exploded, saying something to the effect of "You have no idea how hard it is. You didn't have to do it." She was insulting his effort and integrity. She may have been doing it out of ignorance, but David could not have known that. He felt it was an indictment of him. He experienced her as monumentally unempathic and willfully mean.

Even if we set aside one spectacularly bad teacher, it is psychologically painful for anyone to overcome frustration time and time again in order to be able to complete a task when others can do it relatively easily. Not knowing why it is so frustrating for you, or having a teacher treat you as if you were willfully malingering when you are struggling, is more than a child can bear. A friend and colleague, Ned Hallowell, author of *The Childhood Roots of Adult Happiness,* says that what we fail to remember when we work with children is that everyone lives their life based on their strengths, not on their remediated weaknesses. School, however, presses on a child's weaknesses every day.

When I came to work at a boys' private school, I found that one or two boys a year blew up in anger at the amount of homework they were given. They were so furious at everyone, they were soon regarded as disciplinary problems. Almost without exception, when we had such boys tested we found nonverbal learning disabilities, which the school had unwittingly uncovered through its challenging homework demands. That's what happened to David. It happened much earlier in his school career because his executive functioning problems were compounded by fine-motor-skill difficulties. School was a terrible fit for David. Schools, particularly traditional schools such as Notre Dame, rely heavily on rapid, written production. If your ability to write by hand is 30 percent slower than everyone else's in the class, you are going to be frustrated and feel stupid.

School came to feel like an assault on David's identity. He knew he was smart, yet far too many experiences gave him the sensation that he was stupid. He could either accept the redefinition of himself as dumb and slow, or he could fight the institution and the people who made him feel that way, namely school. The only way around that confrontation is for a child to understand that despite his intelligence, something in his neurological wiring makes school difficult for him, that is, a learning disability.

I ask David if he has thought of himself as learning disabled. His answer: "No, I can't say that I have. *I always just thought of myself as being me.* I'd been referred to as learning disabled by several people, but my figuring was: 'Okay, I get the information the first time, don't need to rehash it, and have the common sense not to waste my time on homework. How, exactly, is that disabled?' Of course, organization was a different story. I was never very well organized."

David resists, perhaps resents, the term *disabled* because it seems to imply that he is handicapped in some vital way. In the statement above, David reveals both that he suffered from organizational difficulties and that he found it almost impossible to understand that he was disabled because he understood the material. That is precisely how a nonverbal learning disability shows up and why they present such a challenge to children, families, and teachers. It is exactly as David describes: A verbally gifted child understands the material, but cannot process it, organize it, or present it as quickly as educators need him to in the classroom. David's internal experience was not that he was learning disabled, because his comprehension was close to perfect. It would make more sense, in a common-sense kind of way, to call him *school disabled.*

More painful than being learning disabled was the reality that David's parents were slowly sucked down into the vortex of his dismal school performance. It is scary to feel as if you are drowning. To have the people who love you jump in to save you and start to drown as well is terrifying. That's what happened to David's parents. No matter what they tried, it didn't seem to work. It wasn't just a matter of being made to feel helpless, or having to attend countless school meetings, or seeing D's on a report card. They came to see David as defined by oppositional behavior and themselves as defined, at least in part, by his school failure. Their "gifted" son became their difficult, underachieving son.

When I ask David if that were the case, he acknowledges that his parents had been pulled in, against their better judgment: "My parents, since they were the ones who raised me, did know better—*but there were times when it seemed like I was nothing more than a guy who refused to do his homework,* even to them. With other people, though . . . Well, when you're that young, there's really not a lot you do outside of school that other people are aware of. *Many people knew me as little more than a bad student.*"

His mother describes how she couldn't help but begin to define herself as "the-mother-who-produced-the-bad-student," or "the-smart-mother-who-couldn't-get-her-child-to-do-anything." As a school psychologist, I have been to enough IEP (Individualized Educational Program) and faculty meetings to know that educators invariably off-load their sense of helplessness onto the mothers of children (rarely the fathers). Educators do indeed sit around the table and silently think, "If only they set limits"; or, "If only they had a realistic view of their child." I'll admit to having had those thoughts myself. When you are faced with a bewildering student like David and you don't have good answers on the tip of your tongue, it takes discipline and reflection to pull yourself out of the tendency to blame someone else for your own sense of helplessness. And David had a particular genius for making everyone around him feel at a loss.

By tenth grade, or even before, school exerted a terrible power over David and his family. It began to undermine both David and his mother's sense of identity. It caused them to fight.

When his school troubles began to invade his home and his relationship with his parents, David was in a terrible bind. He needed to fight school in order to maintain his sense of dignity and worth. At the same time, the more he fought school, the more it seemed to turn his mother against him or lower her opinion of him—or so it must have seemed to him.

I know from Marianne's notes that she was in pain, not knowing at whom to be angry: David or the school. What is also evident to me is that their love is intact, in spite of all the stress of the school years. David's school experience was deeply wounding for him and for his parents, but interestingly, while the adults in his life have voiced hopelessness at times, David insists:

> Hope is the one thing I have always had. I wanted to leave, but my better judgment prevailed. I thought, I'd come this far and if I leave now I'll have wasted the last two years of my life. I didn't really have a third choice so I went along with it. But that's a thing I've noticed. My love of learning is still active. School hasn't managed to suppress it. . . . It's been hard on my parents and on me, but I think down the road we'll be able to look back at it as just a very long argument that we survived. The relationship is bigger than that.

HEATHER—NO ONE LIKES TO FEEL STUPID

"The one piece of advice I wish someone would have given my dad or even my teachers would have been that the harder you push, the more the child gets angry." Heather is dark-haired, tall, and thin. She holds herself like an athlete and is full of passionate moral conviction, the domesticated remnant of the fury that once possessed her.

"No one likes to feel stupid and this is what constantly happens. This for me was a major contributing factor in my rebellion against school. If I already had no one to talk to and felt stupid, why should I try?"

I was interviewing Heather at Rocky Mountain Academy, a therapeutic boarding school in eastern Idaho, near the border with Washington state. She had been at the academy for close to two years. She believes that coming to RMA saved her life. It was not a voluntary decision. When she was brought there in tenth grade she was an angry, out-of-control kid, an alcoholic, and a drug user. She had been an alcoholic since eighth grade. Nine close friends had died from drug-related car accidents or murders during her years in middle school and early high school. She had been gang-raped in eighth grade. Her life was skidding downhill at a terrifying pace.

"I began to feel stupid for a couple of reasons that really started in seventh grade," Heather wrote to me in the weeks after our first meeting. "I found myself being pushed harder and harder by my father to achieve the best grades and perform perfectly. I was unable to talk to him . . . due to his comments on my intelligence."

Heather is anything but stupid. Indeed, she taught herself to read at an early age, watching *Hooked on Phonics* with her twin sisters, who were four years older. However, by the time she arrived at her combined middle school/high school in rural Washington, all three of her sisters had preceded her, and they had all been wonderful students. As the only adopted child in the family she felt different, alone, mistrustful, and unprepared. "Since my teacher in sixth grade was someone who did not really teach, I was ill-equipped to deal with the more demanding workload in the junior and senior high school," she added.

Heather's biological mother was a drug user. She had four children out of wedlock who were taken away from her. Heather's mother's boyfriend molested her older sisters. According to Heather, she and her mother "never bonded"—the reason she was taken away. Heather acknowledges that she may have had attachment difficulties. She lived in eleven foster homes before she was formally adopted by a district superviser for a United States federal agency and his wife. He had three children from a previous marriage, but he and his new wife wanted a child of their own. Heather fulfilled that wish.

She was a little tomboy. Her best friend was Chris, a boy she met in kindergarten. They were the closest of friends. "I was always with the guys. I was like, forget girls." She remembers not talking for periods of time during her elementary school years because she didn't trust women or "mom" figures. She was, however, slowly growing closer to her adoptive mother. Tragically—and that word could be used to describe so many events in her life—her adoptive mother was killed in a car crash when she was eight years old. Heather hadn't said "Good-bye" or "I love you" or anything to her that morning.

"I've been swimming since I was like three. I'm like a little fish, but she woke me up because I was going to be late and so I hurried out of the house . . . I just left." She was halfway through her swim lesson when the owner of the pool came to collect Heather and her sister and take them to their father. She remembers: "My dad was standing there crying."

For a child who had attachment problems, the loss of her adoptive mother was colossal. Following her death, Heather's older sister began to pick on her constantly. Her father began to date another woman a year later, a woman with a "perfect" daughter to whom Heather was often unfavorably compared.

"About seventh grade my father began really spending a lot more time with his girlfriend, and really telling me that Melanie was so much better and I needed to be just like Melanie because I got into so much trouble and I'm such a bad kid."

The new woman in their father's life had the paradoxical effect of driving Heather and her older sisters together. First of all, they were left alone a lot. Her sisters would pick her up at sports and take her out to parties with them. "I did really well my seventh-grade year. I was like, okay, I'll do this. Well, I'm getting good grades and then my sisters starting taking me out to parties with them. Because they don't want me home alone. So then they really start letting me drink. They would be like, 'Here, Heather, have a beer.' Because they thought I was funny when I got drunk."

Did anyone at school notice that Heather, who often came to school sleep-deprived and hungover, was spinning out of control? Maybe, she says, "but the teachers, the teachers were all about their jobs." Some of her teachers invited her to talk with them, but by that time she was too cool for school. "I was like hey, this is what my sisters are doing, we're getting along now." Heather believes that school personnel saw what was happening to her, but because her father was so well known in their small town, no one was willing to confront the issue of her delinquent behavior. There was also the issue of athletics. Heather was a star athlete. Drunk or sober, she showed up for games.

She tried to get good grades in elementary school to keep up with her older sisters. "You know, getting the good grades for my dad because I really wanted him to notice me. I'd be like, 'Hello, I get grades, too, look at me!' " It didn't seem as if that strategy was working, and by sixth and seventh grades she was developing a new strategy. She joined every team on which Melanie—"perfect" Melanie—played, and Heather outplayed her. On the basketball court, on the track field, in the swimming pool, she was markedly more aggressive than she had ever been, and she became the star athlete of her grade. "When I began to play sports for the school, it almost didn't matter what I did because I had found my calling in the athletic field. My grades went up even though I wasn't doing the work and no one seemed to bother me about getting into trouble."

The girl who had lost two mothers, who had had a difficult relationship with her older sisters, and who experienced her father as moving out of her life found two strategies for success: partying with her sisters, and dazzling the fans on the sidelines of her basketball games. One night at a party, after she had resisted the sexual advances of one of her sisters' friends, she overheard this sister telling the boy that she would get Heather drunk and then "she'll do whatever you want." That was a turning point for Heather. "I mean from that moment on I realized that, you know, my sisters really didn't care about me. . . . I mean after that like I just pounded a ton of beers and I just kissed him, I was like whatever." Heather didn't become promiscuous at that point—"Like I hadn't had sex or anything"—but after that she was a compulsive drinker.

The anchor of her life was her kindergarten friend Chris. The two had a profound need for each other. "If Chris couldn't sleep at night, he would leave a note on his pillow saying, 'At Heather's, love you, Mom,' and he'd come in the middle of the night and crawl in bed with me. Like I couldn't sleep, and we'd cuddle up and go to sleep." She did the same. "I mean, if there was a note saying, 'Dad, at Chris's,' my dad was like okay." She says they never held hands, but they "hugged and cuddled all the time because he was like my best friend . . . like a big teddy bear. Never kissed, nothing. Never made a move on me. Perfect gentleman."

She was gang-raped by five men in her sisters' college dorm room when she was thirteen years old. Her sisters were drunk and unconscious at the time. She went to bed without telling them what happened. The next morning she got up at six and went to the airport on her own to go home. She never reported the rape until she went into therapy years later.

By ninth grade, both she and Chris were drinking, smoking marijuana, and taking mushrooms and Ecstasy. Four of their friends, drunk, were killed by a train at a train crossing. Her grades had fallen from A's in elementary school to C's in tenth grade. She was, however, still in good standing with school personnel because she made it to every game. She felt that either no one cared about her or they cared about her only because she was good at sports. Chris died in a car accident in late November of her ninth-grade year. He flipped his vehicle into a pond. The pond iced over that night and his body wasn't found for three days. She saw him pulled out of the water. The rest is a blur.

Like many parents, her father tricked her into going to Rocky Mountain Academy. (Some parents have two security guards wake up a child in the middle of the night to transport her to RMA.) He told her they were going to visit her aunt in Spokane, and instead drove her up the road to the school. Heather reports, "I flipped out on my dad. . . . What are you doing to me? Why am I here? I hate you, don't touch me, don't talk to me!" Like so many RMA parents, he had to mortgage his house and spend all of Heather's college fund to pay for a school that provides far more than an ordinary education: It combines school with drug rehab, therapy, and a demanding emotional curriculum.

It took Heather months to follow the rules and behave in a civil way to the staff and teachers at RMA. She didn't trust teachers, she didn't trust the system, she didn't believe education had anything to do with her identity anymore. After two years she reports:

> My perspective on teachers has changed. Like as in like my elementary school and in my high school, you know, I felt like you couldn't talk to the teachers. The teachers here, they teach you but they don't teach you just class. . . . I can actually talk to them and understand them. I've always been challenged [here] in academics. If I say this is too easy, they'll find something for me. Or if I say this does not interest me at all, but if we do this with it, I'd love to do that. You know and they'll accommodate me and they'll help me get what I need. So I'm actually, I'm learning more than I ever did.

ZOE: FROM SCHOOL NIGHTMARE TO DEFERRED DREAMS

"I'm just not a school kid," Zoe announces matter-of-factly. "No, not from the beginning."

"What does it mean to not be a school kid?" I ask.

"A school kid loves to be in school. You know, loves to do work, loves to be in after-school clubs and oh, *that is so not me!* I tried it at the Blake. I signed up for cheerleading and I was really good at that, but it's just not me." Zoe has a patch over her eye, the result of recent surgery to reattach a retina. She relates that the surgery was incredibly painful, yet her description of the pain of the surgery doesn't seem to compare with the endless agony of school.

"Most kids like school in elementary school and then by middle school and high school they start to have problems. I never liked school, not from the get-go." So I ask, when did you first have the thought that you might drop out of school? Zoe laughs. "Oh . . . every day. I was like, I'm going to drop out." Zoe and I sit in an empty classroom in a unique charter school called Boston Evening Academy. It is open from four-thirty to eight-thirty in the evening. Every single student at BEA is a former dropout who, after a period of months or years out of school, has chosen to return to try to get a high school degree after all. The students have to apply for admission, and explain the changes in their motivation. The process forces them to look at the behavior and motivation that led them to flee school. Many, like Zoe, are nineteen or twenty and still have a year or two to go before they receive a high school degree.

Zoe's dream is to be a fashion designer, and according to the art teachers at BEA, she has talent. She has always visualized clothing designs and her own dress communicates a distinctive sense of style. If she can just do the basic requirements of school and complete high school they are confident she can gain admission to a respected art college where she can pursue her passion. However, like many artists, she experiences the rigid demands of school as an oppressive constraint on her mind and spirit, as chafing as most of us would experience wearing handcuffs as everyday attire. What she has needed is to get into a place where she can throw herself into the area of her talent. She has known it all along, but lacked the power to change her environment and the maturity and insight to change herself or her strategy to accommodate the temporary imposition of school in service of her greater goal.

Her experience of complete school failure and dropping out has given her at least this much power over her own destiny. Her experience, and the natural engine of development, also have given her new insights about herself that make it possible for her to see more clearly the roots of her struggle with school, as well as the commitment she is now prepared to make to achieve her dream. When she talks about her situation, you can hear her angry youth and emerging maturity, her bitterness about school and teachers past, and recognition of something different this time around:

I hate doing anything that I *have* to do. I have to go to school and I
hate that. If they left school as an option, I wouldn't go. So I am
glad that I can appreciate the fact that I have to go now, but I
couldn't appreciate it then. The fact that I had to go and I had to
do my work and I had to pay attention. I hated it. Now it's my
choice but they [the faculty at BEA] still let you know like it is
your choice but we care about you too much to let you not do it.

Kids who drop out have a unique perspective on school because,
unlike the vast majority of students who, happy or not, manage to
stick it out until graduation, dropouts are willing to pay the ultimate
price of losing the chance for a diploma in order to get out of the
building. Other kids may yearn to leave school; dropouts actually do
it. A group of former dropouts from BEA took the time to explain
their experiences to me.

The decisions that these students make are not impulsive, nor are
the students unaware of the risks of leaving. It is just that their hatred
of school, their feelings of anxiety, or their family problems are just
too intense to allow them to continue. One young man explained, "In
second grade my father was passing away and he was getting sick.
Nothing seemed important to me. I thought if people reject me I don't
care. I've already lost everything that I've loved the most so I don't care
no more." He was missing forty-five days a year by fifth grade, failed
to pass seventh and eighth, and dropped out as a sixteen-year-old
ninth-grader.

Another BEA student described starting at a large urban high
school in ninth grade: "The crowd was too big. When you have a big
school like that, you have such a variety that you get lost. It's like a
maze. . . . Most people learn all of their things in high school: drugs,
different types of drugs, stealing cars. All the bad things people say
don't do, you learn in high school."

A talented African-American student from the inner city was recruited for a special program and enrolled in a suburban high school.
He fell for the many temptations he found there: "I went to a white
school. I'm not saying white people are richer than black but they
have cars. So ninth-graders come pulling up or tenth-graders. Everybody has a car. It wasn't like Boston Public, you have to walk in the
cold. You just got in the car and just left, put the heat on."

And indeed, many of them checked in for attendance in the morning and then left the building, meeting their friends and spending the day hanging out and smoking weed.

These must have been tough students to motivate, particularly once they had tasted the pleasures of freedom and pseudo-adulthood. Whatever their reasons for leaving, however, all of the students who dropped out expressed a profound disappointment in their teachers and in the school management. Whatever personal difficulties they were experiencing, and no matter how hard they fought "the system," these young people expected their teachers to reach out to them, and ask more of them. I found this to be a striking paradox. They hated school, yet they hoped the teachers and administrators could find some way to help them achieve success in there. Recognizing that Zoe was having problems with motivation in sixth grade, her father signed her up for a new charter school in Boston starting in seventh. Here is her ambivalent description of the Renaissance School:

> The first two weeks of school were great at the Renaissance. And then it just all goes downhill. Their discipline falls apart. If they have you do something for the first month of school, they don't stick to it. . . . No matter how much kids say "I don't want you to tell me what to do" kids are not good on their own when they are that young. . . . If you don't tell them to do their homework, they don't do it. So you have to stay on top of them. They did not do that at the Renaissance. They just let you do what you want to do and you got into trouble. You did exactly what you want to do, which at the time you are in seventh and eighth grade, it's not anything productive. You want to get in trouble and hang out with your friends.

Zoe is withering in her criticisms of teachers. "The teachers are going to get paid whether we learn or not," she states. "Everybody at the Renaissance, I didn't learn anything while I was there. I got straight F's on my report card, three years in a row. I passed every year. They passed me. I obviously didn't know the stuff 'cause I didn't pass tests, and it's just, they were just crazy."

Most surprisingly, Zoe believes that there is an economic motivation for the teachers' behavior. "They get paid to sit up there and talk and tell us what we need to know. They don't get paid depending on

> "The kids in my grade say we don't have a social ladder, but they arent
> one of the few who are always teased, forgotten, and left out. it really sux
> being one of those, but then i personaly wouldnt give it up for anything.
> Pretty much all the kids in my class dont like me beacuse i'm different
> than they are and dont care about it. i dont try and do the stuff that
> they do or try to be somthing im not. im just me. sometimes i think
> it scares them that im so different." (Eighth-grader)

whether we write it down or whether we pay attention. . . . They could care less whether we are paying attention just as long as we are there. . . . That's why there is overcrowding in schools. The more kids that go there, the more you get paid. And, you don't give a damn what we are doing just as long as we are sitting there."

It might surprise many adults to hear that children conclude that teachers are not invested in them, but rather are more interested in making money off them. The other casualty of large classroom size is teacher motivation, because teachers become exhausted with keeping up with a large number of kids, and so they engage in an informal process of triage, leaving the less motivated, more resistant children on the battlefield to die. Kristen, another Boston Evening Academy student, told me that she was amazed to find a teacher at BEA who had been her history teacher in her previous inner-city high school. At the high school, she had habitually come to his class, put her head down on the desk, and slept. It was an act of academic despair matched by her teacher's demoralized response. As far as she could remember, the teacher, Mr. Shaw, had never addressed the behavior; he never disturbed her sleep. She could not have been more surprised to encounter him again in the small classes at BEA, where putting your head on a desk is not permitted. Because of a change in class size, change of rules, and, no doubt, a change in Mr. Shaw's morale, he would now stop any student from putting his head down on the desk. It was not only Kristen who was changed by BEA: so was her teacher.

Unfortunately, the failure of Zoe's charter middle school, the Renaissance, to hold her accountable for the ninth-grade work she hadn't done put her in a difficult position when she reached high school, "because for once somebody actually cared that when I was at the Renaissance I got all F's." The administration at the Blake decreed that she had to repeat ninth grade.

"They said, 'Well, Zoe, you never passed the ninth grade when you were at the Renaissance,' and I'm like, 'Well, that's not my problem.'" She was now sixteen, almost seventeen, and she experienced them as "trying to put me way back." She wanted to take a test that would prove that she could master ninth-grade work, but her father intervened on the side of the school and insisted she repeat ninth grade. They fought and he refused to budge. She left school on February 12 of her repeat ninth-grade year. At the time she was taking a double course load: ninth- *and* tenth-grade English classes, and ninth- *and* tenth-grade math classes.

Every year, 5 out of 100 students over the age of sixteen drop out of school before receiving their diplomas, approximately 3.8 *million* young people. In the years between sixteen and twenty-one, the absolute number of dropouts increases until the number of high school dropouts reaches a total of 10.6 percent of young people in that age bracket. There are stunning differences among the races in the percentage of children who drop out: 6.9 percent are white (non-Hispanic), 13.1 percent are African-Americans, and—highest of all—27.8 percent are Hispanic. Each of these children has a long story of humiliation and gradual disengagement prior to his departure. For most, the decision to leave was not only a long time coming but visible by middle school. The question in my mind is whether programs of early identification and remediation could have saved their high school careers.

I am a psychologist, not an educational reformer. However, as a psychologist who works at a private school with a tuition of twenty-two thousand dollars, I know that a school's budget for support services, programs, and optimal class size makes an enormous difference in the psychological experience of children. I'm not saying that all potential dropouts can be steered toward completion. There will always be some kids who find themselves too allergic to the structure and demands of school to stay the course. But with the proper intervention early enough in a child's school career—well before eighth grade—it would be possible to help her connect to school before her worldview becomes clouded with failure and humiliation.

I ask Zoe how she felt on the day she decided to leave school. Had she felt relieved or excited? "I was sad the day I dropped out and

I was dropping out because I didn't want to be in the ninth grade and here I was. . . . I wasn't going to be in the ninth grade and have three more years ahead of me."

If we were tempted to judge Zoe as an irresponsible or oppositional kind of girl, it might be important to know that after she left school she and her mother moved in with her grandmother to nurse her in the last year of her life. Despite all of her complaining about school, and her sometimes tough exterior, it is clear that Zoe still has hope for school. Whatever her complaints about her family, she still has hope for them. She devoted herself to family, in fact, in tending to her dying grandmother. She also navigated a painful conflict with her father, who was angry when she dropped out of high school, but he eventually was the one who accompanied her to BEA the day she enrolled:

> Yeah, you know, he was so angry that I moved out and everything and he was just like, "You know I'm just going to go along with you. Whatever you want to do, I'm just going to go along 'cause I don't want to fight with you about school and stuff anymore."

It is impossible not to be inspired by Zoe. As much as she has hated school over many years, she is trying again at Boston Evening Academy. She is working hard to make her school career and her family as good as she can. She just had to do it her way and in her own time.

Some students give up on school. They just cannot bear it. Either they collapse psychologically, trudging listlessly through the system, hoping that a minimal effort will help them scrape by, or—after they turn sixteen—they physically drop out of school. Dropping out of school is the final act of despair on a long journey of frustration. It is almost never a sudden decision. It is a decision taken in fury or despair because every child knows that education is important. We have heard the stories of a few kids who bombed out of school in one way or another, kids most people don't hear much about, except for the labels. It is important for the reader to know from a statistical point of view how common that experience of despair can be and how desperate these young people feel who make that choice.

Teenagers who leave school jump out into a job market where a high school degree is the basic, entry-level requirement for most positions. As a group, they will not earn as much as their peers who stayed in school and received a degree. They make up a disproportionate percentage of the nation's prison and death-row inmates. They are at risk.

The economic and risk statistics for high school dropouts are so unfavorable, it only makes sense for kids to stay in school. Any parent, any teacher, any sensible adult would counsel a child to hang on and "just finish!" Indeed, one can imagine that every child who drops out of school has had exactly that conversation with parents, relatives, guidance counselors, teachers, and even friends. After a student leaves, you can be sure that some people play the blame game. School personnel wish the child had better parental support, parents wish the school had done more to engage the child, and so on.

The socioeconomic factors that support wealthier kids in school work in reverse against poor kids, resulting in their despair about the educational process. Children from families in the bottom 20 percent of family incomes in the United States drop out at a rate six times greater than the children of other classes. In terms of education, the rich get richer and the poor stay poorer.

The United States is the only major industrialized nation to spend more on the education of middle-class white students than it does on the education of poor children of color. All of the profound social divisions in American education and the disparate outcomes for rich and poor have been documented, notably by Jonathan Kozol in his book *Savage Inequalities.* I cannot add to his analysis of the American educational system except by taking the reader inside the psychology of children making the decision to leave school. What I have learned is that the decision starts years before the child actually physically leaves school. Most children who eventually drop out have had the thought by second grade.

In my twenties and early thirties I trained as a child psychologist at two hospitals on the South Side of Chicago—one a major teaching hospital, the other a small children's psychiatric hospital. Virtually every one of my patients at both hospitals was African-American and poor. It didn't matter whether I worked with children on an inpatient or an out-patient basis, whether I was testing them for learning disabilities or evaluating them for psychotic thinking, the majority had already given up on school.

If I asked an eight-year-old how school was, he would shrug his shoulders in a defeated way, look at the floor, and mumble something about school being hard, or not liking it, or even hating it. If I was administering some psychological tests, the boy—and it was mainly angry boys who ended up in the hospital—would be hesitant and ashamed of any task connected with writing. He would look at the pencil as if it were his enemy and he would talk about school as if it were only a place where he got into trouble. The painful truth was that the children I saw had no hope that school would get them anywhere. The former chancellor of the New York public schools, Harold Levy, said that many kids look at the schools that are provided for them and think, "There is nothing for me here. I have to get out as soon as possible."

When a child is black and poor in a racist society, it is not a surprise that he or she should conclude that a shabby school with too few books, peeling paint, and a leaky roof would have little to offer him. For a Hispanic child who feels that her family needs her to help earn money, family loyalty may triumph over her educational aspirations. She may also not have a role model who has finished high school. It is more difficult to explain why a middle-class white child from an educated family would fall into fury and despair and drop out of school.

In all three cases, the reasons are actually the same: The child concludes that she cannot get the sense of connection, recognition, and power that she needs to know that she is truly developing. She finds those things outside of school, and not inside. Perhaps she experiences a sense of recognition within her family instead of in the school environment. Perhaps she wants to get a sense of power by having a baby or by being treated like a grown-up in the workplace.

Right or wrong, students drop out because they do not fit into school and feel powerless to change the circumstances of their own education. While many alternative programs in high schools are designed to give back a sense of power to the powerless, for too many young people it is too late. They have experienced a sense of bad fit in school for too long.

Although many dropouts, like Zoe and her colleagues, eventually choose to resume their education in some kind of school setting, first they are compelled to leave what is, for them, a tortured life in school, and find a way to grow themselves elsewhere.

7

Transitions and Turnarounds

What led to my failure to get A's in school was
my lack of motivation, but I'm seeing the light now.
—*Erik, fifteen*

Smart kids are a dime a dozen. Personality,
perseverance—you need a lot more
than brains to succeed in life.
—*Mrs. Rosenberg, teacher*

"He always has a hard fall," a mother said to me about her son, Ryan, referring to his poor academic performance at the start of each school year. "He tends to pick up after Christmas and he usually has a strong finish in the spring." I was glad to hear that she had perspective, but the doubt in her voice was unmistakable. Would it really happen that way again this year? He currently had D's in three of his courses and his teachers described him as having that "deer in the headlights" look on his face. Could he turn it around?

Ryan was a tenth-grader and his mother was describing a motivational curve that is exactly the opposite of that which most students experience in school. For the majority, academic motivation peaks in September and October, then slides downhill through the winter and into the spring. For Ryan, the beginning of every school year was fraught with anxiety, for both him and his family. It customarily took him two or three months to find traction in his courses. He always received his lowest grades right at the start of the year, and his parents and teachers would start to panic, never sure whether this year he would once again pull up his grades. His style is different from other kids', and therefore alarming. Because he always appears to be digging himself a hole that is going to be tough to climb out of, it seems reasonable for adults to worry, to jump in and try to do something. That's why I had been called in. Ryan was sent to talk to the psychologist in hopes that I could divine the reasons for his perennial slow start.

I expected to find a boy frightened and hopeless. After all, he did have three D's and it was the third week of October. Contrary to my expectations, he appeared reasonably confident.

"I'll do better in the spring," he told me. "I always do."

Is there an explanation for what happens to him in the fall? He told me about himself. He is a shy and socially awkward boy—"I'm not in the cool group" is how he put it—and he tends to fall out of touch with friends over the summer. During July and August he lives in his own imagination, doing things at his own pace. Every year, the return to the demanding social environment of school is a disorienting shock. He has to regain his balance in order to be able to focus on his studies. Despite his confidence, it was nevertheless an uncomfortable pattern, all the more so because he knew that, along with pushing his D's up to C's, he was going to have to deal with the worry of his parents and teachers. For most kids, adult anxiety feels like an additional burden. So he was trying to tell me: "I know what's happening to me. I'll be all right." And he was. By spring, his grades were C's and B's and his teachers were full of admiration for what a steady and hardworking student he was.

Students experience transitions and turnarounds many times during their school years. All students occasionally find themselves struggling, both developmentally and academically. They have to find a way to turn the situation around, perhaps many times during their lives in school. Many of the challenges they face are institutional, others are developmental or social, but the underlying challenge is the same: to adjust.

EXTERNAL AND INTERNAL CHALLENGES

Children are likely to face two kinds of challenges that require them to devise a new strategy: external and internal. Examples of external challenge might be institutional transitions, such as moving to high school, or even moving up from kindergarten to first grade, with an increased demand for reading. Many kids are thrown by the change from a self-contained classroom with a single homeroom teacher to a block schedule where they travel from class to class, or perhaps by getting a new homeroom teacher with whom they don't feel any sense of fit. Moving to a different town or switching schools is an obvious threat to a child's sense of fit. She will have to search in order to find it.

In the years since I wrote *Best Friends, Worst Enemies: Understanding the Social Lives of Children,* I have talked to thousands of children about the social challenges they faced when they entered a community as new students. Happily, many kids report that it did not take long to find a new friend in their new setting. Others say, in April or May of their first year in the new school, "It was hard . . . it's still hard," or, "My old school was easier. I had more friends there," and the ongoing struggle is still evident in their faces.

Any institutional change requires a child to develop a new strategy. It helps when everyone else in the class is making the same transition; there is comfort in having company, and the adults are more attuned to a group shift. Family changes can throw children off their stride: the birth of a new baby, a parental divorce, or a death in the family or among friends. A child may struggle to regain her footing after such an event. A second-grader may feel disrupted by the birth of a new baby, until she finds a friend in class whose mother has also recently given birth. They can talk about being older sisters and bolster each other's sense of identity as competent and mature.

The most difficult changes are the developmental ones, the internal changes that require a child to approach school in a different way, or the developmental delays that keep him from developing at the same pace as other children. Girls who come into puberty much earlier than others and boys who mature later than others may find their school careers disrupted because their identities and their social relationships are changed. Familiar with their own strategies, children are constantly reviewing new approaches to the problems that dog them.

Erik, a sophomore, describes his epiphany: "I'm real aware that right now is when I should be changing from my typically lazy, unmotivated self. I think all throughout my school years I kind of have

just done enough to get by, and now is the time to step it up. If I just
do a whole year like the first few weeks of last year—manage my
time, stay off the phone, and lock myself in my room and get my
work done—I can get A's."

It is helpful to think about all of childhood as a series of transitions and adaptations. It is just that some are negotiated so smoothly
that we don't even notice that a child has bridged these gaps. At other
times, the child doesn't know how to get from here to there. All parents can be certain that their child will hit such a point, but they just
cannot know when in her young life that is going to happen, or necessarily why. The English psychoanalyst Donald Woods Winnicott
wrote that when a child patient was brought to him for treatment, his
aim was to enter the child's life, to try to understand the child and
make her feel safe, and then to get out as soon as development had
taken over again. His model is an excellent one for teachers and parents as well.

THE TURNAROUND: A DO-IT-YOURSELF PROJECT

Whatever got them into trouble, a turnaround is a child's own heroic
story of challenge and victory: No one can do it for them. Anxious
mothers can't find it for them. Overbearing fathers can't force them
to find it or make anyone give it to them. It is the child who discovers
the foothold he will use to recover his bearings and push through the
indignities of school life.

That said, a child's turnaround is not a solitary or isolated event.
It happens in a context, and in every story of a child's turnaround
there are adult actors in what would best be described as supporting
roles. These adults recognize the child's struggle. They either clear
the space, step out of the way, or lend just the right kind of support
(intentionally or not) in a way that enables the child to tap his own
inner resources, modify his strategy, and move forward successfully.
This person may be a parent, but often it is a teacher or family friend
able perhaps to see and hear the child more objectively, one whose relationship with the child is less emotionally charged. It is often the
role that a teacher or psychologist plays, but sometimes a child is able
to articulate the problem and solution herself.

Caroline, a family friend, at thirteen was suffering terribly in school in seventh grade. Her family had moved to a large suburban district from a smaller one a few miles away the year before and, as an artistic but reserved girl with no ready friends, she found the large junior high school environment a deeply lonely, depressing experience. She made good enough grades, but was sullen and angry most of the time at home. With the discouraging prospect of moving on to the even larger high school the next year, Caroline told her parents midyear that she was desperate to find an alternative. They listened sympathetically, but had no easy options. They silently hoped she would outgrow her discomfort, make some friends, and find it possible to stick with the neighborhood school.

> "I am left handed so I learn differently than a lot of people and she taught me the way I learned. That is definitely what I call a great teacher, someone who can open your mind to a subject that you had been so foreign with before."
>
> (Sixth-grader)

One day she got a call from a friend from her old neighborhood—another young artist—who told Caroline about a private fine-arts academy opening downtown that was recruiting its first class of freshmen. She was going to enroll and wondered if Caroline could come, too. Caroline was excited at the prospect of doing something so dramatically different: going to a small art school with just a handful of other students and her old friend, a school just starting up, where she felt she could have an impact in a way not possible in a larger, established institution. Her parents had reservations about the heavy arts focus of the school, but learned that the organizers were respected educators and the curriculum was well thought out. They could see how excited Caroline suddenly was about school and, although money for tuition was an issue, they agreed at least to start the admissions process and see what kind of financial aid might be available. When the school offered Caroline a substantial scholarship, she was ecstatic and her parents scraped together the remaining tuition to allow her to go to the school of her choice.

Her freshman year in the new school was both daunting and exciting. In this smaller, more specialized environment she enjoyed the focus on the arts and took risks in that and in other endeavors in which she had no experience at all and precious little talent. She signed on to play soccer because the school needed every kid in order to field a team. She persevered even in the face of a coach who made jokes about her ability. She took her commitment to the success of the school seriously and felt proud of her contribution as a pioneering freshman.

More relaxed and open at home, she shared with her parents her feeling that, although she enjoyed the focus on the arts, she was disappointed that offerings in more traditional academic subjects she enjoyed—science and foreign languages—were thinner than she had expected. Nonetheless, the year was an important growth year for Caroline, and when at the end of the year her parents encouraged her to return to the public high school for the more expansive overall curriculum, including many art courses, they were surprised when she agreed. The following year she made the transition beautifully.

Who would have predicted that at a small, specialized start-up school Caroline would find the social, athletic, and leadership opportunities that would enable her to grow dramatically in confidence? Who would have thought that after persuading her parents to let her go, and investing herself so completely in the school and social life there, at the end of the year she would look objectively at what she was and wasn't getting there, and choose to leave for the larger school and coursework that was important to her? It wasn't the adults in her life who made the year away so valuable and the transition back so successful. It was Caroline herself who knew intuitively what she needed each time. At the smaller school she felt comfortable and connected enough to take risks and grow in ways that subsequently, a year later, enabled her to feel confident and capable enough to dive into the fray of the larger school environment and successfully pursue those learning opportunities.

In some instances, children convey their struggle in symptoms. They aren't necessarily able or prepared to articulate what they need. My own son, Will, struggles with the neuromuscular demands of handwriting; it is painful for him and his writing is illegible. In general, boys have lousy handwriting in comparison to girls. On average, they aren't as good in small motor abilities as girls are. For Will, the very act of holding a pencil and writing was, and continues to be, exhausting. In kindergarten, he used to get halfway down a worksheet, throw down his pencil, put his head on the desk, and cry. It was unbearably painful for him to meet the ordinary writing challenges of school. His kindergarten teacher discovered that it was easier for him to write standing up, and so she tacked his worksheets to the wall.

At the end of second grade we were told by his teachers that they might not be able to meet his needs in a regular classroom. With the help of an aide, who took dictation, he hung on doing the work in a regular setting until he was able to master the computer keyboard. Now in sixth grade, he uses a laptop to do all of his work. It took many meetings of educational professionals and parents to figure out what to do. He could not have made the transition on his own. His teacher, for example, had to be willing to scan her worksheets into his computer. Throughout this extended educational ordeal, Will insisted that he wanted to stay in the mainstream setting, accountable for the same work. He hung on socially, despite some challenging passages. His has been a portrait in courage, and has resulted in a slow-motion turnaround of his school career over four years.

When children struggle with serious challenges or setbacks and aren't able to articulate the cause or the cure, for whatever reason—confusion, family loyalty, fear of disappointing the parents, fear of being seen as different—it's up to adults to look and listen more closely to discern the true nature of the struggle, to consult the child, and to act just enough to make room for a child (and development) to take over again.

LILA: FROM SCHOOL PHOBIA TO STAGE PRESENCE

Seeing Lila today, watching this beautiful young woman perform onstage in front of an audience of several hundred people, it is almost impossible to believe that she was ever too anxious to come to school. Only two years earlier, in tenth grade, she had stayed in bed many mornings, unable to rise and attend her large urban high school. Now a senior playing the role of Matthew Shepard's mother, Lila provides the climactic moment in a student production of *The Laramie Project,* a play based on the murder of a gay college student who was beaten, tied to a fence, and left to die in Laramie, Wyoming, in 1998.

Lila and the rest of the cast are from an innovative pilot public school, Boston Arts Academy, and they are doing an outreach performance of the play for a couple of hundred of their peers from other Boston public school students at the unlikely hour of ten o'clock on a Monday morning. The majority of the cast is African-American or Hispanic, like Lila, and many have street accents that creep into the rural accents of Wyoming that they use in their characterizations.

The narrator informs us that the prosecutors have left the fate of Aaron McKinney, one of Matthew's two murderers, in the family's hands. It is up to them to decide whether he should receive the death penalty. In the final scene, the entire cast is onstage. The judge sits high in the center, the jury stage left, the defendant in an orange jumpsuit down in front of the judge, the police and townspeople arrayed around the back. Lila sits on the last chair at the right, wearing a white sweater. As she rises, her movements are that of a dignified middle-aged woman in devastating psychological pain. As the mother, Lila delivers the actual statement that Matthew's real father had read to the court. (The director had swapped the gender of some roles.)

Her small gay son, she says, "didn't look like a winner," but he was. She would "like nothing better than to see you die," she tells Aaron McKinney; however, "I am going to grant you life . . . because of Matthew." Every day for the rest of his life, she informs Aaron, he should thank Matthew Shepard for the fact that he is alive. In that moment, Lila is not seventeen years old. She is a mother who has lost her son in a brutal murder and she has a found a way around her own feelings of revenge.

After the play, I go backstage to congratulate Lila. Linda Nathan, the head of Boston Arts Academy, is there, hugging all of the cast members and celebrating their triumph. She knows the name of every

---

"I think that our parents have forgotten how much pressure there is at school with teachers, friends, and homework. Some teachers don't know that it takes longer for some people to do homework than others. They also don't know that sometimes you may try really hard, but you still get a bad grade." (Seventh-grader)

student and feels absolutely comfortable giving them hugs. "Great job," she tells them. "You were wonderful."

Before the show I had heard from Lila's drama teacher that she had received a scholarship to a theater program. I had assumed that it was for a summer internship, because some weeks earlier, when I had first shadowed Lila at BAA, we had heard a pitch from a summer theater-arts program.

"No," says Lila, "it is for Juilliard Week. I'll go to New York for a week and attend events at Juilliard."

"Oh, do you think it will tempt you to apply there?" I ask.

"I don't think so," she states. "I want a more complete college experience."

Her talent, maturity, opportunities, and the beginning of wisdom about herself and her life goals are triumphs that would have seemed unimaginable a few years earlier. Not that there had ever been a lack of effort. Her parents have worried about her education from the time she was little, and have worked hard and fought all along the way for her to have opportunities. They have continued to care about her education in spite of a painful divorce, her father's heart attack, and significant financial problems

Now, in her senior year, Lila leaves her home at six A.M. every weekday to take a subway that will get her to Boston Arts Academy on time. On the day that I followed her through all of her classes I was tired and ready to go home at 4:45 in the afternoon, midway through her three-hour rehearsal for *The Laramie Project*. Lila had a schedule that would take her back on the subway and home by ten P.M., where she would do her homework, sleep perhaps six hours, and repeat the drill the next day. Lila has her parents' determination and ambition, and they share the dream of her getting a good education. Her journey, however, has not always been psychologically easy.

When she was in elementary school, Lila's parents arranged for her to attend a small, private, progressive elementary school on a scholarship. They struggled financially, and the tuition was beyond anything they could afford. However, they had found Sunnyside, which was committed to having a more racially diverse population, and they wanted a good education for their daughter. A match was made. Lila loved the little elementary school, with 19 students per grade, 175 students from grades pre-K through eighth grade. She notes that she was one of only a few children of color in her class, but considered it not so much a hardship as simply a difference. She has warm memories of her seventh- and eighth-grade teacher, Ms. Hill, who was caring and helpful. "She talked to me, she taught me a lot of things, and I just stayed in contact with her," Lila says.

In seventh grade Lila's world began to unravel. Her parents separated that year and moved toward divorce. Things at home were tense. School issues came to a head in ninth grade. Lila had wanted to go to a large school, a public school, and her mother moved them across town so she could attend an innovative public high school of about two thousand students. Unfortunately, delays meant that Lila did not start at the school until four weeks into the year. It made her anxious to start the school year so late; she knew only a few kids from her former school there and they weren't close friends or in her classes.

At the same time, the school went through a massive reorganization that changed the program and aspects of student life profoundly. There was tension and divisiveness within the school community and among the teachers, and a feeling of upheaval for the students, many of whom were already invested in the school's traditional program.

This kind of thing—tug-of-war politics and administrative and program upheavals—happen in every community, and while the budget costs and benefits are often aired at public meetings, rarely do adults stop to take stock of the impact such changes will have on the children who must accommodate them, the children who suffer the consequences.

At the beginning of her ninth-grade year, Lila moved to a new apartment, started a new school, arrived almost a month late, and was immediately told—along with all the other students—that the school was abandoning the very program she had come for. Overwhelmed by family problems at home, and feeling at sea in a new school, she became both school phobic and agoraphobic. Many days she was afraid both to go to school and to go out and meet with her friends.

Lila recalls: "I would like lose my mind for a second and be like, okay, what's going on? I didn't want to go to school. If I made plans with my friends, I'd be like I can't go anymore. They'd be, 'Why not?' . . . I'd just be, like I have to go see my cousin."

Making excuses to hide her fear, Lila avoided both school and, at times, the mall: the modern marketplace, from which the term *agoraphobia* is derived. The anxieties she remembers beginning in seventh and eighth grade grew worse in ninth grade. She worried about school, about her mother, and about her future. Many days, feeling ill, or with heart pounding, she would simply opt out of school and stay home. She visited a therapist and tried medication, but felt both were ineffective and dropped them. She occasionally smoked marijuana. Despite the continued pressures at home and school, about two-thirds through her tenth-grade year her symptoms simply faded away. What happened? "I've grown a lot since [ninth grade]," is her answer. Lila's unraveling and her recovery are indeed a story of growth involving struggle, strategy, and self-knowledge.

> "One thing is never, never forget at least seven assignments. You will get so many detentions, miss so many recesses and have to go to a parent teacher conferences."
>
> (Sixth-grader)

In seventh and eighth grade she had managed well enough despite the breakup of her family, thanks in part to the familiar, supportive school environment she enjoyed, and the history teacher whom she really liked and with whom she talked about many things. Yet Lila had rejected the idea of continuing in the private school setting. Uncertain as she was about her destination, intuitively she knew it was time to leave the small-school nest. As she describes it: "I didn't want to go to another private school for high school because I just didn't want to be going into private school for my whole life. I don't think that was something I'd want to do. Stay in private school for all this time and just be sheltered by everything . . ."

So, leaving all of her close friends, some of them dating back to kindergarten, Lila left the shelter of a small school and went to a big school that was in a state of flux, at a time when her family was in tough shape, both financially and emotionally. The combination of losses and new fears sent her into a downward spiral. She was absent for many days, close to the limit of absences the state would allow without requiring her to repeat ninth grade. Her transcript for ninth grade shows all D's. Without the intervention of a caring administrator, she might not have passed the year at all.

In tenth grade, Lila earned B's and D's; in eleventh grade she received B's and A's. Now, in the fall of her senior year, she has straight A's. (I teased her, noticing that she never mentions C's. Her answer—her knowledge about herself—was that she has never gotten C's. She has either done well or come close to failing.)

Midway through tenth grade, a family friend, Aunt Lottie, began to step into Lila's life as an active adviser. Lottie is not a real aunt, but someone who has been in her life since Sunnyside days. They met when Lottie was looking for someone to baby-sit her children from seven to eight o'clock each morning and take them to school, allowing her to go off to work early. She saw the "Sunnyside" sticker on the back of Lila's mother's car and approached them. Lila got an early-morning baby-sitting job. Aunt Lottie turned out to be a sponsor who cared a lot about Lila's life. Midway through tenth grade, Lottie became more active in advising and supporting Lila and her family.

"I could go over there whenever I wanted to," Lila says. "She would give me advice. She would just talk to me and give me advice, suggestions of what I can do. Just listening to me and asking questions and things like that all the time."

Lottie was a treasured listener and adviser, someone Hispanic—"another person of color," says Lila—and someone with the conviction that Lila should use her acting talent and audition for Boston Arts Academy, the brand-new public school for the visual and performing arts. Lila was a natural for BAA. She had, since elementary school, participated in a respected children's theater program and had appeared in many productions. Once Aunt Lottie had set the wheels in motion for Lila to switch schools, Lila's mother began to search for an apartment in Boston; Lila auditioned for and was accepted into the theater program.

What did Lila lose during ninth grade and what did she recover at the academy? I have said that all adolescents—indeed, all human beings—need three feelings to know that their development is on course, that they are growing up the right way. Those three feelings are connection, recognition, and a sense of power. If we look at what happened to Lila as she transitioned from Sunnyside School to ninth grade at the larger school at a time of organizational upheaval, we can see that all three of those elements for emotional health were at risk.

By leaving Sunnyside and going to a high school where she knew almost no one, she lost most of her friendship connections. When she left the sheltered confines of a small private school, she lost the experience of daily recognition because she no longer attended a place where everyone in the halls knew her name, where everyone had seen her onstage as an actress, and had met her brother and parents.

To a certain extent, every student who leaves a small elementary school for middle school, and in a few years makes the transition to high school, has to deal with the anonymity that comes with a larger school. There aren't many high schools in the United States that are smaller than the elementary schools that feed into them. Learning to go to a larger school, or adjusting to specialist teachers rather than just one homeroom teacher, is part of growing up. Most kids find the size of a school a developmental challenge, and most seem to master it. Some young people seek anonymity, and find the halls of a large high school reassuringly impersonal. Others—perhaps the majority—do not. If you see how teenagers travel in groups, the energy with which they greet one another in the halls, and how they gather at the same tables at lunch, it is obvious that they crave the recognition of the group. They crave being known by both adults and peers. Lila describes the loss she felt when her academic house at the large high school was reorganized and, as she put it, "taken away":

> It was a lot like this, very personalized, very diverse [place] . . . but then they switched it up: too many kids, too much stuff besides school going on. Too many opportunities for me not to do school, not to get consequences for stuff. If I skipped a class, they'd say "You have detention," but they'd never make me go to the detention. It is different in this school [BAA], because if you're not in one class, everyone's going to see you in the hall. The teachers talk to each other. And I care what the teachers think. In my last school, I didn't care what the teachers thought.

Here Lila says that it is the experience of being recognized in the hall, and possibly getting into trouble, that makes her go to class. But it is not just recognition—in the sense of someone knowing your name and face—that Lila is describing. It is the feeling of mutual recognition and connection and caring that works the magic. It is the experience of seeing a teacher you respect, who also knows you, who also cares enough about your education and the rules to give you detention. Giving you a detention? That's caring? You bet it is! Though there are many kinds of caring that adolescents understand, a willingness to confront them with a consequence is sometimes the only kind of caring that adolescents respect. Indeed, I might say that it is essential to their mental health. We all act differently when we're in a large, anonymous environment than we do in a small, caring environment where we are held accountable for our actions by people we know. It is that simple.

All students need a sense of power in their lives. Especially when things in their personal lives are not going well, they need to be able to find some powerful feelings at school. There are few things that make a child feel as powerless as her parents' divorce. One of them is not having a home or enough money to rent one. In my work as a school psychologist, I have watched many boys and girls unravel psychologically because of a divorce, parental illness, the departure of the dad, a fall in income, and the resultant loss of the family house. As we've seen, Lila had a number of those risk factors operating in her life at the same moment.

Lila has found a sense of power at Boston Arts Academy. When I shadowed her for a day at the school, I witnessed a girl enjoying an abundant sense of connection, recognition, and power. Indeed, much of the day seemed designed to give all students a sense of all three.

When I went to meet Lila she was assisting the teacher in a yoga class. Dressed like a teacher in a staff sweatshirt while all of the ninth-graders were in plain theater clothes, she moved among the younger kids, helping them take their yoga positions. The instructor was a woman of about thirty. She kept saying, "What Lila and I are going to do . . ." Though it was clear that she was truly running the class, she shared her power with Lila. That cooperative and caring energy—among students and between students and teachers—was visible throughout the day when I visited.

What was it, ultimately, that turned Lila's high school career around? Was it growth and development? Did she become acclimated to the large high school she attended previously, midway through tenth grade? Was it the therapy and medication? Did her family's troubles subside? Was it the intervention of her aunt Lottie? Was it the promise of coming to a school where her acting ability would be recognized? Is it the quality of teaching and respect for the students she finds at BAA?

Lila sees the seeds of her fall and the seeds of her recovery interspersed, but she also recognizes that her final years in a nurturing environment where she found a fit enabled her to complete her transformation from a terror-struck ninth-grader to a happy, ambitious young high school graduate.

I understand why Matthew Shepard's mother said that her son was her hero. I think so many students are everyday heroes.

HEATHER'S RECOVERY

In the last chapter, we witnessed the horrifying downward spiral of Heather's life during her eighth- and ninth-grade years. By all rights, she should have ended up dead in a car accident or from an overdose. No adult knew the facts of her life and her behavior, which were, she admits now, totally out of control. By the time of my interview with her, she had undergone an amazing turnaround. Indeed, she was applying to colleges and wrote to me about regretting the weakness of her early high school record. It is easy to say that she got off drugs and her behavior was brought under control by being in a therapeutic school, but that only superficially explains her total transformation. (Rehab and therapeutic programs don't work for all kids. Many resist or run away.) The real answer is that she got what she needed in her life. At her old school, she resented the hypocrisy of the teachers with respect to her athletic career and she was angry about the lack of recognition for and interest in her writing.

> When I was receiving those grades for doing nothing I felt disgusted that they would sell themselves out to win recognition for the schools athletics. I looked down upon them which helped me to gain yet another reason to hate school and resent my teachers. When I won the writing award I wasn't recognized when I won the district or the state competitions. It wasn't until I received fourth in the nation that they said anything about the matter at

all. It was a small deal and they said two words about it and that was it. I must say I was very disappointed greatly. Since then I have not written poetry or stories because I have a lot of anxiety about the quality of my writing.

Connection, recognition, and a sense of power: Heather did not feel any of those in her old school. She had no sense of connection with her teachers, she felt she was being recognized for the wrong things (or the right things for the wrong reasons), and she felt utterly powerless to change either her father's opinion of her or his level of interest in her or her self-esteem. Her experience at Rocky Mountain Academy restored all three, but the healing could begin only after she had spent three months behaving, as she says, like a "total bitch."

I have no doubt that she was as difficult, hostile, and paranoid as any teenager could be when she arrived. I just didn't see a trace of it when we met. She had a close and loving relationship with a member of the faculty. "I found that she was honest," Heather stated.

She felt both challenged and recognized as an intellectual person, and she had rediscovered a sense of power that must have been robbed from her by her multiple experiences of loss, abandonment, rape, and adult disinterest.

Here is Heather's description of the return of her self-confidence:

> The most influential experience that I have experienced during my stay here was done in late March to early April. It was called my wilderness challenge. It consists of ten days of being out in the woods with everything you could possibly need on you back. . . . This trip was so moving for me because I was able to see how strong I am physically and emotionally. You have to deal with cold weather, hunger, exhaustion, and other people freaking out. . . . A lot of things became clear and after I returned to school some of the things I thought about helped me to believe in myself enough to try in school.

HELPING A CHILD TURN THINGS AROUND

Some children are naturally more emotionally articulate than others. The linkage between self-knowledge and best action is not precise, but it is always the case that a child is encouraged by a parent or teacher who resists the impulse to criticize or take over, and instead makes the extra effort to understand the nature of the child's struggle. In this way, even serious challenges become more manageable and less frightening (for children and parents alike). For a child, the experience of being heard and responded to, and having adults express confidence in you, is strengthening.

Turnarounds aren't made to order. Child development is not just a miracle but at times a mystery. A strategy that failed in November can sow the seeds for success that shows itself months later. As a child struggles to manage what feels like a disaster, and at the same time searches for a way to make something better happen, what a parent can provide is easy to name and often difficult to implement: attention, resources, space, time, experimentation, and faith.

Children need for us to recognize their struggle and pay attention to it. That doesn't mean to intervene immediately, or to start yelling or panicking, or to come to a premature conclusion. It means recognizing that a child has hit a rough spot in his school life. Heather fell into such trouble in eighth grade following the death of her mother. Her father was unable to pay enough attention to her struggles. He was grief-stricken and overwhelmed. He was also drinking as much as Heather. He wasn't on the job.

Kids need some resources. The most obvious resource is our time, by sitting with the child when she's doing her homework, or by taking the time to talk. If that doesn't start a turnaround—and most often it does—a child might need an extra-help class, a tutor, or some meetings with a guidance counselor or psychologist.

The gift of space is sometimes invaluable, something as simple as giving your child some occasional "mental health" days off from school. Educators may be angry at me for suggesting days off, but I have seen how grateful children can be when they have been given the space to relax and figure things out. (Such a day is not to watch television. It is for sleeping late and having parent and child spend a different kind of day together.) Such days enable many kids to rediscover their courage. I think of it as providing space for development. In any case, the combination of a straightforward acknowledgment by a parent that you see the child locked in a struggle at school, whether it is with the material, the teacher, her own self-esteem, or

"I think adults have forgotten how hard it is. It's really harder than you think."

(Fifth-grader)

the social group, and the offer of some psychic space may be enough for her to find her underlying strength. It isn't always the right thing to do to send a child back into battle the next day.

Experimentation? It is important to refrain from coming to a premature conclusion about the nature of the problem. Parents need to formulate questions and propose (not order) interventions: Does he have a learning disability? Is she depressed? Are these the usual social ups and downs of sixth grade or has she really been rejected by her peers? Does she need a tutor? Once you formulate the questions, use your child as a consultant, and use your child's teachers as consultants. If you come up with hypotheses together, test them out together. You, your child, and your child's teachers should approach this with the thought that you are running experiments to see if you can help your child find a better fit in school.

A tutor can sometimes make a class less scary. A less anxious child is apt to perform better. Sometimes a change of schedule or a change of rewards or consequences at home may work. In dire cases, it needs to be a change of setting, either a change of class or a change of school (if that is feasible). Avoid the temptation of determining a plan of action without sufficient thought or experimentation. Punishments like taking away television can backfire if television wasn't the problem in the first place. Then, if no television doesn't make a child's grades go up, a parent may get angrier and blame the child even more for the failure of a half-baked solution.

A child needs his parents to have faith in his ability to develop and find the solution on his own. That is often the toughest thing for concerned parents to do. However, if a parent believes in a child, that may provide the confidence that the shaky child lacks until he regains it himself. Ultimately, the only sure turnaround remedy is one that emerges from the truth of the child's experience and carries the power of the child's own intentions.

8

"If Only They Could Remember"

———

It's just that parents are really actually childish inside and
I think when people get older and when parents get older
they lose what they used to know about life. If they could
remember, they would see that their kids are turning out
really well, but their kids also aren't ready yet to be
judged like they were done growing up.
—*Emily, fifteen*

Don't ask your poor children those automatic questions . . .
those dull, automatic, querulous, duty questions (almost
the only conversation that most parents have to offer). . . .
And don't say, "How was school today, dear" which
really means: "Please entertain me . . . please give me an
interesting and stimulating account of high marks."
—*Brenda Ueland,* Strength to Your Sword

I was interviewing Flora's mother, Debbie, in her den, sitting on a
comfortable green sofa with numerous pillows stacked around me.
Debbie described the twists and turns of Flora's life in school, occasionally contrasting them with her own and her husband's respective
histories as students. Debbie had been a dutiful and successful student: good grades, and eleven years without an absence until the year
her father died. Her husband had been pretty good in elementary
school as well. However, in high school he started "causing trouble."

Flora's school career has not been a carbon copy of either parent's. Because she had two working parents, Flora had gone to

preschool for long hours, sometimes from 7:30 A.M to 5:30 P.M. However, she had a wonderful teacher who made it extremely easy for her and she began to like school. There were occasional surprises, such as the time Flora punched a classmate in the face. The outcome was also unexpected: The two girls went on to become best friends and remained so through elementary school. And then there was the first-grade teacher who decided that Flora was mean. It was painful for Flora's parents to have their six-year-old in a class with a teacher who clearly did not like her.

As Debbie talked to me over the course of several hours, she went through the challenges that Flora had presented at every age. They had all been somewhat different from what Debbie had expected from her little girl. Now that Flora is a high school junior, Debbie has new concerns. Flora has encountered a lot of conflict with girlfriends in high school, in part because of gossip generated when she started dating a high-status nineteen-year-old senior when she was fifteen and just a tenth-grader. Her mother knows they have a sexual relationship. She is also deeply worried that Flora's boyfriend has hit her on occasion. Debbie talked to lawyers about getting him prosecuted for statutory rape when she discovered that they were sexually active. She thought she had a case because he was four years older. "It's not that easy," she told me. Still, throughout high school, Flora has maintained a B average in her courses and has an excellent attendance record.

I recite this almost random selection of Flora's developmental twists and turns to illustrate the dilemma of every parent. You cannot predict your child's future in school nor can you control it. No parent who sends a beautiful child to preschool anticipates that her daughter will hit another girl in the eye, any more than she might predict the two would go on to become fast friends. No parent who sends her child to school could predict that she would fall in love with a boyfriend who physically abuses her (though it happens with great frequency, sadly). Few of the parents of children you have met in this book could have predicted the challenges their children faced in their school careers and the ways in which they grew and changed through their experiences in school.

Most of us don't even know the experiences or people our children value the most from their journey, or the ones who have wounded them the most deeply. Has your child shared that with you? The inability to anticipate and to control the future, however, is only one of the many tough realities parents must face when they send a child off on that first bus ride. And the older they get, the more their separate existence plays out at school and the less you are likely to see of it.

I have worked with parents for years in school settings and I have sat with them through their most painful fears and irrational minor anxieties. In fact, I interrupted my writing of this chapter to talk to an anxious father about his tenth-grade son's emotional meltdown over the previous weekend in which the boy had complained bitterly about the overwhelming demands of school, endless quizzes, tests, and papers. The explosion of feeling ended with his son's despairing assertion: "I just cannot do it anymore."

> **"The last time I tried to tell them about school we got in a fight. Otherwise I talk to them about it, but not much."**
>
> (Seventh-grader)

After that declaration, the father had allowed him to skip school and sleep in on a Monday morning and was prepared to allow him another mental-health day on Tuesday. He called me wanting the answers to five questions: Was his son suicidal? Was his son seriously depressed? (He had been diagnosed with it and put on medication a year earlier. On medication, his grades had improved from C's to B's and he had emerged from the depression. Now off the medication, was this a relapse?) What was behind this terrible weekend? How much of his son's distress was related to the possibility that he might go on an exchange program to Costa Rica for his junior year? (This was something his son really wanted to do. He had taken all the initiative to apply to the program, while his parents had deep reservations about the plan. Was his son lobbying to go abroad by announcing his dissatisfaction with his present school, or was he indicating some uncertainty about going abroad, now that he had been formally accepted into the program?) The father struggled to read his son's distress accurately.

Parenting is, without question, the hardest thing most people do

in their lives. Following a child's journey through school can be ago-
nizing at times. No one is really prepared for the power of the love
they feel for their children, and the feelings of profound vulnerability
to which having children make you susceptible. Few of us are ready
for how different our children's lives and temperaments are from our
own. I believe that the central task of raising a child is to understand
who that child is, what her strengths and limitations are, and the
myriad of ways in which she is different from her parents. What
makes watching a child trot off to school so tough for a parent is that
there is perhaps no setting that drives home a parent's sense of helplessness as acutely, nor any place that emphasizes the stylistic differences between parent and child, the way school does. Having a child
in school hammers home the discrepancies between a parent's dreams
and the sometimes ruthless reality of a child's abilities and experience. Each child must construct her own school journey, according to
her own abilities and temperament, and in light of the pressures and
personnel she encounters. Even if we have a child extraordinarily like
us in temperament, so many other variables will certainly be different. We cannot predict what is going to happen when our children go
to school.

As parents, we often fuss at our children that they're doing themselves some disservice, sabotaging their own best interests with some
pattern of behavior: impulsiveness, wishful thinking, runaway fears,
perfectionism, or other unrealistic expectations. The truth is that parents, too, bring some behaviors to their child's school journey that
may impede or undermine the child's development or strategy for
success. Parental impulses and behaviors may add to the burden and
complexity of what a child must manage.

UNREALISTIC DREAMS AND HOPES

Every loving parent hopes that his child will do well in school and be
happy there. Our dreams for our children are an expression of our
best, most loving selves. It is unbearably sad to meet a parent who
does not have any aspirations for his child. If dreams are the best and
most normal part of parenting, in my experience every parent's
dreams are a bit unrealistic. When I first saw my daughter in a gymnastics class at age four I fantasized for several minutes about sitting

in the stands watching her compete in the Olympics—a father's pride, completely disconnected from reality. Our dreams for our children spring from love, not from a rational assessment of ability.

Our dreams for our children come straight from the parental heart and are pristine; it is difficult for a parent to imagine that her dreams could be destructive for the child. Unfortunately, they sometimes can be. We wish for our children to be achievers because we want them to succeed in the rank-ordered system in which they are going to spend so much of their young lives. I remember a father who plagued a school because he had his heart set on his daughter being a doctor and she was not strong academically. She was always at risk of disappointing her father, whom she loved very much. I know a father who went into a depression when his son didn't make the varsity basketball team. As much as the mother tried to reassure her son that it was "all the coach's problem," that could not erase the son's profound sense that if he were better at sports, his father would be happy.

Problems with unrealistic dreams arise when children cannot meet their parents' expectations. The journey for our children is always more of a struggle than our hopes and dreams allow us to imagine. When our dreams remain fixed, untempered by our children's reality, our children pay the price.

A school social worker asked me to help her prepare for an upcoming meeting with the parents of a ninth-grade boy who was learning disabled—he had striking difficulties with math—and had some of the symptoms of Asperger's syndrome, a form of high-functioning autism that makes it extraordinarily difficult for a child to connect socially with other children. The boy had no friends in school. The parents, both recent immigrants, told the social worker on the phone that they hoped their son would be able to attend Yale University. Thus, they were reluctant to sign him up for special-education services in math. Unrealistic dreams for their son, combined with resistance to academic support, made the social worker want to scream at them, "He's not going to Yale! Forget about it! Can't you see he needs special help?"

I reminded her that all parents want the best for their children. All parents are compelled to dream big dreams for their children, and those dreams often have cultural labels on them. Parents from fancy private schools and parents struggling in inner-city ghettos have told me, "I'd like my child to go to Harvard," even when this clearly was not a fit for their child's interests or academic abilities. Caleb, the struggling eighth-grader at Nativity Prep whom we met in chapter 5, told me that he intended to go to Harvard. When I asked him why, he said, "Because it is the best." Whether it is true or not, that's his answer. As parents, *we all want the best for our children.*

I suggested to the school social worker that she take the parents' wish for Yale as a metaphor, an expression of their desire to be told that their son was okay, not defective. They hoped, as all parents do, that he could have a good life. I advised her to ask them about their hopes and dreams for their move to America, and what they hoped specifically for their son. I wanted them to have a chance to tell her how much they loved this boy. After they were done, I suggested that she ask them if they had worries about him. My guess was that they would be relieved to tell her about their worries. Parents always have them, but they wouldn't be able to express their worries until they had been able to detail their dreams. Indeed, that turned out to be exactly the sequence of the conversation at the meeting. They ended up asking her to arrange for special-education services for their son.

Ambitious parents, as well as anxious parents, constantly fret about the future. They compare their child's performance to their dream of what it should be, or, worse yet, to her more outwardly accomplished siblings or children down the street. I encounter parents all the time who imagine that if they concentrate on what they want hard enough, they can will their child to accomplish exactly that. The problem with this strategy: It does not work and it makes a child feel like a chronic failure.

One boy told me, sadly: "My family has a family portrait, this picture of how they want everything to turn out, and I don't think I'm going to fit into it." Wise parents know that you have to accept the child you have been given and paint a different picture in your mind if it does not accommodate that child. However, changing an internal image is not easy. If we were mediocre students, we'd like our children to be far better than we were. Most people, when surveyed, report that they wish they had worked harder in high school. If we tasted the satisfactions and recognitions of honor society, it is hard not to want that for our children. However, you do not get to replay the tape of your life through your own child for the simple reason that your life was complex and unique. So is your child's.

HELPLESSNESS, ANXIETY, AND IRRATIONAL FEARS

It is a universal human instinct to want to protect your child from danger and pain. Every parent feels it. We've all felt that spike of anxiety when our child runs toward a busy street or walks too close to the edge of a drop-off. We've all experienced the sudden rising up of our outrage and fury if something threatens our child. Like a mother grizzly bear, we swing around menacingly if we hear any distress in our cubs and we're prepared to attack anyone who comes too near. The desire to protect leads inevitably to the fear that we will *not be able* to protect our children from harm. The birth of a child opens us up to a huge number of fears we may never have felt before. Years ago, I knew an incredibly anxious mother who called her pediatrician once or twice a day for the first two months of her child's life. Finally, the pediatrician sat her down and said, "Mrs. Smith, you have given birth to a baby. You have opened yourself up to a lifetime of anxiety. You're going to have to pace yourself."

Parental fears come in two flavors: the reasonable and the irrational. Some fears are well founded, worries about your child venturing out onto untested ice covering a lake in the early part of the winter, for example, or fears about his being bullied by bigger boys at school, or fears about his future should he do poorly in school. Others are the products of overactive imaginations or fearful memories of our own childhoods. In their pasts, most parents have had a turn on the scary end of a bully's taunt or a mean teacher's withering criticism. As a result of parents' unresolved traumas children may grow up in an atmosphere of anxiety, without being able to identify what they should be afraid of and why.

Children are naturally resilient, not fragile. Yet too many parents with whom I speak believe that children can be easily broken by an upsetting encounter with an angry friend or unsympathetic teacher. A parent's calm concern and expression of confidence can help; a parent's anxiety and fears never do. Children frequently say, "Mom, Dad, don't worry so much," and they are usually right. They don't want us to worry so much because our irrational fears are annoying and un-helpful. Kids often feel undermined. Instead of thinking, "My mother is just nuts," they think, "I must be doing something wrong to have my father be so worried about this." Kids can experience an anxious parent as a vote of no confidence in them and it confuses them. They may feel they have to not only surmount the challenge at school but also now calm parental anxiety.

Children want us to worry about their school careers when *they* (not we) are suffering and anxious. Otherwise, they almost never want us to worry more than they do. "It's not that big a deal," my daughter says to me. This makes me stop and think about whether I have just gotten my—as the English say—underwear in a twist for no particular reason. Sometimes, I press on because it is an issue about which my teenager is not anxious enough. Other times, I realize she is right.

> **"i like to talk to my dad about stuff when i get home and he helps me with social problems."**
>
> (Eighth-grader)

It is perhaps obvious to state that the hardest thing that any parent must bear is helplessness, whether or not it relates to school. We are all helpless to make our children more athletic or smarter or so-cially more capable. If we could do it, we would. We cannot. We cannot control how tall our children are going to be or whether they are musical, nor can we force them to cultivate an academic passion. Most poignantly, we cannot protect them from most childhood illnesses or accidents of chance. But there is some-thing different about the helplessness and loss of control we experi-ence when they are in school. There they are in the care of other adults who we hope know and will care for our children. Sometimes—all too often—that doesn't happen for our kids.

In my experience fathers are often pretty accepting of the school's academic assessment of their sons. However, they become inflamed and feel incredibly helpless when a varsity coach views the ability of their sons differently than they do. For the last seven years I have worked at an all-boys school. Year after year angry parents write let-ters to the headmaster about one issue above all others: cuts from var-sity ice hockey. Not being chosen for the varsity team hurts boys who have been playing hockey since they were four. The rejection crushes a dream that many of these kids have held in their minds for years, as have their fathers. The dads have paid for hockey camps and equipment, they have supported their sons, they have driven to distant games, and, suddenly, they are helpless to protect their boys from hurt at the hands of the school. It enrages some and saddens others.

The dilemma for the child is simply this: He has a pretty realistic idea of what kind of hockey player he is—far more realistic than his dad does. A boy may wish to make the team, but because he had to skate against other boys, he could feel their strength and speed. He doesn't have the same sense of helplessness that his father has, standing on the other side of the boards. The boy experiences being outraced to the puck. The father cannot feel the speed of another skater, or he may not see it accurately. What the parent feels is his own sense of pride in his son, wish for his son's success, and helplessness when he cannot ensure that his son will play varsity.

When a parent is trying to overcome her sense of helplessness by attacking a school, the child is put in a painful position. Obviously, the nature of that position depends on the age of a child; having a parent intervene in the life of a first-grader is different than it would be for a varsity athlete, who, naturally, has more autonomy and dignity issues. However, because children are so acutely tuned in to the skill levels of other children, the child almost always knows if the parent is acting unreasonably in the situation. A child is equally sensitive to the issue of having his "weakness" or "failure" made into a major issue by his parent. A child can always feel when the parent is treating her own sense of helplessness rather than addressing the child's pain.

I asked a mother to list the five most difficult things about having a child in school. Three of the items she mentioned spoke to her inability to protect her child from being hurt, either by students or by "dealing with the child regarding bullies and antisocial behavior that 'isn't seen' by school personnel . . . dealing with the dangerous behavior of another child [bringing a gun onto school property and showing it to another child] . . . [and] keeping your child's self-esteem high when they learn differently than other students and when teachers don't appreciate or recognize their skills or gifts."

Each of her concerns screams out: "My child could get hurt in school. I would know what to do if I were there. . . . If I could see for myself what was happening, I would be able to protect her from harm."

Protecting a child from pain is fundamental to the identity of any loving parent. The impulse is so strong, if we could do so, we might be tempted to try to raise our children entirely without struggle or suffering. I have been asked by principals of affluent suburban schools and headmasters of private schools to speak on the subject of "Pain is inevitable" because there are so many parents who have no tolerance or perspective for their child's pain. The educators want me to emphasize that there is a certain irreducible minimum of pain in childhood. Because school is hard and frustrating and not custom-tailored to fit every child perfectly, it is going to be painful at times.

It is paradoxical how protective some parents are of their children where others are concerned, while being unconscious of the ways in which they themselves can hurt them—a truth known to every psychologist and psychiatrist. It is important to remember that at times we hurt our own children by mistake, by misguided efforts to do the right thing, because we are condemned to repeat some painful thing that was done to us by our parents, or even in the tragic belief that it is "for the child's own good."

Our children often forgive us these parenting errors. None of us could function without our children's generous ability to forgive. "It's okay, Dad," my daughter says to me when I've screwed up, and she means it. Yet, we cannot forgive when someone else hurts our child. Any parent who has had a child in an elementary school classroom in which the teacher did not warm to her or actively disliked her will recall the fury and frustration of not being able to protect her from the "other" who dominated her life every day for a year.

Our desire to protect can get in the way of our children learning invaluable lessons from mistakes and failure, or simply from reality. I once spoke to a PTA audience about allowing a child to make mistakes and to learn from them. After my talk a woman came up to me and said, "But you don't mean allowing them to fail courses, do you?"

"What do you mean by 'fail'?" I inquired.

"Well, allowing him to get low grades that would hurt him on his transcript."

"How low a grade?" I asked.

"He mostly gets A's and B's," she said. "But a C would really hurt his college chances. I wouldn't want him to get a C." She implied that a concerned parent would do absolutely anything in her power: pressure, tutors, more pressure, inducements, and whatever else it took to keep her son from getting that dreaded C.

It just so happened that in the previous month a freshman student at MIT had committed suicide after receiving a low grade—the first C grade he had ever received in his life. I suggested to this mother that it might put her son at risk psychologically to have never had the experience of failing in high school. It was possible, I suggested, that he might get into the elite college on which she had set her sights, and once there he would face a level of competition he had never encountered before.

"I would rather have my child fail in high school, when I'm around to help him deal with it," I said in a coaxing sort of way.

"I understand what you are saying," she said, "but he needs the grades to get into a good college."

School is a place for children to make mistakes, yet some parents cannot bear the helplessness of watching it happen. What happens when you are so afraid of a child making a mistake that you don't allow him to be authentic in his self-expression and work? Here is a seventh-grade girl writing about her experience of a poetry assignment:

> They don't give you any room to be creative—even in art class they tell you what to do. We're in a poetry unit now and she gave us an assignment where it's practically fill in the blank. It's supposed to be about what poetry is all about. But it HAS to be 17 lines, it HAS to have alliteration every other line, it HAS to have seven metaphors, and it has to have this and it has to have that. By the time you get through, it's just a bunch of words that aren't anything about what poetry is for you . . .

It isn't just parents who often feel compelled to rig the moment for a child's fail-safe experience. Teachers do it, too, when, perhaps under pressure themselves, their need for a child to succeed overpowers the wisdom that children need to learn by trial *and* error.

If we can't manage our own sense of helplessness and find ourselves unable to let our children go, we will destroy their sense of autonomy and they will hate us for it. Alternatively, they will never develop a sense of independence. They will never fully develop as people. A thirty-five-year-old woman reported to me that her mother never let her have friendships independent of the household when she was a child. She now feels as if she doesn't know how to make friends. Her mother would not let her daughter go out into the world, and as a result the daughter felt as if she missed some vital early learning that could no longer be made up.

The stakes are high for the kids and it is not easy to get it right. I have seen children whose parents let them go too early, overestimating their competence and self-control. I have also seen parents who held on to their kids too long. The process of parenting is always one of figuring out how close and how far away to stand, from the moment they begin to walk on their own. I have always argued that the job of a parent is to create a large enough framework around the child so that she feels contained and looked after, but also has a continual experience of space.

A mother wrote to me that the hardest thing for her as a parent was watching her child move into a larger world where she cannot restrict what she sees:

> And then there is all the growing-up stuff that would happen in any community setting—exposure to different values, beliefs, people than we might choose to bring into our home. Of course, the flip side is exposure to different values, beliefs and people! We want our children exposed to the world, but sometimes we wish we could turn their heads a little quicker and hold their hands a little tighter along the way.

In all these cases, we stand on the distant sidelines, enraged and impotent, yet sometimes amazed at the unexpected growth we witness in our child's ability to manage the situation. "He's an asshole," players observe philosophically about their out-of-control coaches, "but he's the coach."

PARENTAL HISTORY AND PROJECTIONS: WHEN THE PAST OBSCURES THE PRESENT

Parents often tell me that one of the most startling discoveries of parenting is that their children turn out to be so different from what they expected—and especially different from themselves. In my opinion, discussing how different your children are from you should be the number-one topic of conversation among parents at all times. Why do I say that? When I talk to their children, the point they usually emphasize is about difference: "My father doesn't understand. I don't like sports the way he does"; or, "She was good in school. I'm not"; or, "My father always knew he wanted to be a doctor"; or, "They don't get it."

These are such clichés by now. I imagine the reader mentally turning away and saying, "Of course. Children always say those things about their parents." The truth is that they do not. Most children are much like their parents in a variety of ways. Most children feel understood by their parents most of the time. Any boy will tell me when I ask him who in the world knows him the best: "My mom," he states without hesitation. Problems arise when similarities in appearance and temperament disguise the profound differences between parent and child.

One of the advantages of having adopted children is that when you look at them you are visually reminded that they are not from your own genetic stock. My blond-haired daughter, who tans easily, is from a German background and my black-haired son is half-Mexican. When we go on a summer vacation, the two of them get brown in the sun, while my wife and I—both of us are from Irish-English backgrounds—become pink and sometimes red. No doubt we have been deprived of whatever pleasure there is in having children who look just like us. At the same time, their obvious differences keep us from falling into the trap of imagining that they could be "just like us." They're not like us. That's perfectly clear in an adoptive family, but—surprisingly—that's true in every family.

The truth is that professor parents don't always give birth to future professors; race-car drivers don't usually raise race-car–driving children, even though they have spent a lot more time around race-

> **"My mom just hugs me and then tells me how much better i have it because her mother ruined her years as a child."**
>
> (Eighth-grader)

tracks than the ordinary person does. The media make a big fuss when the son of a former big-leaguer makes it to the major leagues. However, that, too, is the exception that proves the rule. How many children of professional ballplayers have followed in their fathers' footsteps? Children are often born with temperaments that are unlike either parent. Even the child who shares some personality traits and interests with her parents has her own ways of being, and will rightly bristle (at least in childhood) at attempts to portray her as a clone of her parents, even when it's meant as a compliment.

The German poet Rainer Maria Rilke described this difficulty between human beings as the challenge of learning to "love the difference between them." He says that the ultimate aim of any love relationship is to "see the other whole against the sky." That is particularly difficult for parents, so wound up in their children's lives and so full of love for them.

Because parents care so much about their children, their deepest feelings about themselves and their own lives are inevitably involved, albeit unconsciously, in the mix. In psychology, we call any transfer of old feelings from one person's history to another new situation "projection." This projection of the parent's experience onto the child can oftentimes be burdensome, precisely because it is so subtle. If we are overly anxious, our child can recognize it, tell us to back off, or just write us off. Projected feelings are unconscious on the parent's part, and pernicious. It is almost impossible for the child to articulate, much less rebut, the projection; it would involve rubbing the parent's nose in something she doesn't want to admit. Instead, the child is left with the vague feeling that "this isn't me who my mom is talking about," but he cannot articulate why his mother is seeing the situation so differently and so wrong.

Parents may have trouble interpreting their child's school experience because they may have had dramatically different school histories. Both mother and father view the child's troubles through their own lens, which may be the lens of gender, school type, or temperament.

Perhaps more difficult is when there is a huge differential between the couple in how happy or unhappy they were in school. I met with a Catholic man who had endured numerous painful experiences in an old-fashioned parochial school. He was always the "bad boy," was always being disciplined, always getting his knuckles rapped with a ruler. His wife had a far more benevolent experience in her public school district. She had felt cherished by the well-trained teachers who had the time to spend with her because the class sizes were so small in her town.

She and her husband came to their children's school with entirely different expectations. He was suspicious and skeptical that the school could provide a healthy, supportive experience for their children. She was open and trusting, assuming that the teachers would be wonderful. Neither approach took into account the complexities of their children's experiences in school. Both were a collection of reflexes that had relatively little to do with the child and everything to do with their own personal histories.

SHEPHERDING A SPECIAL-NEEDS
CHILD THROUGH SCHOOL

Whenever I speak to a parent audience in this country, some parents wait to speak privately to me at the end. They are almost always parents of learning-disabled kids. These parents apologize for buttonholing me privately, but they absolutely need to tell their stories. A mother in Oregon described her boys' heartbreaking social experiences in school. Her eight-year-old has a serious speech defect, but is capable of doing grade-level work. Her ten-year-old has neurological problems, either pervasive developmental disorder or obsessive-compulsive disorder or both. She wept when describing the years they had endured without friends, the total absence of birthday invitations. She turned bitter as she told me, "I got so desperate I asked other families to invite my boys to parties, but they wouldn't," adding, "The administrators either don't know how to help or they don't want to help."

A father stood up at a PTA meeting and began to weep about his fifth-grade son with Asperger's syndrome who had never been invited to a play date. Parents of overweight children describe the daily teasing their children suffer at school.

Parenting a child who is "different" changes your life. Seeing the world through the eyes of a learning-disabled child who struggles in school cannot help but shape your days and your perceptions. Indeed, it can take over a family's life. I have seen it transform hopeful parents into desperate people, turn shy parents into ferocious advocates, and make competent people feel totally lost. I guess it is theoretically possible for parents to deny the disabilities and resist being changed by pretending that everything is fine, but in the contemporary school system such a stance would be tough to maintain. School personnel notify you if they find your child is different, and then you have to deal with how they choose to serve—or not serve—your child.

If wanting to feel in control and wanting to protect their children from harm are two of the core desires of parents, then having an especially vulnerable child heightens these parental feelings. The tricky part is that these children do need more services and it is essential that their parents advocate for them. Because of the inevitable financial pressures on any school system, it is likely that without an advocate, a special-needs child will get only minimal services. That is the simple truth. Therefore, the psychological challenges for the parent are to figure out how much fighting is enough and when it is time for a child to fight his own battles, because even though the school shoe doesn't really fit, the child will still have his own developmental imperatives and school journey. Obviously, if the child has an extreme disability—Down syndrome or cerebral palsy or serious autism, a disorder that distorts normal development so profoundly—he will need advocacy forever. However, it is possible for parents to become such dedicated and ferocious advocates that they confuse their child's relationship with the school with *their* (the parents') fights with the school. The parents' work becomes foremost.

The special-needs child wants what every other child wants from school: to get through intact, to feel his or her own success, and to finish. The trick for the parent is, after all the fighting and advocacy are done, to focus on the child's growth and celebrate her development.

X-TREME PARENTS PUSH A CHILD TO THE LIMIT

If ordinary parental impulses and behaviors can become burdensome to a child attempting to manage the complex developmental and logistic challenges of school, extreme behavior by parents can be crushing. I see the "micromanagers," parents who are overinvolved, endlessly controlling, and—at the deepest level—unable to trust their child or the school.

There are the "helicopter moms" who constantly hover, ready to drop down and rescue their child. Such a mother is an embarrassment to her children. The child can see that she is annoying to school personnel, fighting over issues that are, in fact, inconsequential. She is also undermining her child's confidence. It is vital to remember that a child interprets a parent's attack on a school over some issue as a judgment of the child's management of school tasks. Too often an anxious parent conveys the message "You're not doing very well" to her child when she intended to convey it only to the school principal. The child concludes, "If I weren't such a screwup, my mother wouldn't have to be fighting for me this way all the time."

If mothers often err on the side of protection, fathers often do so as "hypercompetitors," endlessly measuring their child's performance in athletics and academics by comparison to other children or to performance standards. The dad experiences himself as being aware and alert, on the job: a dedicated parent intensely interested in his child's progress. Unfortunately, this kind of hyperfocus can make an average child feel like a chronic disappointment. It can make a high-achieving child chronically stressed.

The "chronic critic" mistakenly believes that expressing dissatisfaction with a child is a good motivational technique. It is not. It puts the relationship between parent and child at risk. The child feels, with justification, "No matter what I do, I can't please my father," and he begins to withdraw.

The "invisible parent" is physically absent, uncaring, preoccupied, or pseudoengaged. That might seem like a blessing, considering the excesses of those who are overinvolved, but a child with disengaged parents carries a burden of self-doubt and shame similar to that of children who blame themselves for their parents' divorce. "I'm not good enough or they'd stick around," a child thinks. Because the thought is so shameful and painful, she certainly cannot say it and sometimes cannot even acknowledge it to herself. She'll create another story to explain the invisible parent and to account for her shame; the substitute story never works. Feeling chronically abandoned makes a child feel chronically ashamed. That is simply true.

Children also do work in school because they love their parents. If their parents never notice, over time a child may lose the motivation to work. "What's the point of knocking myself out?" they think. Often the child of an invisible parent finds a substitute parent, a coach, or a teacher, who gives him the recognition of which he is deprived.

A PHILOSOPHICAL VIEWPOINT: FLARSHEIM'S H

Many years ago, when I was in training at Michael Reese Hospital in Chicago, I had as a teacher a brilliant child psychiatrist named Alfred Flarsheim. He was a tall, thin, eccentric man with an extraordinarily loving heart. He taught me a great deal about children and about being an effective therapist. More than anything else he taught me how to think philosophically about the dilemmas of children's lives. When we met, he was the psychiatric consultant to Bruno Bettelheim's Orthogenic School on the campus of the University of Chicago. His influence is apparent throughout this book. Now I want to share a central tenet of Flarsheim's philosophy with you.

During one seminar, Flarsheim walked to the blackboard and drew a large H on it. He then pointed to the horizontal line and said, "This is a child's level of functioning." He then drew a line about four inches above the solid horizontal line and another, dotted line about four inches below it. Pointing to the topmost line he said, "This is where people would like the child to be." He elaborated, still pointing to the line at the top: "Any damn fool can look at a person and say he should be up here. We say it to kids all the time: 'Pull your socks up! Study harder! You can do better!' However, if you want to truly understand people, you have to understand what they have to do every day to get from here [he pointed to the lowest line] to here [the solid line representing a child's usual level of functioning]."

He then made an observation that I found stunning at the time, and that I still think is radical. It flies in the face of common assumptions we hold about children. Flarsheim said, *"Every child is doing the best he or she can at every moment."* Stop and consider that statement. Can it possibly be true? It seems to imply that children don't mess up, that they don't make bad decisions, that they are in control of themselves all the time. That is not true and that is not what Flarsheim claimed. What he was saying was that every child is doing her developmental best at any given moment in time; that no child intentionally does a bad job at her own development.

Pride, a desire to be loved, the wish to be competent—a child is doing his best at all times to manage these pressures. Sometimes a child's best doesn't look so good to us. A child who is going along with the bullying of a vulnerable victim in fifth grade is not showing us his best behavior, but in that moment he is doing all he is prepared to do under the circumstances. We may not like a child's choices—a seventh-grader failing to study for a test, for example—but it is the child's best strategy in that moment. A seventh-grader who doesn't study either is doing something he prefers or is afraid to come to grips with academic material that frustrates him or makes him feel stupid.

Research shows that children sometimes react to school situations with self-destructive behavior. What dictates the behavior is not the character of the child but the situation in which she finds herself, and her assessment of what the best possible reaction might be to the particular stresses she is encountering in the environment. A disrespectful, tuned-out student is coping with something we do not perceive in the same way. She is doing her best to manage the classroom, the teacher, or her peers. An adult might dislike what she's doing, but it is her strategy. After twenty years of consulting to schools, I have

---

"Well, I think that my parents know to a certain extent of what goes on in school as far as reading books and watching shows about children. I just don't think that they can really relate to us even though they were once a child. Once they become adults, all the stupid things that matter when you're younger seem to make no sense to them and they don't understand me when I talk about my friends and me and all our problems." (Ninth-grader)

come to understand that a child's perception of school is always valid, though never complete. Her strategy is always an attempt to succeed, even if it doesn't appear as such to us.

Your child is never doing badly on purpose. He is trying as hard as he can. When you are full of helpless feelings, you don't have to scream, "You're not putting any effort into your homework," because he is, in some way, trying his hardest—trying hard not to be humiliated, not to hit the limits of his knowledge, to be a buddy to his buddies, or look like a manly guy who doesn't care about school.

A child always has a strategy and it is always that child's best strategy at that moment. *If* we respect it as such, we take the first step to understanding what might work for the child in school. *If* we try to understand the child's reasons for her choices, we may be able to change the circumstances in which she learns, make our hopes clearer, or in many other ways influence the course of her journey. But I can assure you that if a child feels we do not respect that she is making her best effort (at the moment), then she will inevitably feel misunderstood by adults. What I know with certainty is that when children feel understood by their parents, they are often able to adopt a new strategy. They almost never change course when they have angry, helpless parents exhorting them to "do better!"

9

College Craziness
Reclaiming Senior Year

———

I'm taking this class because my parents say I need to
learn to organize my thoughts for when I go to college.
—*Second-grade boy at lunchtime book-discussion group*

Education is a private matter between the person and
the world of knowledge and experience, and has little
to do with school or college.
—*Lillian Smith*

Looking at the college admissions process and its impact on children, parents, *and* schools, I think that the gods must have been
mad to have invented this process. Having a college degree has become more important in the economic life of the country than it was
thirty years ago. However, it has achieved a symbolic importance so
out of proportion to its actual meaning, and the admissions process
has evolved into such a Byzantine ritual and chariot race (forgive the
mixed metaphor), that it can make normal people nutty and people
who were a bit flaky to begin with completely crazy. It pushes every
panic button for parents: hopes and dreams for their child and the
family, ambition and fear of failure (their child's and their own), and
anxiety over separation, finances, and the inevitable uncertainties of
process and outcome.

A high school senior told me that one early-fall afternoon she
came home from school and walked into her family's kitchen where,

on the table, were all of the college applications she had collected in her desk drawer until she was ready to fill them out. Someone had taken them from her desk and filled them out completely, not the essays, of course, but all of the blanks requiring information. The girl's mother, clearly nervous, was standing in the corner of the kitchen awaiting her daughter's reaction. It wasn't long in coming. The senior walked over to the stack of applications, picked them up, dropped them in the trash barrel, and departed for her room. She sat at her computer, went to each of the college Web sites, and printed out new copies of the applications. When she had collected them all, she walked back into the kitchen, held them up to her mother, and, turning on her heel, returned to her room and put them back in her desk drawer. This was all done silently; the daughter never said a word. That night the mother came to hear my college admissions talk and announced herself as "the crazy mother who filled out her daughter's college applications."

A senior in New York City told me that his parents had hired an SAT tutor for his entire tenth- and eleventh-grade years, and that during his junior year he had taken thirty practice SAT exams in preparation for the SAT exam in the fall of his senior year, the one that really counts. Teachers in Pasadena, California, tell me that well-to-do parents are sending their children to "juku" schools, modeled on the ubiquitous cram schools that are a standard feature of high school life in Japan. When one of the teachers suggested to a father that the juku schools rely on rote learning, that they cannot teach analytic thinking, the father acknowledged her point. "That's true," he said, "but her SAT scores really went up." Recently an SAT tutor in Boston was profiled in the local paper. He promises the families of high school seniors that if they send their children to him (for $250 per hour) he can raise their English SAT scores by having them write and rewrite a generic essay, which they can then memorize and reproduce on the exam itself. A mother in San Antonio, Texas, asked me the following question: "Should I encourage my son to work on rounding out his résumé for college, or should I encourage him to do the things he loves." I asked the age of her son and she said, "Ninth grade."

After fifteen years of traveling around the United States and working with high school juniors and seniors, I am deeply worried about the college admissions process in this country and its impact on students and on the senior year itself. Typically (but not always) I have visited elite schools: powerful suburban high schools and academically challenging private schools where a high proportion of children—sometimes 98 percent—are college-bound. My invitations to address seniors come from the college counselors, themselves worried about the impact of the process on students. They witness the stress that the college competition causes for the kids and the unrealistic expectations that dreams of college stimulate in the parents. College admissions counselors at struggling high schools are also worried about the impact of the process on their kids. Their students may not be academically prepared to compete, they might not be able to pay the college tuitions, and the college process makes them feel like failures.

Two years ago I ran a daylong seminar for the college counselors at the eight largest private boarding schools in the Northeast. These counselors came from schools with famous names: Exeter, Andover, and Deerfield, among others. Such schools exist on a rarefied plateau; their average tuition is higher than at most colleges' in the country and 100 percent of their graduates go on to fine colleges. However, like specially-bred mice used in science experiments, they provide an interesting laboratory in which to view the forces at work in the transition from high school to college. When I asked the college counselors to do an individual exercise in imagination, without reference to reality, and propose two changes to the college admissions process that would really benefit students, they all came back with the same suggestions: eliminate early decision, and have students take two years off between high school and college.

I am not the only person who is concerned about the impact of the college admissions race in the United States. Most discussions, however, focus on the technical aspects of the admissions process: the nature of the tests, SAT or ACT, that are used in admissions; and on the demographics of access to college. In the last two years, the president of Yale and *The Wall Street Journal* have addressed the way in which the early decision favors children from wealthier families. And there is always the almost universal recognition that college is unaffordable for too many families. These are all valid concerns. However, mine are somewhat different, based in psychology rather than economics. The college admissions process is harmful to students and their families for three fundamental reasons: It does not address and often obscures the developmental needs of children and families; it distorts and can devalue the experience of going to school; and it comes close to ruining the developmental value of senior year in high school.

ADOLESCENTS ARE SEPARATING
AND BECOMING INDIVIDUALS

For seventeen- and eighteen-year-olds in high school there are two powerful imperatives in their lives: graduating—they are more likely to describe it as "getting out of high school"—and growing into self-sufficient young adults. The college admissions process can some-times so distract adults that it is difficult for parents to remember that the developmental challenge at this age is becoming a whole person, not getting into a good college. We launch children into adulthood in the hope of seeing them blossom into productive, moral citizens. Sometimes parents become totally confused and think that getting into a good college is *proof* that their child is a successful person, or that going to the "right" college will *make* him a productive, moral adult. Being able to handle college-level work independently may be a piece of evidence that a child is growing into adulthood, but it is not and can never be *the* test of adulthood for a number of obvious rea-sons. Many people grow up to be the best kind of people—mature, authentic, inspired, productive, contributing, happy people, even *great* people—without going to college at all, and there are certainly a lot of immature, unproductive, small-minded, and unhappy people with college degrees. College and adulthood are not the same thing and they are not even reached by the same path.

In late adolescence, students are in a period psychologists call "separation and individuation," in which they are fully differentiating from their family and parents. It is a stressful time. It surprises most people to learn that the late-adolescent years are the time of the most psychological breakdowns in human life. Erik Erikson used the term *identity formation* to describe the late-adolescent child's busy task of consolidating a sense of herself as unique, capable, and independent. There are times when young people fall into confusion or identity conflict and require a period of "moratorium" in order to answer the questions "Who am I?" and "What kind of an adult do I want to be?" Sadly, this is a time when some late adolescents break down into psychotic and schizophrenic illnesses. The process of separating from one's family of origin and developing into a separate person is so demanding that some kids become casualties.

Even among healthy kids, the separation-individuation process doesn't always look so attractive from a parental point of view. A mother asked me, "Why is it that seventeen-year-old boys can be so rude to their parents?" Most of the time the answer is that the boy— or young man—wants his parents to back off. He experiences their concern, their orders, even their love, as pulling him backward into the family, back to boyhood. What he is pulling away from is the infantilizing influence of the parent. That is exactly what teenagers are feeling when they say to us: "Don't treat me like a baby." We can take umbrage and say, "I'm still responsible for you!" or reply that they are not yet fully adult, that they do not yet possess the experience and judgment of adults. We are not wrong about that. However, they experience themselves as being close to adulthood, usually closer than we know, and they do not want to be pulled backward by a parent fussing.

Many high school students are already functioning as adults in the world well before they graduate. They are physically fully grown up. They possess licenses and drive cars. A large percentage of them have held responsible after-school or summer jobs. A majority have had sexual experiences. Some have active love lives and have experienced passion, commitment, and disappointment. They have also compared notes and learned about the problems in the lives of their peers' parents: alcoholism, sexual abuse, bad marriages, and disengaged parents. There are relatively few secrets left among high school students. The majority of seniors, close to 80 percent, have used drugs and alcohol, which means that they have made the decision to break the law, sometimes repeatedly. Though we may not always like it, they *are* smarter than we think, and we have to acknowledge that, as a practical matter, late adolescents function as adults. If we cannot accept that fact, they treat us rudely. That push-me-pull-you experience of raising adolescents is exactly what the separation-individuation process of late adolescence feels like, for both children and parents.

I make this sound as if the child is moving in only one direction—out—and the parent is doing only one thing—holding on. It is more complicated than that. Late adolescents are scared to be leaving home, frightened of giving up their parents' support, aware that they are not yet as competent as they hope to be one day. Though many parents are grieving the departure of their babies into adulthood, some parents are more than ready to have their children leave and give them—the parents—their old lives back. Children and parents have mixed feelings about this developmental departure dance and yet they must find a way to let each other go. I have had many parents express anger at the way their children were separating from them. I have had many more cry as they talked about their children leaving. The majority of students I talk to express a deep restlessness and readiness to go, while simultaneously experiencing a growing sense of uncertainty and anticipatory homesickness.

During all this, high school seniors have to go to school every day and act like children. They have to sit in rows and pay attention and meet arbitrary requirements. They have to be on time and act as if they respect some adults whom they do not, in fact, respect. If there is a constant tension in every high school, it is precisely about the conflict between the adult strivings of the students and the inevitable infantilizing aspects of the school culture. The cure for that tension is, of course, graduation. And that's why one senior boy, admitted early to his first-choice college, didn't talk much about it all year. He kept telling his friends: "All I want to do is graduate from this place!"

THE GOAL IS GROWING UP, NOT COLLEGE

I want to repeat my previous assertion that growing up and getting out of school are the true developmental goals of every late adolescent. College is not, in and of itself, an intrinsic goal. After all, viewed from the point of view of students, college is just more school. Getting into another school is a momentary achievement, while feeling grown up is something substantial that is part of you. When you hear students talk about college with excitement in their voices, it is often only when they talk about certain aspects of college life because they see it as a place where they can realize their own developmental strivings. "I can sleep late," they proclaim, "I can take

"To my family and my teachers from my old public school the best and
only college I can go to is Harvard. I will feel like a failure if I don't get in
to an Ivy league college. I feel it is the least that I owe my mother
after all we have been through together. Tell me something to put it
all in perspective, please." (Twelfth-grader)

afternoon classes," or, "I can cut classes." Often when parents over-hear this they jump to the conclusion that their children are not truly mature or will not be serious about college. I conclude the opposite: The kids are eager to feel mature and anxious to try out their free-dom; they want the chance to shape the educational environment to the needs of their own lives. The way they express those ambitions is by celebrating the overthrow of adult restrictions.

They will, no doubt, face academic challenges. Equally difficult will be developing the skill to get along with a selfish roommate, simply being in a dorm (if they've never gone to sleepaway camp), or negotiat-ing with drunken classmates who play their music too loudly in the mid-dle of the night. For many young adults, such moments are the most challenging and most educational in their college careers. They go to the heart of the identity question. As juniors or seniors in high school, they may not be able to articulate these ideas to their parents, but they have an intuitive feeling about them.

Parents, by contrast, are comforted when their children talk about their proposed major area of study or the strength of the departments at the college or the beauty of the campus. Those are the kinds of things that seem rational and reasonable to adults; good reasons to pick a school. No wonder the college admissions process often leads to misunderstandings. Parents say miserably: "He visited for a week-end and he came back and said he loved the place, but he didn't *see anything*. All he did was stay in the dorm and talk to other kids. He doesn't know much about the university, he didn't meet any of the professors." No, but he intuited something that fit with his idea of his identity.

Time and again, the student who picks a college because of a gut feeling emanating from exactly such a visit has made the right choice and enjoys his college years there. This is because students are asking:

What place feels like the right place to live my independent life? Parents are likely to be asking: What place will give my child the best preparation for life? Once again, the implicit parental assumption is that life begins for a child after school has ended. Kids don't think that way because they are living their lives every day and their lives are changing all the time. For a young adult, the act of choosing where you're going to live and study, feeling genuine ownership of that decision and the consequences, are powerful experiences of blossoming maturity. Surrendering to parental pressure and aspirations offers no such gain.

If you give high school seniors the chance to talk about the meaning of their departure, both for their lives and the lives of family members, you will often get a shrug. They don't want to talk about the matter just then. However, I can guarantee you that it is on their minds, and it is largely the same whether they are headed for college or not. There will be a moment when they open up and tell you their true agenda as they are ready to leave high school, either for the job market or for college. What is in the hearts and minds of college juniors and seniors, the developmental challenges they know they face, in a rough order of priority:

They will leave their friends and a safe, known community.
They will risk their self-esteem and self-confidence in the
     college admissions process.
They know that their departure from the family will, in some
     unpredictable way, change the nature of their relationship
     with all family members.
They have to make good on all of their assertions of
     independence by functioning as a self-sufficient adult when
     they leave high school or when they get to college.

For almost every graduate-to-be there is a moment when she is heading out the door one evening only to have her mother say, "Honey, why don't you stay and have dinner with us?" Almost at the front door, she will turn and say, "I was going to have dinner with my friends." The mother will reply, "I know, sweetie, but we have plenty and, after all, this is your last year with us." Her daughter, simultaneously sad and exasperated, will convey the following message that she may not be able to say: "Mom, I'll always have you and Dad. This is really my last year with my friends." Though her mother cannot feel it that way, her daughter is correct. Barring a tragic event, the relationship with her parents has many chapters left, but she will never again be with the entire cohort of friends with whom she has gone to school for as many as thirteen years. Imagine for a second how it would feel to move to another city and leave your circle of closest friends and longtime colleagues. That is what a departing teenager faces.

Ben, who told us earlier how social and academic life are lived as one, already knows the value of friendship and already has an intuitive sense of the parting ahead when he adds: "I think that it's important to go to school and be around people you like to hang around with, because I think that as you grow, you lose touch with a lot of your friends. In high school you could have dozens of friends you see every day and then as you separate and go to college and on to jobs, it's harder to stay in touch."

Knowing that the college where he is headed is a "good" college doesn't reduce any of the pain of these losses. A student who intends to live and work in his hometown after high school graduation may do so, in part, to be able to hold on to his all-important group of buddies.

The administrative process of college applications is grueling enough, but imagine the parallel universe of emotional tension. The seventeen-year-old student has to summarize everything he has ever done, put it on a piece of paper, and send it off to a bunch of strangers who will look it over and perhaps sniff at his ambition. No matter how he tries to distance himself from the process, it still feels as if he is asking an anonymous group of people, "Do you love me?" If he has applied to any kind of competitive college, he risks receiving no for an answer. For a short period of time it will feel as if he has been rejected as a person, and no matter how many times a student hears that the process is arbitrary and highly competitive, it hurts. It hurts just the way it hurts to be turned down for a job; it feels as if society—not just a college—has no place for you.

Perhaps the most important factor of all affecting any child's high school graduation is the impact of her growth and development on her family. Some parents blanch at this reminder of their child's independence and their own loss of control. It is equally true, however, that when the child departs the family, either for college or for living independently, family life goes on without her and she is no longer part of the daily drama. That has an impact on every senior's thinking.

The separation-individuation process we glimpsed earlier is not a solo act by the child. It is not a developmental achievement of the child surrounded by static family members. It is a family dance. Everyone is readjusting to make room for the growing autonomy of the high school senior. The parents are managing their sadness at the eventual departure of their child, and the feelings of helplessness that accompany giving up their day-to-day parenting. Siblings, especially much younger siblings, grapple with the anxious worry that their older brother or sister is leaving the family—disappearing from it completely and forever. "Will he remember me after he goes to college?" they worry. More competitive brothers and sisters may be thinking, "Once he leaves, I'll get his room and I'll repaint it!" Whatever the case, the emotional system of the family is going to be rearranged by the departure of the child. Everyone feels it, everyone anticipates it, and no one is more aware of the change than the outgoing senior himself.

A senior boy once waited until the end of my speech to his class before saying, "Dr. Thompson, I don't think I can go to college next year." Why not? I inquired. "Well, my father died last year and I'm an only child. I don't think my mother is ready for me to leave."

A girl who had been desperate for years to move on from her abusive mother, a single parent, suddenly expressed second thoughts about leaving her: "I'm afraid if I leave she won't be able to make it," she said. "I want to be a good daughter. I want to do the right thing."

Many college-bound seniors have said to me, "I know my parents' marriage won't last after I leave. They've just been staying to-

---

"We hear about college every day, and how we have to do umpteen million things in order to get into a good school. They don't understand how irritating and stressful that can be, how facts about the best schools and students are shoved in our faces everyday and we're left to wonder how we're ever going to get into college. They don't understand why it causes so much anxiety for some students." (Eleventh-grader)

gether until I finish high school." Parents rarely tell their children such things, but children usually know what kind of shape their parents' marriage is in. They may feel guilty and responsible and have a wish to stay to hold the family together. A wish to stay nearby and keep the family intact influences many children's college choice.

Because American culture worships independence and individuality above all other values, children also share the wish to be individuals. They look forward to adolescence because they will be free and on their own. Children in the United States expect to deviate from their parents' wishes and values, at least during their adolescence; they anticipate having to fight for their freedom. When my daughter was ten she said to me, "Dad, I love you now, but when I'm twelve I'll hate you." That did not turn out to be the case. We had many loving moments and some angry moments (still do). However, the idea of adolescence that she absorbed from her peers and the popular culture was one of opposition to oppression and a rebellion against authority: a peculiarly American idea of growing up in which each child recapitulates the Revolution in her own life. Most adolescents have said to their parents: "Why don't you trust me?"; "I want a later curfew"; "You're too strict"; or, "Get off my back!"

I once asked a group of seniors, "What are you worried about happening to you in college?" One young man said, "I'm afraid I'll go totally wild!" He feared having too much freedom, too much aloneness, too little self-control. Girls often report that they are going to miss the closeness and conversations they have had with their mothers. Boys may not be allowed to admit to such feelings, at least not in public. Both boys and girls express openly the sadness of being apart from younger siblings who have sometimes been their most reliable companions and friends through childhood.

Growing up and becoming a loving, independent, moral young adult is truly a big deal. Getting into college is just one aspect of the process of maturation. We forget that when we focus so heavily on a child's collegiate future, we ignore or devalue the experience of the life they are living right now.

"This is the year that counts!" More recently, ninth-graders have been reporting to me that their ambitious (or perhaps simply anxious) parents say, "Every year in high school now counts. That didn't use to be the case, but *they* look at the *whole* high school record now" ("they" being college admissions folks). Last year Colorado lawmakers discussed doing away with twelfth grade altogether and using the money to expand preschool programs to better prepare students for college by giving them an early start. Florida adopted a plan to let students skip senior year by graduating with fewer credits. When you think more deeply about it, perhaps the kindergarten year is the most important. After all, that is the year when most children start to read. Or perhaps it is the year before school formally begins. Head Start was founded on the premise that the preschool years are critical for underprivileged children. They need support in order to develop pre-reading skills. Or perhaps the freshman year in college is the most important because it establishes whether a student can function on his own.

There is no "most important year" of education. They are all potentially crucial because every child's developmental pace is different. A disastrously bad year can affect many years to follow. We could say that the elementary years are more crucial than the later years, but then I remember the many boys I have known—indifferent students—who went to college and found something they loved in the curriculum, something deeply meaningful that they could pursue as a career. Passion in learning can arise at any time, from pre-K through college. Since we can't predict when that will happen, we must not think that one year is intrinsically more important than another.

Someone might argue that having a goal motivates students. Hearing from educators that their transcript matters is good for them and helps them strive for excellence. If there are no consequences for a weak high school transcript, why should children work hard? While I agree that it helps children to know what they are working toward, that is only a very small part of what motivates them to succeed in school.

The problem with holding out the threat and/or the promise of college to students is that it assumes that all children are motivated by the same things that their parents are. They are not. A parent's most precious dreams may prove a huge burden to the child. An Asian-American boy who attended a private school in California told me, "My parents will be so disappointed if I don't get into one of four colleges. They are both working two jobs to send me here and they want a return on their investment." While I am certain that those parents never used that language with their son—they undoubtedly told him that they wanted only the best for him—he interpreted it as their wanting a return on their investment.

The principal of a school told me that after a senior did not get into an Ivy League college, her physician father was seen weeping outside the school. The principal called him into her office, where he confessed that every day of her life since the day she was born he had prayed that his daughter would get into Harvard. Besides being incredibly sad—how can this girl ever feel that she is not a disappointment to her father—there is something wrong when parents of young children are thinking and talking about college from their birth. The idea of college then shapes and inevitably distorts the process of education and development from the beginning of a child's school life. When parents of kindergarten students discuss college placement, they cultivate a view of school that makes it into a race with a big payoff at the end. They do not understand what is actually going to get their children through thirteen years of school—from age five to age eighteen—with their souls and intellectual enthusiasms intact. They risk turning school for their children into a grueling full-time job of fulfilling their parents' fantasies of trophy lives, or, perhaps, living out their unlived lives.

I know a school where the only measure of worth for teachers became the success their students had on the AP exam. The teachers began to behave in punitive ways toward the students who weren't taking AP courses or were not taking them "seriously enough." The school developed a driven, compulsive atmosphere that was downright grim. In such an environment, instead of enjoying learning or exercising their leadership ability, students feel the pressure to tailor a résumé, grind out the grades, sign up for extracurricular activities they don't really care about, and, above all, never take academic risks.

THE MOST IMPORTANT (SENIOR) YEAR

If we could remove the college admissions lens from the senior year, if the adults could focus on their child's present instead of so relentlessly on their projected future, we would see a rich expanse of time and place and opportunity for our children to learn some of the most important lessons they can take into adult life.

The senior year should provide students with five opportunities that they cannot get almost any other time in the life cycle. First, they should have a chance to practice their leadership skills. They have literally earned their seniority by putting in so many years in school. Now they need the opportunities that will challenge them to lead and mentor others. They need to be held accountable as leaders. They find that opportunity as leaders on the basketball team, the yearbook, or the debate team, or as the steady voices of experience in the cast for the spring musical. One of the biggest problems about school, for students, is that they feel useless and do not have enough meaningful community responsibilities. Senior year should provide a partial cure for such feelings of uselessness.

Often students who did not feel confident enough to show their leadership ability as sophomores or juniors come into their own in the senior year. We may believe that leaders are born or that they arise naturally when the opportunity presents itself, but it doesn't always work that way. Some kids need to be put into a leadership position in order to find the skills within themselves. I have seen many boys, considered immature by their teachers during their junior year, who then stepped up to the plate in their last year of high school. That's what the senior year should provide. If it fails to do so, kids will either find that leadership aspect of their development delayed, or they will look outside of school for it, to the workplace, which is fine— I'm glad they've found a venue—but they become disengaged from school because their feelings of competence come from outside the school building.

Unfortunately, the demands of the college admissions process sometimes cause seniors to psychologically check out of their schools in the fall in order to file their early-decision applications. The system gives students the message that the senior year is just a way station, and so they perform their leadership jobs with one foot out the door. That's just one reason to hate the early-decision process.

The second opportunity the senior year should provide is time for self-discovery. Ideally, a senior would have the better part of a year to look over the universe of possible colleges to find the right fit for his personality and learning style. Though obviously economics is a central factor in college choice, most kids think through other choices as well: big versus small, urban versus rural. Such questions always come down to identity questions: "Who am I? What fits my personality?" Done right, the college admissions process should have a refining effect on the late-adolescent sense of identity, where a senior thinks, "I know better who I am because I have decided to go to this college rather than that one." That insight occurs in conversations with adults who know something about the student and are willing to share some of their own wisdom.

I remember a high school basketball player who thought of her coach as hyperfocused on basketball. She assumed that her coach would respect her only if she, too, applied to the roughest, toughest college-basketball program that would accept her. However, in a series of conversations with her coach about the differences between Division I and Division III schools, she learned about her coach's dissatisfaction with having played Division I sports. That allowed the girl to confess to her own worries about big-time college sports. This series of conversations ultimately allowed her to go to a Division III school with her coach's blessing. It also helped bring her sports-obsessed father to heel, because, despite his ambitions, he wanted his daughter to be happy. I hope conversations like that are going on between senior athletes and coaches in all schools.

Varsity athletes are likely to have a coach who takes an interest in their college athletic careers. Other kids might find they have no one with whom to discuss their college thoughts and worries. These conversations should take place with parents, certainly, but it is extremely helpful if a senior can talk to someone objective, someone knowledgeable, outside the family, a person who isn't as anxious and involved as a parent tends to be.

The third opportunity the senior year should give a student is the chance to take stock of her talents and accomplishments; this should be a time of satisfaction and personal consolidation. I hope that for every senior there is a moment when she can say more than "Thank God, I've finished," but, rather, can mutter something such as "Damn, I'm good." If that happens only with the receipt of a college acceptance letter, then the system has failed to recognize the young person for who she really is. And it has definitely failed the child who isn't heading to college, whose skills and interests logically lead elsewhere.

There are seniors who are ready for adulthood, who don't want the continued infantilization and uncertainty of student life, who feel that they can achieve what they want and need by entering the job market. I once spoke to a man who had started managing bands in South Africa when he was eighteen years old and eventually founded a record company. He asked me whether MIT was a good college. Startled, I replied, "Of course, why do you even ask?" He replied that his son wanted to go there but that he, the father, felt as if his son would be stuck in college during the most energetic and productive years of his life. He was certain that the years eighteen to twenty-two were the prime years in a person's adulthood. I could not argue with his life experience.

> "I've got plans, but they act like if you're not going to college, there's something wrong with you. I know I'm not the only one, but I feel like it."
>
> (Twelfth-grader)

The fourth opportunity the senior year should offer students is a chance to give something meaningful back to their communities. I feel strongly that if seniors aren't given the chance to express their gratitude to the community of adults that has surrounded them, and do not have a chance to make a real contribution, they are likely to become annoyances instead. The late-adolescent attitude of "We can't wait to get out of here" is often a cover for a deeper feeling: "We're afraid you'll never see us as valuable and adult in this town." It is essential that the school values seniors through the spring, right up until graduation, and that seniors be given many chances to provide service to the community in meaningful public and independent ways.

It is equally important for adults to have a chance to say thanks for their contributions. Many seniors tell me how meaningful it was for them to see teachers cry at their graduation. Kids need to know that they were important and will be missed—both as important parts of school life and as individuals about whom teachers have cared. Every child should come away from each school year feeling useful, as someone who knows that he or she can make a contribution to society.

Seniors need a great deal of ritual, and that is the fifth opportunity they should be provided with. The departure from high school is the closest thing we have to a rite of passage in our ritual-starved culture. The rituals should work the same way for both the college-bound and the work-bound. Adults often think that adolescents are going to be so cynical about any kind of ceremony that there is no point in attempting to put together a meaningful graduation. They could not be more wrong. Adolescents are deeply moved by graduation-connected ceremonies that are traditional and personal.

I was talking to a group of seniors from a girls' school. Many had been classmates for ten or twelve years. When I asked if they had any worries about graduation, one said, "What if you can't stop crying at graduation?" Other girls nodded their heads. They knew they were going to be moved. They had seen the seniors before them experience strong feelings at parting from one another.

From a psychological point of view, one graduation ceremony isn't enough. There need to be smaller, more intimate ceremonies that prepare the way to the formal celebration. At my daughter's school there is a "capping ceremony" held five days before graduation, for when the kids receive their gowns from the rental company. They hold a brief assembly in which each senior invites the faculty member who, in the student's mind, is most responsible for getting him to graduation, and that teacher symbolically "caps" the soon-to-be graduate. Besides celebrating the bond between teacher and student—something truly worth celebrating—the capping ceremony puts the student in charge, because he chooses to honor a teacher or coach, not the other way around. For that reason it is also one of the most genuine and positive forms of teacher evaluation an educator could ever hope to receive.

COLLEGE TALK:
REPLACING THE RACE WITH REFLECTION

For college-bound students, college considerations and decision-making are an inevitable part of their high school years. Ideally, the college conversation can be a valuable learning experience for children (about themselves) *and* parents (about their children). A few ways to protect the value of your child's senior year and keep the college conversation from becoming college craziness:

Remember who is going to college. Don't fill out your child's applications, don't write her essays for her, don't fall in love with a college for her, and don't pick a college for her. If you more or less go through the application process *for* your child, you have deprived her of an important learning experience. If you micromanage the college admissions process, the only thing she will take from it is the sense that she is too young or too incompetent to have done it herself. Or she will resent her parents. No matter how much they love their child, parents need to stay focused on the fact that it is actually the child who is going to attend college. The child will live the life, will put up with the disorientation and the homesickness, will have to make new friends, and will have to stay up late at night to study for exams. The child will have to master calculus, not the parent. If the young person has to do all of that, she should be able to do it in a place of her own choosing.

Ask your child how you might be helpful. There is no one in the world better qualified to consult with about the college process than your child. There is no possible harm in asking, "Do you want help with this?" or, "Am I talking about college too much?" The hardest part for caring (and controlling) parents is to back off when they have received specific instructions from their child to do so. They fear that if they don't make it happen, it isn't going to happen.

Use an adult friend, a college counselor, or a wise educator friend to help you maintain perspective. You may need someone to talk to during this period, preferably someone who has been through it. Such a person has a hundred stories and would be glad to ration them out in response to your anxiety.

Don't compare your child to other children. Don't gossip about college. Innocent parental conversations reported back to kids often have a detrimental effect. Many seniors have told me that hearing their parents discuss everyone's college choices makes them feel uncomfortable. If you really want to know, ask your child, "What do you think of the choices some of your friends are making?"

Practice moderation. If you are thinking and talking about college every day of the week, you are certainly becoming a bore and perhaps a burden to your child. Put yourself on a "college diet." I heard this suggestion from the dean of admissions at Bates College and I thought it wonderfully sensible: Talk about college only two days per week during your child's senior year.

Don't let a college admissions office tell you the worth of your child. I once sat with a boy and his mother at an expensive private school and witnessed her saying to him, "If I had known that you were only going to get into two colleges like this, I would never have paid the tuition money for you to go to this school." Her son, faced with the choice of a college on the East Coast—close to home and his bitterly disappointed mother—and the West Coast, was on the next plane to the West Coast. I couldn't blame him. His mother had allowed a college admissions committee to define his value to her.

If your child gets turned down at a college, as a parent there are only a few notes you should strike: "I'm so sorry. They missed a great kid"; "I hope you are not too disappointed"; "It was a bit of a reach for you"; "It is the college's loss"; "You'll do well wherever you go because you are a great person."

Take time to savor the developmental gains your child is making month by month in his senior year. Look at who he is becoming and the challenges he has met and moved through to get there. If you believe that your child has grown into a loving, interesting, productive, moral adult, then, whether or not a college admissions committee can see that, just make sure your child knows that *you* do.

10

Best Wisdom

—

When you look at a lifetime as a whole, the bits of
wisdom you require, how to live, what really matters in
life is something different people learn at different rates,
at different times and places in their life. It varies from
person to person. I just picked that bit up pretty early.
—*Dan, sixteen*

Who is wise? He who learns from all men, as it is said,
from all my teachers have I gotten understanding.
—*Ben Zoma,* Ethics of the Fathers *(first century A.D.)*

I consider myself a lucky person. I started teaching school the year I
graduated from college and, thirty-five years later, I am still—in
spite of my speaking, traveling, and writing—the psychologist for a
school community. I consider that a lucky thing because everyone in
schools—children and adults alike—is searching for wisdom, and
many have shared their journeys with me, whether intentionally or
not, and I have learned so much from them. Everyone in school struggles every day with issues of morality, citizenship, and democracy.
Everyone is on a quest for meaning, scientific and humanistic.

Children are always asking the big questions, like: "Do we have
to read this? It's boring"; "Why do we have a dress code. It's so stupid"; "Can I be first in line?"; "Can we start a gay-straight alliance?";
"That's not fair." They don't sound like important questions, but they
are. They don't sound philosophical, but they surely are. Indeed,
schools are an ongoing course in practical philosophy. When a

kindergartner with hurt feelings says, "That's not fair," he is asking these questions: "Is this teasing inevitable? Do other kids have to leave me out? Is there anything adults can do about this, or do I have to find my own solution to this problem? Is this what life is all about, teasing and harassment?"

A tenth-grader may challenge his teacher by asking: "Jeez, why do we have to read *Macbeth*? Shakespeare is weird. It's impossible to read." If a high school teacher does not have an answer for that question other than some boring response such as "It's required," or "It's on the APs," or "You'll need it in college," then she has failed the test of wisdom. Any teenager who challenges an English teacher in this way is actually asking: "Do adults have anything to teach me? What is the relevance of enduring values and timeless literature for my life?" When a teacher accepts the challenges implicit in the original question, "Do we have to read *Macbeth*?" she is forced to articulate once again the importance of great writing, of great art. I hope she has an unexpected answer that will catch a tenth-grader off guard, something about her personal response to Shakespeare, something gripping and bloody rather than bureaucratic. That's the way to pique a teenager's interest in Shakespeare.

I like things to be gripping and bloody. That's why I became a psychologist. I wanted to hear secrets. I wanted to see raw emotion. I was curious to know what was in other people's dreams. (I wanted to know if other people were as crazy as I felt.) Over the years I have been drawn to life in schools because they, too, are vivid places, full of surprises and revelations every bit as powerful as those heard in my private office. I remember a kindergarten teacher who used a "peace blanket" to help students solve disputes. If two children were fighting, the teacher would pull out her blanket and require them to sit on it and discuss their problems. She achieved an extraordinary record in resolving problems this way. One day a kindergarten boy came to her and asked if he could borrow the blanket.

"Why?" she asked.

"I want my parents to use it," he said.

Stunned by this sudden insight into his family, she lent it to him. He came in sadly the next day and returned it to her.

"It didn't work," he said. There are few secrets in schools.

Above all, schools are challenging places. Kids force their teachers to examine their assumptions. They make adults feel stupid and help-less, and often pull back the curtain on certain individuals, exposing them as frauds. When a teenage boy scorns a teacher as a "jerk," he is sometimes just frustrated or in a bad mood. But all too frequently, he is right on the money. When a teacher is burned out, his students know it. It is painfully obvious to them because they sit with his lack of passion every day. Time and time again I have heard students' ter-rifyingly accurate appraisals of their teachers. As a speaker, I would feel safer giving a mediocre speech to a group of adults than to an assembly room full of children. Grown-ups tend to be polite when you are wasting their time; kids are not.

Because children can be so tough on grown-ups, and because teachers make such incessant demands on children, and have so much power over them, school is a high-stakes game. They have the power to hurt one another, and teachers can fail, as we have heard from the dropouts as well as the most successful students we have followed in this book. My job as a psychologist brings me together with the most frustrated administrators, confused teachers, and angri-est students. The most successful kids in the school rarely find them-selves in the psychologist's office. I have consulted with principals facing the decision to expel a child from school and, as a result, per-haps blighting the child's life. I have sat with the student facing the punishment of expulsion, filled with defiance and shame, afraid he will lose his friends, the love of his family, and his future. I have watched them struggle with fundamental human problems: the indi-vidual versus the group, moral standards versus mercy, the merci-less reality of difference and unequal ability in the face of academic standards. My friend Edward Hallowell once said to me, "People think school is a protection from real life. There is no protection at all. School is every bit as harsh as life."

You are tested in schools, tested in the most profound sense, and if you engage creatively, you have a chance of becoming wise. The reader might conclude after reading this book that I think schools are deeply flawed places, where kids are bored and misunderstood a great deal of the time. I do. I also experience schools as being among the most interesting, passionate, productive, and intense places I have ever known.

Winston Churchill famously described democracy as follows:

"No one pretends that democracy is perfect or all-wise. Indeed, it has been said that democracy is the worst form of Government except all those other forms that have been tried from time to time." I would describe schools much the same way. As deeply flawed as they are, we haven't yet invented anything better for educating an entire population of children: not homeschooling, not the apprentice system, not online courses, and certainly not a lack of education.

THE WISDOM OF STUDENTS

Throughout this book I have asked the reader to recognize what so often gets lost in the everyday pressure of parenting and teaching children: we need to listen to what children say and take their observations seriously. Now, I'll take it a step further and say, if you remember these particular things that children say, you will be a better parent and teacher. If I have wisdom about what works and what doesn't work for kids in school, it has come to me from listening to children, talented educators, and parents. I want to share that wisdom with you here.

The five most important things I have learned from students, which I believe apply to all students, are: (1) they are always searching for feelings of success; (2) they come equipped with great "crap detectors"; (3) they do not lie about the nature of their experiences in school; (4) they crave meaningful, reciprocal relationships with adults in school; and (5) they want to feel useful.

These five characteristics are true of every student—whether she is academically gifted or learning disabled, whether he comes from a family that values school or not. Teachers sometimes angrily complain, "The kids don't come to school ready to learn." It's true that not all kids come from homes that give them middle-class, school-friendly values. However, every child draws from these five qualities in the psychological journey of school.

Children want to feel successful. This craving is so powerful that you can always count on it. Adults sometimes lose track of this fact and start to believe that kids don't want to succeed in school. Children may confuse us by doing self-destructive things. Because they are scared of being humiliated they don't study for tests. They fail to "try." In some cases when they get older, they become truant and drop out.

How can I say that children are always searching for success when at times they seem to turn their backs on it? The critical idea here is that they are always searching for *feelings* of mastery, and if they don't feel them in school, they will leave—either psychologically or physically. They seek success in their social lives, in an out-of-school job, or even in disturbed states of mind. Like Heather, enraged by the teachers in her school who valued her only as an athlete, students are capable of going on strike if they are valued for the wrong things. You can neither understand nor motivate children unless you understand in what arena they have chosen to feel successful and why.

Think about some of the kids we have heard from in this book: the most embittered students, the ones who left their schools in disgust. Even if they didn't always show it, all of them wanted more of something. A girl, a former dropout, at Boston Evening Academy described to me how she avoided classes. "Nobody cares. Let me tell you. We had three lunch periods. You're only supposed to go to one. I went to all three lunches. The principal sat in my face and told me, 'You go to three lunches,' but he didn't do nothing about it. He didn't care [so] I didn't want nothing." If you look past her negativity, at her core this girl wanted a sign that someone was interested in her being a success in school. When she couldn't find it, not even in the principal's behavior, she left school persuaded that she could feel more successful elsewhere.

Do you remember David, the boy whom I described as "allergic" to school? In the last year of his to-the-death battle with school, he made a relationship with a teacher who kept him in the program for emotionally disordered students so that he could finish. As oppositional as he was, as embittered as he felt, he still wanted some experience of success and was willing to relax his fury at school in order to let this woman touch his life.

To me, the story of a child's school journey is always inspiring, as it is for any hiker who finishes the Appalachian trail, no matter how long it took. From the class valedictorian to the child who barely managed to squeak through the system, there is always something to be learned from what a child overcame in order to finish. I know a man who barely graduated from high school. In fact, in order to walk at graduation a teacher gave him a chance to make up for a failing final exam by taking a makeup exam the night before graduation. The

> **"School isn't just grades. It's making and keeping friends, learning how to act around friends, establishing a reputation, and just trying to keep up with all the changes that are going on around you."** (Eighth-grader)

teacher graded it on the spot and gave him the green light to graduate. The boy's classmates recognized he was a weak student; they knew of his last-minute recovery, and when he walked up to receive his diploma they gave him their biggest cheer at graduation. There was nothing patronizing about their hurrahs. No matter how successful or unsuccessful they were in school, they all identified with his struggle and his triumph.

Because children are always seeking success, it is our job as adults to provide them with meaningful experiences of mastery. The real tragedies occur when adults forget that kids want to succeed, when teachers write students off by saying, "They don't care. They don't come to school ready to learn," as if all children know what the academic enterprise requires. It is essential to tap into a child's desire for success. It is there.

In schools, I have also learned that every child comes equipped with an adult "crap detector." Being taught by someone is a good way to get to know them as a person; their character, or lack of it, shines through. Children in general are such good judges of character. I have learned to trust their long-term judgments of teachers and administrators. They know the score. It is a mistake to dismiss the judgments of children just because they are sometimes disrespectful or unbalanced. Being rude does not mean you are wrong. Since children are not always kind about adults who have power over them, and because they may react with momentary frustration when challenged, I would not put children in charge of the process of teacher evaluation. It might be too harsh. It would, however, be honest.

Over time, children take the measure of a teacher, of a program, and of a school. They come to respect the quiet, demanding Latin teacher who was not remotely "cool" at the beginning of the year, and they come to distrust the immature, showy teacher who swept them off their feet in the fall. They know which teachers are disciplined about correcting papers and which ones are not. They intuitively understand which teachers rely on fear to control kids and which of their teachers deeply love children. Above all, they know who the hypocrites are (and are kind enough to not always say so). Remember your school days? Have you changed your opinions about the character of the teachers who taught you?

When I was an undergraduate in college I relied heavily on a student-written and student-published confidential guide to courses and professors in order to choose my courses. I did not always agree totally with the published conclusions after I had taken the course myself—after all, I had to come to an independent judgment—but the assessments of my peers were never from left field. I have come to rely on the critical assessments of children, even elementary school children. If a second-grade child says a teacher is scary, and has found the teacher scary more than once, either I am dealing with an unusually anxious child or I have a scary teacher on my faculty—or perhaps both. It is often the anxious (or learning-disabled, or unusual) child who identifies some teacher's character flaw that is subtle but real. When I subsequently observe that teacher, I often can see what the child experienced.

Children do not lie about their school experiences. Of course, if you check on them, they do sometimes report that they have finished their homework when they haven't, or they may lie about smoking a cigarette at school. But I am talking about their core experiences of school. Sometimes they exaggerate, they may dramatize, perhaps they are trapped by their developmental concerns, but they do not lie. My biggest problem with teachers is that they sometimes draw conclusions about kids that flatly contradict what those children are saying.

I once counseled a boy who was a "poster child" for ADHD (attention-deficit/hyperactivity disorder). As a result of his unusual neurology, he had difficulty following school rules. During the period of time that I met with this boy, at one point I talked with an angry teacher who wanted him out of the school. I told the teacher that the boy loved the school. The teacher, full of skepticism, replied, "Well, he doesn't show it." The tone implied that the teacher did not believe me. I argued, "He says he loves the school. He tells everybody how proud he is of being here." The teacher replied, "I've heard him say that, but if he loves the school, why doesn't he follow the rules?" This so-called adult logic makes me crazy. The truth is that the boy loved the school *and* he had trouble following rules.

All the reports I received from students for this book had the ring of truth. Of course children may lie about what goes on in school if they fear parental disapproval and disciplinary action, but in my experience, over time and if you create safe circumstances for sharing, children plainly tell you what impact school has on their souls and psyches.

You should worry if your child says nothing at all about her school experience. That suggests three possibilities: (1) Something bad is happening to your child at school; (2) you have a naturally private child; or, most likely, (3) your child has come to distrust your responses because you do not really listen to her or like what you hear when she does open up. A boy said to me once, "There's no point in talking to my mother. She gets bent out of shape about everything I say. There's no way not to hurt her feelings, so I don't tell her anything anymore."

Children don't always know what is necessary for them on an educational basis, but they always know what is good for their souls. That is to say, though they may not know the sequence of math courses that lead to calculus, they always know when they are uncomfortable in school. Like babies who sort the world into "me" experiences and "not me" experiences, kids in school sort their experiences into those exact same categories. As they grow older, the judgments become more nuanced. They can sort them into many different piles, some of which might be called "intolerable"; others might merit the name "used to be hideous, but now bearable"; still others, "not too bad." As adults, we cannot contradict these categories of experience. They are, by definition, valid and beyond appeal. Here is a ninth-grader describing her intense discomfort in English history class and a teacher-led discussion of sexuality:

> Right now, in English history class, we are reading the book *The Epic of Gilgamesh* to go along with our study of ancient cultures. Well, on the second page of this book is a lovely description of the town prostitute having sex with a hairy forest man. . . . This whole scene was shocking enough to read in a usually dry school

book, but to discuss it? . . . Both teachers then started to laugh at how we were acting. Reading scenes like these with teachers is not a fun thing to do.

Her humorous tone tells you that she survived the embarrassment, and there may be something in an adult reader that says, "Oh, get over it. It wasn't that bad," but I ask you to remember how reactive you were to every little thing that happened in school and how much it counted. Frequently a mother will say to me, "Oh, my child is so sensitive," implying that her child is different from her classmates (mothers of boys often apologize for having sensitive sons). Every child is sensitive every day. That is the way we were made. That is why, if you can create the conditions in which a child can speak about his truth, he will tell you what you need to know.

Finally, children have taught me that no matter what they say, they are always searching for a relationship with an adult that is challenging and supportive for them. It's also crucial that it's clear the relationship *means something to the grown-up, too.* The teacher has to look forward to seeing the student and the student has to feel that sense of mutuality. Every child wants to be important to someone in the building. They seek out that relationship and recognize it when they have it. You should have heard the former dropouts at Boston Evening Academy talk about Meg Maccini, the head of their school. They all remembered their initial interview with her. To a person, they registered the depth of her interest in them, and, more important, they felt that first meeting was the beginning of a relationship in which they counted.

In all schools, teachers greet children warmly. They often report that they love children, but it is obvious to me that they do not and cannot love them all. The best elementary school teachers do manage to "love their class." I have just been looking at the photos of the final party for my son, Will's, classroom, and you can see in the snapshots that the teacher, Mary, adores this group. Just as adults in any workplace come to treasure a colleague, most teachers develop a special affection for some children who light up their day. I am not speaking here of the teacher's pet or the child with the best grades in the class. It is a mistake to believe that teachers love only the "smart" or the "good" kids. Some teachers love outlaws, others love artists, or athletes, and still others find themselves drawn to the quietest kids. Such relationships between kids and adults are ineffable, unpredictable, and precious beyond words. *Every child is looking for a teacher who finds her special.*

When I am sitting with a discouraged, angry, hopeless student, I always ask whether he has made a relationship with a teacher in the school, someone who looks out for him, someone who understands him. If I receive a yes to that question, I know there is hope for the child's school career. If I get a no, that child's school career is in psychological jeopardy—no matter how smart or talented he may be.

Do you think I am overstating this matter? When I look back on my own high school career, I believe that I had two teachers with whom I had a special relationship. One, with my biology teacher, was obvious and acknowledged by both of us. He was my mentor and biology was my passion. The other was more distant, formal, and unacknowledged, but real nonetheless. All the rest of my high school teachers—good, bad, or indifferent—have faded into the background. The influence on my life of these two men continues in my dedication to kids and my devotion to schools.

> **"I learned I could make a difference. That is important because it makes me feel important."**
>
> (Eighth-grader)

It is wonderful when a teacher really lets a child into his life. My wife, Theresa, did her Ph.D. dissertation years ago on close relationships between teachers and eighth-grade boys, and in it she examined the structural aspects of such relationships. She found that they contained all the same elements that characterize mentor-mentee relationships in the business world: mutual respect, mutual support, and both parties feeling their careers are enhanced by the relationship. That may seem odd to say about a student-teacher relationship. You have to spend a good deal of time in schools to see how reciprocal relationships can be between kids and adults. I have seen many responsible adults cry at graduation because they are losing relationships that mean a lot to them. One of the bittersweet memories I have of teaching is the annual pain of departure.

Through sixth grade, the relationships tend to be more one-sided. Love flows both ways, but it is the teacher who, like a parent, provides support. However, after seventh grade, the reciprocal elements of student-teacher relationships grow more apparent. When I followed Lila around the Boston Arts Academy I saw that she enjoyed such relationships with a couple of her teachers. They counted on her. Some teachers at her previous school had reached out and offered her a relationship, but Lila had not been available, or perhaps it just was not the right match. She found it at the Arts Academy.

The crucial element in this special relationship is the child's feeling that she can be useful, that she matters to the teacher in some way. For a small child, that might involve completing an in-class job or taking papers down to the office. For a teenager, it may be helping to set up a science experiment or simply acting as a sounding board for a teacher's ideas. The form of the connection between child and teacher does not matter; what's important is that the student feels useful to the adult in a practical or psychological way.

The biggest problem for children in school is the many years of enforced uselessness brought about by our extended educational process. As countries become more industrialized, the age at which children can leave school becomes postponed. Children can leave school at twelve in South Africa, fourteen in Thailand, sixteen in the United States. Recently, some politicians in this country have agitated to increase the age at which children can leave school to eighteen. Though I understand the impulse, like so many ideas that politicians have about education it is misguided—unless we create more opportunities for children to obtain excellent vocational training or to perform community-service work (often called "service learning"). If we rely on the law to confine the 10 percent of the population that ordinarily drops out of school in their junior or senior year, we will be turning schools into psychological jails. Students often leave because they cannot find the success they need in school, or they cannot bear the chronic feeling of being immature and useless when they have the bodies and dreams of adults. I wish politicians would listen to children, because my experience is that they are completely clear about the ways in which school does and does not work for them.

THE WISDOM OF EDUCATORS

I recently consulted to a high school and was still around at four o'clock in the afternoon, late enough to observe a respected veteran teacher join two junior girls for an informal jog. The teacher excused himself from our conversation, went to change his clothes, and jogged down the road with the two girls, who had, he told me, ambitions to become more regular runners. Because they knew how disciplined he was about exercise—he always ran at the end of the school day—they had approached him to ask whether he would serve as their inspiration to get their running regimen under way. As I left the school I passed the trio on the road. The teacher, a thin, tall man with long legs, had shortened his stride and undoubtedly slowed his pace so that the girls could keep up. He was at their side, perhaps only an eighth of a step ahead, looking at them with an encouraging smile, which the girls reciprocated. From what I could see, it was the perfect teaching moment, a voluntary act on all parts: The girls wanted the knowledge that the teacher possessed, and the teacher was willing to set aside his own level of skill (in this case, his running speed) in order to match their pace, and yet he was setting a standard.

There are more doctoral degrees awarded in education annually in the United States than in any other field. There is a mountain of empirical research about what makes a good teacher as well as some extraordinary and inspiring books on the subject, such as Parker Palmer's *The Courage to Teach.* I do not feel it is my place either to critique teachers or to tell them how to do their jobs better. There are plenty of people in the United States critiquing teachers. Indeed, everyone seems to think they know all there is to know about teaching simply because they attended school. My experience watching teachers work has humbled me in this department. I think great teaching—the inspired, passionate connection between kids and adults in the classroom—is exceedingly rare. The educator Edward Pulling once defined teaching as "The transmission of knowledge through personality." His characterization suggests the unique act of creativity that is at the core of a great teacher.

Teachers are excellent judges of other teachers and though they are usually diplomatic in their criticisms of a colleague, it is not difficult in our conversations to tell what they value and what they dislike in one another. Their observations, along with others form master teachers who have shared with me what they do and why, have sharpened my own view of the teaching process and the way it shapes a child's experience in school.

For me, it comes down to four points: (1) The finest teachers love and trust the age of the children they teach (and kids know it!); (2) good teachers understand that over the long haul you cannot motivate children effectively through fear—you must create a safe community for learning; (3) the wisest teachers understand that there are many sources of knowledge besides schools and books; (4) the great teachers understand that teaching and learning are singular acts of self-exposure on the part of both adults and children.

Children adore a teacher who trusts them and trusts in their developmental age. Joe Daly wrote the following appreciation of a teacher and family friend, Ginger Chappel, when he was in second grade: "The thing I like about Ginger is that she respects me."

Over the years I have seen teachers who have clearly celebrated the age of the children they teach. The gifted English teacher Tom Doelger told me: "Part of my teaching load has traditionally been sophomores. I've done a number of other things, but always two sections of sophomores. . . . It's a lovely age. The more they sneer, the better I like it." I am stunned when I see other teachers who appear to be chronically impatient, even annoyed, with the maturity level of the children in their class. As a moral matter, (not a contract matter), how could a teacher not love the age of the children with whom she spends her entire day? When a teacher is constantly characterizing her students' behavior as bad or immature I want to scream, "They are eighth-graders (or kindergartners, or fifth-graders)! What do you expect?" Lousy teachers fail to understand that if you declare war on children's developmental level, they are compelled to dig in and defend themselves—"We are who we are"—by asserting their alleged "immaturity" as their right. You cannot expect sixth-grade girls not to giggle and conspire against one another. You must not imagine that eighteen-year-olds will work hard through the spring of senior year. The best teachers treat children with respect for their developmental level.

Hurrah for teachers like these! Their students feel they are known and cared about.

After the much-reported school shootings of the nineties, everyone understands that schools must be kept safe from threats and guns. That's obvious. However, there are even more pervasive fears that inhabit schools: fear of failure, fear of being unknown, fear of not being

> "She might not realize how much she has helped me, but with out
> her, and with what I'm going through school wise and personal wise, I
> would be a lot different—a wreck. She isn't just the best teacher
> I have ever had, but the way I see it she is the best thing
> that ever has happened to me." (Eighth-grader)

cared about. So many of the dropouts I interviewed said, "The teachers did not care." They described teachers who either did not show an interest in the individual—"Don't put your head on the desk"—or could not effectively discipline the other students in order to create a learning environment. Metal detectors at the doors of urban schools do not begin to make schools safe.

What hooks children on school is a sense of community culture and adult investment. That takes many forms, from money to constant support. If everyone in the building—adults and children alike—feels trapped by their circumstances, no sustained learning can take place there no matter how much politicians threaten "failing" schools. A learning-disabled child lives in fear every day because the very enterprise of school pushes on her weaknesses.

Teachers who succeed in helping kids learn in terrible circumstances, whether economic or cognitive, do so with heroic efforts to make children feel cared for and safe. Six percent of teachers in the United States reach into their own purses to provide books, paper, and pencils to help make their underfunded classrooms a decent place for children. Children know which teachers are willing to do that and which ones are not. They have little regard and even less trust for the system that puts teachers—and students—in that position in the first place.

Children appreciate a teacher who understands that book learning is not the only kind of learning. I once shadowed a new seventh-grade boy around my school, Belmont Hill, on his second day of school. Glued to Alan's side and attempting to see the world through his perspective, I still did not "get it" from a child's point of view when one of his teachers ignored the subject matter—indeed, practically tossed it aside—and informed the class that he was going to teach them to develop character. I thought the teacher was extraordinarily digressive.

At the end of the day, Alan, my companion, said that he liked that teacher's class the best. "He talks about things that other teachers don't talk about" was his straightforward explanation.

I have worked for years with a man I respect very much, Cliff Goodband, the director of the Upper School at Belmont Hill School. Knowing that he had attended good schools and had enjoyed a successful athletic career, I once asked what the most important learning experiences of his life were, expecting that he would mention a teacher or a coach. He cited two experiences.

The first was going to his father's veterinary hospital every weekend to clean out the cages. Though he and his brother hated this chore and always tried to stick each other with the crappiest cages, on a weekly basis he was witness to his father's seven-days-a-week work ethic and his dedication to animals. His other meaningful experience was walking behind a garbage truck one summer in his home town. Seeing the world through the eyes of a blue-collar garbage man, and experiencing the heat as well as the absolute necessity for starting early in order to be finished by noon, had a huge impact on Cliff. Just recently Cliff wrote me an e-mail from his sabbatical saying that we ought to find a way to get boys at Belmont Hill more involved with animals. After more than thirty years in a traditional boys' school enforcing discipline, Cliff has continued to rise above the bureaucratic aspects of the job. He is still thinking hard about how to really reach kids.

Linda Nathan, the founding headmaster and principal at the Boston Arts Academy, refers to the school as an ongoing experiment. A remarkable educator, Linda previously cofounded another pilot school in Boston and has, for the last decade, played a large leadership role in a consortium of twenty such schools within the larger

> "My 6th grade teacher was my favorite because that year my sister was diagnosed with diabetes and she was completely understanding. There were times when i couldnt remember anything and she said it was ok and she understood that my family and I were going through a hard time. Her understanding got me through that year." (Eighth-grader)

public system. Linda is a self-declared "revolutionary" who—as a young teacher in the Boston public schools—declared she wanted to "blow up" the system. Instead, she stayed and brought about change from within. She embodies an unusual combination of traits: educational creativity, focus, political sophistication, a love of teenagers, and an unstoppable desire to see her ideas put into practice. It was Linda who was recruited by the ProArts Consortium, an association of internationally known institutions of higher learning specializing in the arts, to collaborate with the Boston schools in helping to create a "laboratory of innovation and education for the entire school system."

Linda Nathan advocates for smaller-size high schools, preferably no larger than four hundred students. It is a radical thing to say when there are, and have always been, successful large high schools in the United States that have produced outstanding graduates. However, as American society becomes more atomized, as the divorce rate rises, as the suburbs become more anonymous and parents spend less time with their children, perhaps the need for smaller schools has increased. Certainly, moving to BAA worked for Lila: She feels connected and known there.

Our society devalues learning that takes place outside of schools; I think this is a terrible mistake. Whenever I am giving a speech about boys to a PTA group, I ask whether there is someone in the audience who was raised on a farm. There are fewer and fewer, but if a person raises his hand I ask him by what age he learned to drive farm machinery and he gives me a huge smile, delighted to be able to tell his story to a school-focused group of parents: "A small tractor at nine, the big tractor at fourteen." Learning does not begin and end with schools. Learning starts with your parents, continues with imitating your peers, sometimes listening to teachers, and it eventually opens into your own experiences working behind the counter scooping cones at your local ice-cream parlor. (I have known teens who never learned their times tables in elementary school, but instead mastered computation working as cashiers. Sadly, computers that make it unnecessary for kids to add and subtract have eliminated much of this learning.)

Teachers who act as if school is the be-all and end-all of education lose credibility with kids because they are wrong. On the other hand, teachers who respect the learning that children do on their own, who respect the skills that kids develop on computers or through their personal reading, win the appreciation and respect of students. (Don't get me started on teachers who express disapproval of boys who read comic books or who, unbelievably, criticize girls for doing too much "outside reading." Are they nuts?)

The best teachers understand that the twin acts of teaching and learning are acts of personal daring and self-exposure. I am not speaking here of the kind of showy, immature, "I'm your friend," pander-to-the-kids kind of teaching. No, I am talking about the monumentally adult act of standing up in front of a group of children and maintaining one's adulthood while still connecting with children. It is an extremely difficult thing to do day after day. I recommend to the reader that if you have not in recent years tried to organize a group of kids and attempted to demonstrate some complex task, you should try it.

I was a seventh-grade classroom teacher before I became a psychologist. I am here to testify that being a psychologist provides you with many more protections, many more places to hide, than classroom teaching does. As exposed as a teacher is, children are just as vulnerable. I hope that the reader has seen in this book that being a student means you are sometimes at the mercy of the material, the power of your peers, and the power of teachers.

Once again, my friend Tom Doelger puts his finger on the central task of teaching. He remembers attending the bar mitzvah of a boy in one of his classes. During the ceremony the boy read a Torah portion that said (here Tom reminded me that he was paraphrasing), "The duty of every individual is love and kindness . . . all the rest is commentary." Tom takes that to heart in his teaching: "Now, I realize that teaching reading and writing is hard enough in itself, but to teach [love and kindness] in addition . . . that's hopelessly ambitious. But that's what I'm trying to do. . . . One of the ways I teach is through storytelling. Most of the colleagues that I've ever taught with don't. I'm a little bit puzzled by that because storytelling can be so powerful."

What Tom means by storytelling is not retelling the same old war stories. He means sitting down every night with a blank sheet of paper and the text of *Macbeth* and letting his own life come to him, to suggest a story that connects with the kids in this particular class and with Shakespeare's words. "More often than not I don't say, 'Here's the connection between the story that I just told you and the text.' We'll just go right to the text. And I'll leave it up to them to establish connection."

Here is a teacher who takes a risk in *every* class *every* day of the school year. Because he is willing to do so, his students reward him with their own risk-taking, their own guesses, their own willingness to embrace new and unfamiliar material. How does he do it? "The whole thing is still a complete mystery to me. So at the end of my prayer in the morning—and literally I pray every morning—I pray that the grace of God will be in my teaching." He reports that his ability to love kids has been given to him as a gift. "The computers randomly put these teenagers in my classroom and I love them. It's not my choice, it just happens. This, to me, is interesting. I am a more attentive listener to students than I am any other time during my waking hours." Tom reported with some regret that when his wife visited him in class, he seemed so dynamic and spirited that she said she did not recognize the exhausted, introverted man who arrives home at the end of most school days. Great teaching is demanding.

"The best thing a teacher can do is love what they do," observed Adam, the passionate picker and chooser in chapter 4. Much as he considered his music teachers his most significant mentors, his appreciation for teachers went beyond that. "A really good teacher actively enjoys their subject. You can tell. All my music teachers love their subject and love teaching. My math teacher, too; it's blatantly obvious he loves what he's doing, he's interested in what he's teaching you, and you can't help but like his class."

In fact, they have served as the role models for the "passionate picker and chooser" Adam has become.

THE WISDOM OF PARENTS

There are times when I am sitting with a mother or father and I realize they are doing exactly the right thing with respect to their child's schooling. I have two reactions: respect and envy. Respect because parenting is often muddy and confusing, so when someone gets it exactly right, my impulse is to applaud. The envy part comes because as a parent I do not always do the right thing. I want to share with the reader some of the things I see over and over in talented parents.

Wise parents prove again and again that nothing takes the place of being a model for your child. You cannot hope to produce a hardworking student if you send her up to her room to do her homework while you sit downstairs and watch TV. You cannot make a child into a sterling student by doing his homework for him or helping him produce the most impressive science-fair experiment. Good parenting doesn't just demand conscientious behavior and pride in learning; it embodies those qualities.

One of the most memorable families in my years of consulting had a nightly routine in which they ate dinner together at the kitchen table, cleaned it off, and did the dishes as a team. After, they all sat down at the same table, the children to do their homework and the parents to read books of their own choosing. There was conversation. There was back-and-forth banter. The older brother had already had some of the same teachers his younger sister had now and he could recollect attacking some of the same assignments. Working in the presence of one another was what the family did every weekday night. As a result, the parents did not need to hover. They did not need to demand that the homework be checked. They did not need to call it "study hall," nor did they need to enforce it in any way. It was what the family did and who they were. Would it surprise you that these children grew up to be superb students—and loving, family-oriented adults?

The question I hear from wise parents is never "Will he go to _____ University?" The question they ask instead is: "Is school working for him right now?" Wise parents take their child's schooling one year at a time, one day at a time.

The parents I most admire are the ones who manage to stay that half-step behind their child when things are going well, and who scout out more information when things are going badly. If you are too far out in front—talking about exams or college or whatever—you won't be able to hear what your daughter is saying about her daily experience. You may miss something important. Besides, in the battle of school, if you get out too far in front of your child, you start to look like the enemy and your child will start treating you like one!

A friend of mine recalls her father as a cherished mentor, and hearkens back to the summer she was seven years old and learning to ride a bicycle. She remembers him running patiently along just to the side and a step behind, at first holding the seat as she pumped the pedals. Round and round the block they went. Each time she pumped a little harder and his hold grew lighter. Finally, mid-block in one sprint, she shouted happily to him that on the next time around she was ready to try it alone. He didn't respond, and when she turned to tell him again, she was surprised to see him standing in the distance, back at their starting point, grinning and waving her on. He knew when it was time to let go and watch her make her own way.

Conversations between parents and teachers can make a huge difference in the school life of a child. I have thirty years of experience to back up that statement, but I still must point out that these meetings do not always result in dramatic change: the change of a teacher or a revised schedule. While that happens sometimes, most often what the parents or teachers learn is that (returning to my earlier metaphor of the long-distance hiker) the child's shoes hurt. Sometimes the parents had no idea. More often, they suspected it. They knew *something* wasn't right. The shoes that fit last year do not fit this year. Why? Where does it hurt? Your child knows. If we listen, he will tell us.

The wisest parents celebrate their child's development every step of the way. None of us is going to have the privilege of walking this path again with our children. I am writing this paragraph the week after my son, Will, finished sixth grade and my daughter, Joanna, finished eleventh grade. I don't know whether Joanna will play sports in college. She has talent in two sports and it seems as if she has the drive, but I know that only a tiny fraction of high school athletes compete in college. In any case, it isn't my choice. I do not decide which college she goes to, not which coach she likes, or whether her own feelings of satisfaction come from playing on the field or bringing home a paycheck from a part-time job. Her academic journey has been radically different from my own. At times, her dyslexia has made things tough for her and scary for us. Her way of negotiating school has brought with it enormous worries and immense pleasure. What's my role now? I am checking my calendar to make sure that I am available for every soccer, ice hockey, and tennis game next year.

> **"I never worry about my parents reaction because I think I do very well in school and my parents love me no matter what."**
>
> (Seventh-grader)

What about my son, Will? What about his remaining years in school? I cannot predict how it is going to be for him. Seventh grade can be pretty tough, at least socially. I worry about that and am keenly aware that I do not have much control in that department. What I do know is that two weeks ago I watched him give a ten-minute presentation on ancient Greece, his sixth-grade project, to an audience of close to forty people, children and adults. My son, who used to get overwhelmed by crowds, who used to have to leave school assemblies when he was in kindergarten and first grade because they were too noisy and overstimulating, who declined to partici-pate onstage in class plays, opting to work on scenery and backstage, got up in front of an audience and made a wonderful, erudite presen-tation on ancient Greece. Now, I thought his model of the Parthenon was a bit crude, thought that with a little assistance it could have been more presentable, but, then, he did not ask for my help. In any case I'm terrible at building models and I don't know that I could have im-proved upon what he did.

If you had asked me when Will was in third grade, "Can you see your son getting up and giving a speech in front of an audience when he is in sixth grade?" I would have said, "No way." But he got up there and he did a damn good job of it. I'm glad I was there to see it. It reminded me—once again, for the umpteenth time—that I am not in control of his development and his learning and that he and his teach-ers have made some amazing things happen for him in school. I am also reminded that development is a miracle. As parents, our job is to advocate for schools that will foster the miracle of children's growth and development, create loving homes with ample time for learn-ing and sharing with family, and be present at the many moments when their new growth becomes apparent.

I should mention that I was incredibly nervous for Will in the two days leading up to his presentation. I checked with him several times. Did he want to practice it with me? Was he okay about the speech? Every time I asked, he reassured me, "Dad, don't worry. It's fine." And he was right.

Epilogue

The reader may wish to know what has happened to the nine students whose personal stories have been at the heart of this book. As this book was going to press, twelve to eighteen months after I initially interviewed or shadowed them, I certainly wanted to hear how their lives were going.

Helena, the foreign language–loving high school junior whom we shadowed on a snowy, wet day in December, is now a senior at Kensington High School. She is applying for early admission to college, baby-sitting frequently, and working at Gold's Gym. She puts half of her baby-sitting money and her entire Gold's Gym check in a savings account toward college expenses. As for school: "I have learned to accept the behavior of other kids. They have a high school mentality and I'm thinking about the future. I'm a little more patient with them than I was."

Cameron, the determined young man who left behind a drug-addicted mother and abusive father to live with an aunt and pursue his high school career in another state, faced the college search with severely limited financial resources. Though he had hoped to attend a college in New York City, he didn't imagine that he could get in, or that he could afford it if he did. Happily, his work helping other high schools start gay-straight alliances (as a student member of the Gay, Lesbian, Straight Educators Network) made him shine in the admissions process, and he was awarded a hefty financial scholarship, along with others from corporate and community sponsors. As a college freshman now, he posits: "Is college ever really what we expect? It's not the radical place I imagined, but I'm dealing with it."

Adam, the passionate picker and chooser, is attending a large public university that he chose for its strong psychology program, in which he is majoring, and for the specific array of high-level music courses available to him as a nonmajor. In his first meeting with his department adviser, after he told her how much music he intended to take in addition to his psych courses, she reacted conservatively, warning him against such an extensive commitment. His initial reaction was to dump her as an adviser, but his forgiving nature prevailed. "You have to work with them, mold them, shape them, to get what you want," he told me. "I'm in four ensembles," he added.

Joanna is a senior at Cushing Academy and continues to profess her love for Cushing, if not for school itself. Her boyfriend and her soccer team, of which she is captain, are at the center of her life. She has mixed feelings about college. Though she would like to play soccer at a Division II college, she is deeply tired of being a student. One night, while trying to complete an essay on Dante's *Inferno,* she called to say: "This is really tough. It is hard to like literature when you get so little out of it."

Nativity Prep helped find Caleb, from Nigeria, a place at a Catholic boarding school in Connecticut. He struggles with writing and with physics, but a Nativity Prep adviser who supports Nativity graduates even after they have left the school reports that "he says he is very happy." His new school has recognized that he has leadership ability and a sense of humor.

David, who once summed up his school career as "one long argument," nonetheless stayed the course through a modified program and graduated, working for a time as a package sorter for UPS. He then volunteered for internships with service organizations, including Habitat for Humanity and the Heifer Project. Now he is taking a few classes of his own choosing at a community college, looking for employment and a way to move forward with his life. "Time off has given me more perspective," he told me. When I expressed surprise at his new interest in classes, he said, "I'm willing this time, which completely changes things."

Despite her long-standing hatred of schools, Zoe has stuck with Boston Evening Academy and is now a senior. In fact, she has been offered a scholarship at an art school to pursue her interest in clothing design.

Heather writes from Oregon that her life since graduating from

Rocky Mountain Academy has been "one turn after another, some leading to good, others to bad." She has started drinking again, but it is "more under control than I thought possible." She became a wildlands firefighter and reported that it teaches you "how strong you really are." She fought several serious fires until she injured her knee. She is doing office work and hoping that her knee will heal sufficiently so she can return to the field. Her relationship with her father has healed significantly, and she has found love in her life.

Lila had hoped to gain admission to a conservatory as an actor, as some of her classmates at Boston Arts Academy were able to do, but her grade point average kept her from being competitive at the places, like Juilliard, to which she aspired. She is attending a small women's college in suburban Boston. She is somewhat disappointed in her experience there and is trying to build an academic record that will allow her to transfer to a conservatory. She has friends at college and she is, of course, involved in theater. Like any aspiring actor, she is throwing herself out into the world with energy and confidence, e-mailing her widening circle of friends and fans with regular notifications that begin, "Dear Everyone, Just writing to let you know the specific dates I will be performing. . . ."

We will give the last word to Alexandra, whose story was one of painful perseverance in a chronic struggle with a variety of learning difficulties, the demands of school, and what was, for a time in her junior year, a debilitating anxiety problem. Contacted for an update, now a struggling senior, she wrote, "Sometimes I won't deny that with all the work and pressures handed to me this year I feel the need to give up on my education altogether just to relieve all the stress, but I won't give in to failure. I have dreams I want to come true." She is aware that her low grade point average disqualifies her from applying to any four-year colleges, but she is ready to attend a junior college. "I used to look down on that idea, but there's nowhere else to go but up from here," she says, adding that she feels she will be successful in whatever direction her learning takes her. "Hopefully, I'll be able to write a few books of my own one day and publish them."

Then she expresses some hopes for school. "I hope one day school won't be taught using tests which need to be taken within a room full of other students and a chalkboard. I love to learn, but not with so much work that it can feel like you're being driven up a wall. I hope one day it will advance and be . . . a more suitable environment for teachers and kids. Until then I urge any wanting to give up, not to."

Bibliography

Bettelheim, B. *The Uses of Enchantment: The Meaning and Importance of Fairy Tales*. New York: Vintage, 1975.

Bigelow, B., Hall, L., Moroney, T. *Just Let the Kids Play: How to Stop Other Adults from Ruining Your Child's Fun and Success in Youth Sports*. Deerfield Beach, Fla.: Health Communications, 2001.

Bizar, M., Daniels, H., Zemelman, S. *Rethinking High School: Best Practice in Teaching, Learning and Leadership*. Portsmouth, N.H.: Heinemann, 2001.

Brumbaugh, R. S., Lawrence, N. M. *Six Essays on the Foundations of Western Thought*. Boston: Houghton Mifflin, 1963.

Chess, S., Hassibi, M. *Temperament and Development*. New York: Brunner/Mazel, 1977.

Chess, S., Thomas, A. *Origins and Evolution of Behavior Disorders: From Infancy to Early Adult Life*. New York: Brunner/Mazel, 1984.

Coles, R. *The Moral Life of Children*. Boston: Atlantic Monthly Press, 1986.

———. *The Spiritual Life of Children*. Boston: Houghton Mifflin, 1990.

Damon, W. *Social and Personality Development*. New York: Norton, 1983.

Elkind, D. *Children and Adolescents: Interpretive Essays on Jean Piaget*. 2nd Edition. New York: Oxford University Press, 1974.

———. *The Hurried Child: Growing Up Too Fast Too Soon*. Reading, Mass.: Addison-Wesley, 1981.

Erikson, E. H., *Identity Youth and Crisis*. New York: Norton, 1968.

Feiler, B. S. *Learning to Bow*. Boston: Houghton Mifflin, 1991.

Fraiberg, S. H. *The Magic Years: Understanding and Handling the Problems of Early Childhood*. New York: Charles Scribner's Sons, 1959.

Freud, A. *The Ego and the Mechanisms of Defense*. New York: International Universities Press, 1966.

———. *The Writings of Anna Freud*. Volume VIII, 1970–1980: *Psychoanalytic Psychology of Normal Development*. New York: International Universities Press, 1981.

Garbarino, J., Stott, F. M., Faculty of the Erikson Institute. *What Children Can Tell Us*. San Francisco: Jossey-Bass, 1989.

Gardner, H. *Frames of Mind: The Theory of Multiple Intelligences*. New York: Basic Books, 1983.

———. *Multiple Intelligences: The Theory in Practice*. New York: Basic Books, 1993.

Goodlad, J. I. *A Place Called School: Prospects for the Future*. New York: McGraw-Hill, 1984.

Hallowell, E. M. *The Childhood Roots of Adult Happiness*. New York: Ballantine Books, 2002.

Holt, J. *How Children Fail*. New York: Dell, 1964.

Hymowitz, K. S. *Liberation's Children: Parents and Kids in a Postmodern Era*. Chicago: Ivan R. Dee, 2003.

Kagan, J., Moss, H. A. *Birth to Maturity: A Study in Psychological Development*. New York: John Wiley and Sons, 1962.

Katch, J. *Under Deadman's Skin: Discovering the Meaning of Children's Violent Play*. Boston: Beacon Press, 2001.

Kessler, R. *The Soul of Education: Helping Students Find Connection, Compassion and Character at School*. Alexandria, Va.: Association for Supervision and Curriculum Development, 2000.

Kuroyanagi, T. *Totto-Chan: The Little Girl at the Window*. Tokyo: Kodansha International, 1981.

Leonard, G. B. *Education and Ecstasy*. New York: Delacorte Press, 1968.

Meier, D. *The Power of Their Ideas: Lessons for America from a Small School in Harlem*. Boston: Beacon Press, 1995.

———. *In Schools We Trust—Creating Communities of Learning in an Era of Testing and Standardization*. Boston: Beacon Press, 2002.

Meltz, B. F. *Put Yourself in Their Shoes*. New York: Dell, 1999.

Northrop Collegiate School, The Blake Country Day School for Boys, and The Blake School. *Treasures in Our Lives: A Celebration of Our Teachers*. Hopkins, Minneapolis, and Waysata, Minn.: The Blake School, 2001.

Ohanian, S. *Caught in the Middle*. Portsmouth, N.H.: Heinemann, 2001.

Palmer, Parker J. *Let Your Life Speak: Listening for the Voice of Vocation*. Jossey-Bass, 1999.

——— *The Courage to Teach: Exploring the Inner Landscape of a Teacher's Life*. Jossey-Bass, 1997.

Pope, D. C. *"Doing School": How We Are Creating a Generation of Stressed Out, Materialistic, and Miseducated Students*. New Haven: Yale University Press, 2001.

Riera, M. *Uncommon Sense for Parents with Teenagers.* Berkeley, Calif.: Celestial Arts, 1995.

Sizer, N. F., Sizer, T. R. *The Students Are Watching: Schools and the Moral Contract.* Boston: Beacon Press, 1999.

Sizer, T. R. *Horace's Compromise: The Dilemma of the American High School.* Boston: Houghton Mifflin, 1984.

————. *Horace's School: Redesigning the American High School.* New York: Houghton Mifflin, 1992.

Steinberg, L. *Beyond the Classroom: Why School Reform Has Failed and What Parents Need to Do.* New York: Simon & Schuster, 1996.

Tatum, B. D. *"Why Are All the Black Kids Sitting Together in the Cafeteria?":* *And Other Conversations About Race.* New York: Basic Books, 1997.

Tompkins, J. *A Life in School: What the Teacher Learned.* Cambridge, Mass.: Perseus, 1996.

Winnicott, D. W. *The Family and Individual Development.* London: Tavistock, 1965.

————. *The Maturational Processes and the Facilitating Environment.* New York: International Universities Press, 1965.

————. *Thinking About Children.* Reading, Mass.: Addison-Wesley, 1996.

The National Center for Education Statistics (NCES). http://nces.gov/pubs2002/droppub_2001

Hoffmann, Lynn M. "What Students Need in the Restructured High School." *Education Week,* October 16, 2002.

Turner, J. C., Midgely, C., Meyer, D. K., Green, M., Anderman, E. M., Kang, Y., Patrick, H. "The Classroom Environment and Students' Reports of Avoidance Strategies in Mathematics: A Multimethod Study." *Journal of Educational Psychology* 94 (2002), 88–106.

Turner, J. C., Thorpe, P. K., Meyer, D. K. "Students' Reports of Motivation and Negative Affect: A Theoretical and Empirical Analysis." *Journal of Educational Psychology* 90 (1998), 758–71.

About the Authors

MICHAEL THOMPSON, PH.D., is a clinical psychologist, lecturer, consultant, and former seventh-grade teacher. He conducts workshops across the United States on social cruelty, children's friendships, and boys' development. With Catherine O'Neill Grace and Lawrence J. Cohen, Ph.D., he co-authored *Best Friends, Worst Enemies: Understanding the Social Lives of Children* and *Mom, They're Teasing Me: Helping Your Child Solve Social Problems.* With Dan Kindlon, Ph.D., he co-authored the *New York Times* bestseller *Raising Cain: Protecting the Emotional Life of Boys.* He is also the author of *Speaking of Boys: Answers to the Most-Asked Questions About Raising Sons.* He lives in Arlington, Massachusetts, with his wife and two teenage children.

TERESA BARKER, who collaborated with Thompson on *Raising Cain* and *Speaking of Boys,* is a journalist and mother of three school-age children. She lives in Wilmette, Illinois.